STORIES OF IRELAND'S PAST

Stories of Ireland's Past

Knowledge gained from NRA roads archaeology

Edited by Michael Stanley, Rónán Swan & Aidan O'Sullivan

TII Heritage 5

First published in 2017 by
Transport Infrastructure Ireland
Parkgate Business Centre, Parkgate Street, Dublin 8, D08 DK10
Copyright © Transport Infrastructure Ireland and the authors

Library of Congress Cataloguing-in-Publication Data are available for this book.
A CIP catalogue record for this book is available from the British Library.

Material from Ordnance Survey Ireland is reproduced with the permission of the Government of Ireland and Ordnance Survey Ireland under permit number EN0045216.

ISBN 978-0-9932315-5-1
ISSN 2009-8480
TII Heritage 5

Copy-editing: Wordwell Ltd
Cover design, typesetting and layout: Wordwell Ltd
Index: Geraldine Begley

Printed by: Digital Print Dynamics, Dublin

Front cover—A selection of archaeological discoveries from national road schemes. Top left to bottom right: an Edward I silver long-cross penny, c. AD 1279–1307, from a moated site at Busherstown, Co. Offaly; a burial at an early medieval cemetery-settlement at Owenbristy, Co. Galway; the decorated handle of an early medieval ladle from Ballypark, Co. Wicklow; an Early Bronze Age 'vase food vessel' from a pit at Ballynacarriga, Co. Cork; late 18th-/early 19th-century clay pipes from a tenant farm at Lavally, Co. Galway; a Late Mesolithic basket fish-trap from Clowanstown, Co. Meath; an Early Bronze Age barbed-and-tanged flint arrowhead from Coldwood, Co. Galway; an Early Neolithic house at Dunsinane, Co. Wexford; and a Late Iron Age/early medieval glass bead from a cereal-drying kiln at Lismullin, Co. Meath (bottom centre photo by AirShots Ltd; all other photos by John Sunderland).

Back cover—Reconstruction showing how the Late Mesolithic basket fish-traps from Clowanstown, Co. Meath, may have been used (JG O'Donoghue).

CONTENTS

FOREWORD

In 2014 the Archaeology Section of the National Roads Authority (NRA)[1] sought to mark the 20th anniversary of the establishment of the NRA by organising a nationally important public event to appraise and celebrate the many significant archaeological discoveries that had been made on the country's national roads. Leading scholars were invited to critically evaluate the contribution of 'roads archaeology' to our understanding of Ireland's prehistoric and historic past, and to present their findings at a one-day public seminar held in Dublin during Heritage Week. In surveying some 10,000 years of human habitation on the island and assessing the new knowledge acquired through NRA-funded archaeological investigations, the authors have delivered a truly significant publication.

A number of words linger in the mind as one reads *Stories of Ireland's Past: knowledge gained from NRA roads archaeology*. 'Legacy' and 'transformation' are two that stand out in particular. The book speaks to the legacy not only of our ancestors but also of the hundreds of field archaeologists from many countries who have toiled throughout Ireland to unearth, record and understand the traces of our shared past. Over the last two decades or so, their work, and that of a multitude of specialists and academic researchers, can justly be claimed to have transformed to some extent our knowledge of every archaeological period. For certain periods these transformations have fundamentally altered our understanding of past society. As two of the authors put it, 'the great strength of the work carried out by archaeologists and archaeological consultancies working on national road schemes' is that the 'road excavations have opened up to scholarship an entirely different view of Irish archaeology'.

The archaeological legacy of the programme of past works is rightly celebrated in *Stories of Ireland's Past* but the book is not devoid of constructive criticism. In some cases, authors have highlighted the challenges that datasets derived from development-led archaeology can present. *Stories of Ireland's Past* will no doubt prompt our archaeologists (and the wider profession) to reflect on future practice so as to benefit from the lessons learned over the years and from the insights generated by this scholarly synthesis of the excavated evidence. This volume is a significant accomplishment and is unlikely to be eclipsed for some time. While its publication should be seen as a tribute to the profession as a whole, the authors deserve our particular thanks for responding to our invitation and bringing their academic rigour and considerable communication skills to bear on two decades of archaeological discovery.

Michael Nolan
Chief Executive Officer
Transport Infrastructure Ireland

---

[1] Following the merger of the NRA with the Railway Procurement Agency in August 2015, the NRA has operated as Transport Infrastructure Ireland (TII).

ACKNOWLEDGEMENTS

The papers published herein stem from a Heritage Week seminar entitled 'Stories of Ireland's Past: knowledge gained from NRA roads archaeology', which was held at the Wood Quay Venue, Dublin Civic Offices, on 28 August 2014. This one-day seminar was organised by Lillian Butler, Michael Stanley and Rónán Swan of TII. TII are grateful for the participation of Dr Ann Lynch, National Monuments Service, Department of Arts, Heritage, Regional, Rural and Gaeltacht Affairs, and Dr Edel Bhreathnach, Chief Executive Officer of the Discovery Programme, who chaired two of the seminar sessions. TII is particularly grateful to the seminar speakers, who generously took time out from their teaching and research schedules to contribute to the seminar and the subsequent publication. Our thanks to Professor Ian Armit, Dr Katharina Becker, Dr Neil Carlin, Professor Gabriel Cooney, Dr Mark Gardiner, Dr Eoin Grogan, Dr Finbar McCormick, Dr Kieran O'Conor, Professor Tadhg O'Keeffe, Professor Aidan O'Sullivan, Dr Graeme Swindles and Dr Graeme Warren. Each of the papers has benefited from a process of anonymous peer review and TII would like to express its warm thanks to each of the reviewers. The book was copy-edited by Emer Condit and was designed and typeset by Wordwell Ltd.

NOTE ON RADIOCARBON DATES

All of the radiocarbon dates cited in the following papers are calibrated date ranges equivalent to the probable calendrical age of the sample and are expressed as BC or AD dates, calibrated at the two-sigma (2σ) (98% probability) level of confidence.

LIST OF CONTRIBUTORS

Professor Ian Armit is a Professor in the School of Archaeological and Forensic Sciences, University of Bradford.

Dr Katharina Becker is a Lecturer in the Department of Archaeology, University College Cork.

Dr Neil Carlin is a Teaching Fellow in the UCD School of Archaeology, University College Dublin.

Professor Gabriel Cooney is a Professor in the UCD School of Archaeology, University College Dublin.

Dr Mark Gardiner is a Reader in Heritage in the School of History and Heritage, University of Lincoln.

Dr Eoin Grogan is a Lecturer in the Centre for Irish Cultural Heritage/Department of Sean-Ghaeilge, Maynooth University.

Dr Finbar McCormick is a Senior Lecturer in the School of Natural and Built Environment, Queen's University, Belfast.

Dr Kieran O'Conor is a Senior Lecturer in the Department of Archaeology, NUI Galway.

Professor Tadhg O'Keeffe is a Professor in the UCD School of Archaeology, University College Dublin.

Professor Aidan O'Sullivan is a Professor in the UCD School of Archaeology, University College Dublin.

Michael Stanley is an Archaeologist with TII.

Rónán Swan is Head of Archaeology and Heritage with TII.

Dr Graeme Swindles is an Associate Professor in the School of Geography, University of Leeds.

Dr Graeme Warren is an Associate Professor in the UCD School of Archaeology, University College Dublin.

I

TRANSFORMATIONS: KNOWLEDGE GAINED FROM ROADS ARCHAEOLOGY

Aidan O'Sullivan, Michael Stanley & Rónán Swan

Introduction

Transformation. It is a word that can be defined in dictionary terms as a 'marked change in form, nature or appearance'. It is certainly a word that recurs in this book—with the authors using such versions or synonyms as 'transformed', 'transforming', 'changed', 'altered', 'shift', 'renewed', 'revolution' and so on. In archaeological terms, as we shall see, the word could encompass the changing of modern archaeological practices as new technologies, theoretical approaches and insights come on stream, as the discipline keeps track with innovations in the sciences and humanities. It could also be about the transformation of archaeological evidence itself, in terms of its quantity, quality and range, as large-scale archaeological investigations in advance of roadways uncover large numbers of new sites and features. Finally, and most importantly, it could be taken to refer to our own changing archaeological understandings and interpretations of past societies, and indeed how these societies themselves changed (or were 'transformed') across vast spans of time, such as within chronological periods like the Mesolithic, or suddenly enough, as with the arrival of Neolithic farming in Ireland sometime around 3750 BC. The archaeological evidence for the past is not always about change, of course; it can also be about tradition, continuity and repetition, such as the striking conservatism of burial practice that essentially endured through the Bronze Age. There is also much else that endures across time. People lived, worked and died in the same places across centuries and even millennia, inhabiting dwellings or burying their dead in places that would have been well known to previous generations. They often worked the land and lived with their environments in broadly similar ways, managing livestock or growing oats, barley and wheat in cultivated fields. Had prehistoric or early medieval farmers come forward in time and wandered as time-travellers through late medieval or early modern Ireland they would not have been heartily surprised by everything they saw.

Archaeology itself can be defined as the reconstruction of past societies from their material remains, or more succinctly as 'the discipline of things'. As a discipline, it explores how people make their own societies through their material engagement with the world, and sometimes how this changes. It investigates how people live together, work the land, bury their dead, make and use things, and establish and negotiate relationships with other people and with places, times, plants and animals. For some archaeologists it is about identity, exploring how people—and peoples—established and performed social identities of ethnicity, kinship, status, rank and gender through their landscapes, their dwellings, their bodily dress and costume, their technologies and material culture (their 'things'), and their relationships with and uses of materials, plants and animals. Archaeologists exploiting this evidence aim to reconstruct societies as they were: investigating what people did, what they thought they were doing and to what end. Archaeologists try to do lots of things with the evidence that they uncover. In some cases the aim is to curate and preserve archaeological evidence for future generations. They might use LiDAR, geophysics, aerial photography, digital mapping and other approaches to build up an understanding of the archaeological landscape as it survives today and, using that awareness, to devise methods for its protection and management into the future. Indeed, for some archaeologists the practice of the discipline is about society today: how is it that people lived together in the past, and how should we live together? How might we identify structures of power, or inequality, in the past and the present? Who owns archaeology and cultural heritage, and what is it for? What decisions should we make about it, now and in the future?

Archaeology, however, is also about finding things out, and telling stories about the past. For that we need to look at evidence. There is probably no stronger metaphor for what archaeologists do than excavation. Archaeologists in the popular perception, and metaphorically, 'dig into the past'; they 'uncover the past', they reveal 'hidden' places and things, and they travel back down and into time. As important as other archaeological landscape or scientific laboratory approaches are, and whatever the role of archaeology is in modern society, it is archaeological excavations that bring us closest to the people of the past, the dirt under their fingernails as they engaged with each other and their own worlds. And it is archaeological excavations that lie at the heart of this book.

NRA archaeological policy and its transformations

If archaeological excavations, and their potential to continue the investigation of Ireland's long story of human activity over the last 10,000 years (and perhaps more), lie at the heart of this book, we should consider first the context in which all these excavations happened. In reflecting on the contribution of the NRA (now TII) to the enhancement of our knowledge and understanding of Ireland's archaeological heritage, it is important to contextualise the approach taken to archaeology within the body's overall mission. In the late 1990s the Republic of Ireland decided to upgrade, develop and expand its motorway network. Unlike other countries in western Europe, Ireland's motorway network had been largely undeveloped, with limited works in the 1980s and early 1990s. In Ireland archaeological sites are afforded protection through legislation and associated government policy, and developers have a duty to minimise their impact on archaeological sites through avoidance, preservation *in situ* or, as a last resort, preservation by record (i.e. by scientific archaeological excavation). The original strategy for dealing with archaeological sites on the early motorway projects was that known sites identified during the environmental impact assessment would be excavated prior to construction, while the discovery of previously undocumented sites would be left to monitoring during the main construction works. Such an approach was unsatisfactory for several reasons. Archaeologically, it meant that significant sites might not be discovered until construction had commenced, with archaeological layers being truncated and damaged by the heavy machinery, and perhaps leading to a loss of archaeological sites and the potential information they could yield. It also resulted in claims from the construction companies arising from delays and additional costs relating to their work programme.

Cognisant of these challenges and of the need to address archaeology in a responsible manner, the NRA and the Minister for Arts, Heritage, Gaeltacht and the Islands developed a Code of Practice in 2000 which created a framework for the treatment of archaeology on national road schemes. As a consequence, Project Archaeologists were appointed as members of the local authority road design teams to advise on the archaeological implications of decisions as they happened throughout the lifetime of the project. The Code of Practice also set out the duties and responsibilities of both parties, as well as of the Project Archaeologists themselves.

In the intervening period since the adoption of the Code of Practice, there has been considerable archaeological work undertaken on national road schemes. Over 1,500 km of planned roads have been investigated, providing a significant sample for the study of the archaeology of Ireland. For each road project a detailed programme of advance archaeological assessment was undertaken to ensure early identification and full excavation of previously unknown sites, comprising a multi-faceted and multi-phased approach of desk-top assessment, topographical analysis and archaeo-geophysical survey, leading to subsequent machine investigation. The latter assessment methodology entails the entire road corridor being investigated by tracked machines excavating longitudinal trenches and offsets under close archaeological supervision. Approximately 12.5% of each route would be sampled in this fashion. One of the key benefits of undertaking such comprehensive assessment is that sufficient time and resources can be allotted to fully excavate these sites and to prepare and submit the required archaeological excavation reports. As outlined below, making the information gleaned from these archaeological works publicly accessible has been a vital component of the NRA's approach to archaeology. In recent years, in response to requests from both the public and the profession, the focus has been on making the primary data of the excavation reports available.

Interestingly, these national roads were designed, for the most part, to avoid known archaeological sites (a point that is explored in the subsequent papers). Indeed, it is important to note that NRA-funded archaeological investigations have not been a 'random' selection of the Irish landscape. The roads were mostly constructed in the lowlands, generally avoided uplands and mountainous areas, and also rarely went into wetlands (revealing much of importance when they did, of course), and so it is the landscape between that has largely been sampled. Nevertheless, in the course of these archaeological works it has become apparent that the previously undocumented archaeology is every bit as rich as the monumental archaeology that so often characterises Ireland, with sites dating from the very earliest settlement of the island up to the modern period being discovered, excavated, reported on and published. This volume raises many interesting points that should stimulate much reflection within the profession and, more specifically, among TII archaeologists, particularly when considering future policies, practices and methodologies.

This book

This book is the culmination of a project that began in late 2013 when the Archaeology Section of the NRA was making preparations for its contribution to Heritage Week 2014. At that time the section generally marked this annual celebration of our national heritage with a one-day archaeology seminar held in Dublin City. The 2014 event had added significance in that it coincided with the 20th anniversary of the establishment of the NRA, affording a useful opportunity to reflect on its contribution to our understanding of Ireland's archaeological heritage. With this in mind, some of Ireland's leading archaeological scholars were invited to critically assess the impact of 'roads archaeology' on current thinking about each of the major periods of human settlement on the island. The result was a seminar entitled 'Stories of Ireland's Past: knowledge gained from NRA roads archaeology', which was held at the Wood Quay Venue, Dublin Civic Offices, on 28 August 2014.

The authors had much to do. Owing to the NRA policy on dissemination, the results of pre-construction archaeological excavations on national roads have been made widely available to the archaeological profession and the general public. This has been achieved through the publication of numerous books and *Seanda* magazine, as well as the creation of resources such as the on-line NRA Archaeological Sites Database, which was operational from 2008 to 2015 and has since been superseded by the TII Digital Heritage Collections (https://repository.dri.ie/catalog/v6936m966). In addition to this, the NRA routinely granted researchers access to the large corpus of archaeological excavation reports that it has commissioned. (These are the unpublished technical reports often referred to as 'grey literature', prepared by archaeologists shortly after their excavations and prior to more considered publication.) The academic and wider archaeological community have been engaging with these results (and those of Celtic Tiger-era, development-led archaeology generally) for many years now, with particularly fruitful research outcomes being achieved through, for example, the Heritage Council's Irish National Strategic Archaeological Research (INSTAR) Programme and its many projects. Indeed, perhaps the most successful of the INSTAR projects were those that directly engaged with the synthesis of archaeological evidence from road scheme excavations (mostly) for the Neolithic, Iron Age and early medieval periods. Direct funding for doctoral research was also provided through the NRA Research Fellowship Programme, as well as other studies such as the Ballyhanna Research Project, with its analysis of past lives through osteological analyses of human skeletons from that site. Wide dissemination of, and active engagement with, the results of NRA-funded investigations has ensured that the archaeological dividend of road construction has been considerable and has generated clear benefits in terms of knowledge gained. The 'Stories of Ireland's Past' seminar sought to critically assess the scale and nature of this increase in knowledge.

The papers that follow represent diverse responses to a specific challenge, and all the authors have taken time to consider in more depth the impact of NRA-funded archaeological excavations on our knowledge of Ireland's past, and its place in the world beyond. In addition to whatever impressions they may have formed about the influence of pre-development archaeology in recent years, the contributors were invited specifically to evaluate and reflect on the impact of roads archaeology. To assist in this process, each participant was presented with a full suite of NRA publications in hard and soft copy. In addition, they received an external hard drive containing all of the excavation reports available up to December 2013—this amounted to almost 2,000 reports to probe and appraise. Each scholar was afforded an entirely free hand as to how to engage with this material. The resultant papers range from what might be termed the empirically analytical to the theoretically reflective, but all engage with the topic of transformation. What has changed in our knowledge? What changed (or stayed the same) in the past? Recognising that archaeological knowledge is constantly being renewed and updated, it is worth emphasising that each paper reflects the excavation reports and published literature available up to 2015 or so, with limited scope to cite publications that have appeared during the intervening years.

How did the NRA's archaeological practices effect change in our knowledge of the past? The authors outline their individual perspectives, but there are a number of things that can be considered. In the first place, there is the obvious sheer scale of endeavours, and the transformation of the scope of archaeological investigations that ensued. NRA Project Archaeologists and their colleagues working in commercial archaeological companies ensured change through alterations to both policy and practice, and thus Irish archaeology started to work differently in advance of actual road construction. Aerial photography, geophysical survey and test-trenching became standard approaches, so sites were known about long before road construction and could be dealt with in a timely fashion. Archaeological excavation projects were designed and implemented that were much more ambitious in terms of time, scale of operations and complexity of investigations. Highly experienced, younger (for the most part) professional archaeologists became adept at digging Irish soils, in varying conditions, and were capable of recognising, recording and interpreting features that would not have been seen or dealt with by previous generations. Large areas were opened up to their view, so dwelling places, cemeteries and industrial features were exposed in the context of local and wider landscapes. Instead of the narrow views offered by the slot-trenches of previous generations, entire settlements, burial grounds and other spaces were now visible in large, open-area excavations that were often the subject of many months of work by experienced teams. Moreover, the ways in which sites were investigated through post-excavation analyses changed. The NRA were the first to devise and adopt policies and guidelines for the investigation of environmental archaeology, for example, and so, rather than specialist analyses of animal bone, plant remains and insects being a luxury, it became a given to 'do the environmental archaeology'. Finally, as has been mentioned, there were publications. Books, papers, popular articles, posters, websites and more were all produced, and everybody had increased access to the archaeological knowledge that was being discovered.

It will become evident while reading through this book that specialists in each chronological period felt that it was important to offer criticisms of NRA practice and to suggest beneficial changes for the future. For example, among many other things to consider is the treatment of topsoil (wherein archaeological evidence of small finds, or even geoarchaeological or geochemical data, might lie suspended), the lack of sieving for lithics and the consequent likely loss of evidence. This is particularly the case for the Mesolithic, perhaps, but is relevant for other periods too. Might archaeological objects relating to the uses of a medieval house, for example, not be in the topsoil above it? Another criticism that some might make would concern radiocarbon dating—or, more to the point, that more of it could have been done. As some authors below comment, we now have in our archaeological excavation records a plethora of undated pits, gullies, ditches and other features which we will probably never really understand (recognising that in some cases such features held no datable materials). The radiocarbon dating of skeletal assemblages in cemeteries might have been more ambitious. In some cases—early medieval or medieval cemetery populations, for example—the fact that only a selected sample of skeletons were radiocarbon-dated means that the chronology of the cemetery population is and will remain unclear, and we might not be able, currently, to interpret patterns in changing population health, diet and disease across time (these human remains, curated in the National Museum and other collections, could, of course, be further dated in future).

Archaeological methods have moved on again since the 2000s, when most of the archaeological excavations interpreted in this book were carried out (by and large), and we might also note simple changes in archaeological practices, such as the increasing use of LiDAR and the growing use of aerial drones in site photography, capable of photogrammetric recording of excavated site topography. These and other innovative approaches coming on stream will undoubtedly enhance our knowledge both before and during future TII archaeological excavations. There are also recent innovations in archaeological sciences that are really only now starting to make an impact on post-excavation practice, and so were unavailable at the time of the excavations reviewed herein; these might include such investigations as aDNA (ancient DNA) and genomics of human and animal skeletons, organic residue analyses of ceramics, large-scale radiocarbon dating and Bayesian statistical analyses of the chronology of site occupations and histories. These are all starting now, and are beginning to influence archaeological interpretations.

Perhaps the most striking of all the tasks ahead relates to the sheer number of objects from the past that have been recovered and, for the most part, placed in the National Museum of Ireland's collections. These will mostly have been briefly catalogued or listed in grey literature, or illustrated in publications. Although many books and papers have been written about different aspects of material culture uncovered during NRA-funded excavations, it is fair to say that 'the tip of the iceberg', although a cliché, is a useful metaphor here. This recovered material culture of objects and waste products made of stone, flint, clay, bronze, iron, wood, leather, plant materials and other organics will now require a generation of research, and skilled researchers using innovative archaeological sciences. Future artefact studies, drawing on this material, will be undoubtedly transformative (that word again) of our knowledge of the making, use and disposal of things by people in Ireland across time. The book draws attention, then, to techniques and approaches that will be of benefit to researchers and practitioners alike, and highlights numerous opportunities for new research.

In conclusion, the papers presented here are timely and testify to the state of archaeological knowledge at a key point in the discipline's history, as practitioners endeavour to digest, understand and interpret the mass of data unearthed during the unprecedented development boom of recent years. The NRA's archaeological programmes, including its excavations, have been transformative of our knowledge of Ireland's past; and, change being a constant in human affairs, these transformations will undoubtedly continue.

2

ROADS TO AFFLUENCE?
NRA ROADS ARCHAEOLOGY
AND THE MESOLITHIC IN IRELAND

Graeme Warren

This paper reviews the influence of NRA roads archaeology on our understanding of the Mesolithic period (c. 8000–4000 BC) in Ireland. The Mesolithic sees the first clear evidence of the widespread settlement of Ireland by hunter-gatherer communities. The archaeology of the period has long been dominated by comparatively ephemeral sites, and especially by the archaeology of stone tools (for a review of the character of Mesolithic archaeology in Ireland see Waddell 1998 and Woodman 2015).[1] Important Mesolithic sites have been discovered on NRA schemes, such as the well-known fish-traps and associated platform at Clowanstown 1, Co. Meath (Mossop 2009) (Illus. 1). Lesser-known sites discovered by NRA-funded investigations have also been argued to be of great significance; for example, the 'importance of the Early Mesolithic assemblage from Dowdstown 2 [in County Meath] cannot be overestimated' (Sternke 2009, 32). Other reviewers have highlighted the significance of NRA work in particular regions rather than at the level of individual sites: Woodman (2011, 202), for example, argues that the N25 lithic assemblages are an 'important contribution'.

There is, it appears, much to be excited about. But there is little sense as yet either of the character and significance of the Mesolithic evidence recovered from NRA schemes as a whole, or of the impact of developer-funded archaeology more widely on our understanding of the period (but see Woodman 2015). Assessing this Mesolithic evidence and the impact of developer-funded archaeology on the period is a substantial task, and this short paper can only outline some preliminary observations. My argument begins by considering the relationship between the discovery of Mesolithic materials, our expectations of what might be found and the methodologies used. The substance of the paper is comprised of a review of the Mesolithic material recovered in a sample of 24.6% of all NRA-funded excavations, including an outline of the range and character of the evidence and the landscape location of this material. Finally, I consider the influence of NRA Mesolithic archaeology on broader models of the period through quantified textual analyses of key archaeological texts from immediately before and after the 'boom' of archaeological fieldwork.

---

[1] This paper was submitted prior to the publication of Woodman's 2015 synthesis, which could not therefore be incorporated in appropriate detail without completely rewriting the paper.

Illus. 1—
Reconstruction
showing how the
basket fish-traps from
Clowanstown, Co.
Meath, may have been
used (JG
O'Donoghue).

Roads to affluence?

In 1968 Marshall Sahlins argued that the apparent material poverty of hunter–gatherer communities should not be seen as an indicator that they were less well off than people living in the modern metropolitan West. Sahlins (1968, 85) suggested that 'there are two possible courses to affluence. Wants may be "easily satisfied" either by producing much or desiring little, and there are, accordingly, two possible roads to affluence.' In contrast to the Western model of maximising production, there was also a 'Zen solution to scarcity and affluence ... that human material ends are few and finite and technical means unchanging but on the whole adequate. Adopting the Zen strategy, a people can enjoy an unparalleled material plenty—though perhaps only a low standard of living' (ibid.). Sahlins's polemical argument served to make wider comments about contemporary society and it resonated strongly with the counter-cultures of the late 1960s. The 'original affluent society' of hunter-gatherers that he proposed was influential in hunter-gatherer studies, which expanded significantly in the following decades—often with researchers disproving aspects of his model. The 'original affluent society' is resonant with many common assumptions about how hunter-gatherers behave: that they live in small groups, move around a lot and have few material possessions. One of the key themes of hunter-gatherer studies today, however, is recognition of the diversity of social and economic practices found amongst people we call 'hunter-gatherers' (Kelly 1995), and not all hunter-gatherers match the stereotypes. This is especially important in archaeology, where we must beware of the influence of stereotypes on our expectations of the nature and character of the evidence recovered and the interpretations we derive from this.

Sahlins's comments about 'roads to affluence' have another meaning in the current context: how easy is it to assess whether we should be satisfied with how much Mesolithic material has been recovered from NRA road schemes? If we start with an assumption that there is very little of this material and that it is of a restricted range and character, we will be satisfied with the addition of a small number of new sites. If, however, we think that this material is widespread across Ireland, that it is varied in character and that it is often a challenging and slightly different kind of archaeology than that of later periods of prehistory, we might be less easily satisfied with a small number of new sites. This is important because, while accepting the generally high standards of archaeological interventions and the difficult conditions within which colleagues work, there are long-standing concerns about the suitability of some of the methodologies used in developer-funded archaeology for the recovery and high-quality excavation of Mesolithic sites and other ephemeral classes of archaeological evidence. These issues were explored in a series of discussions with researchers in academic and commercial contexts during the boom (Warren 2013); key issues arising from these discussions included neglect of the potential of the topsoil, absence of sieving for lithic assemblages, recognition of the potential significance of very ephemeral features and absence of on-site expertise in stone tools, especially in non-flint materials. It is worth making the comparison to the Netherlands, where in the commercial sector 'methods of fieldwork that are regarded as standard now for the excavation of Mesolithic sites, involv(e) the wet sieving of sediments in squares of 25 x 25 cm or 50 x 50 cm and in layers of 5 or 10 cm' (Rensink 2006, 108). These standardised approaches facilitate comparisons between sites in a way that simply is not possible in Ireland. NRA-funded excavations have found important sites, but there is still scope for a careful evaluation of the impact of different recovery methodologies on the nature and extent of the data recovered.

The particular demands of Mesolithic archaeology are especially important given the lack of agreed standards for archaeological excavation and the general scarcity of Mesolithic specialists. For example, the Dowdstown 2 assemblage mentioned above as being of such significance for our understanding of the Early Mesolithic does not include a single microlith (a very small stone tool characteristic of the Early Mesolithic), probably because there was no sieving of spoil employed on site (Sternke 2009). The lithic assemblage must therefore be understood as a partial sample of the potential of the site.

NRA road schemes and the Mesolithic

A total of 1,957 reports from road scheme sites were kindly provided by the NRA and formed the basis for analysis. Owing to time constraints it was not possible to analyse all schemes, but a sample of 24.6% of the total was examined. This sample was based on seven road schemes (Table 1): a variety of locations across the country were selected to ensure geographic coverage and the sample focused on road schemes with larger numbers of archaeological sites to facilitate statistical analysis. No attempt was made to select schemes on the basis of archaeological consultancies, specialists, etc.

Table 1—Sample of NRA reports analysed.

Road schemes	Total sites
A1/N1 Newry–Dundalk (Dundalk to Border)	23
M3 Clonee–North of Kells	173
N5 Charlestown Bypass	42
N6 Kilbeggan–Athlone	57
N7 Nenagh–Limerick	70
N8 Rathcormac–Fermoy	50
N11 Arklow–Rathnew	66
Total	481
Sample as % of 1,957 total reports	24.6%

All sites on these schemes were assessed for the presence of 'Mesolithic' material. Defining the end of the Mesolithic is difficult and an arbitrary 4000 BC cut-off point was used in assessing radiocarbon-dated sites (Whitehouse et al. 2014). Several sites with pits and spreads of activity ('occupation soils') in the very late fifth and early fourth millennia (i.e. including Early Neolithic I as defined by Whitehouse et al. 2014) show the difficulties with our conventional period boundaries: a detailed review of NRA data focusing on this period would be very worthwhile but was beyond the scope of this paper.

The sites identified as Mesolithic were classified as either 'definite' or 'possible', based on an assessment of radiocarbon and other evidence, where possible. For some sites a combination of large lithic assemblages and radiocarbon dates facilitated confidence in the period attribution. Some sites, however, were identified as Mesolithic on the basis of a small number of lithic artefacts, and in some cases the typological and technological basis for the classification was unclear and/or the analysts themselves only described the attribution as 'likely' or 'most likely' to be Mesolithic.

In many cases single large blades are assigned a Mesolithic date, despite long-standing evidence that large blades also appear in the Early Neolithic (Woodman & Johnson 1996). In fact, butt-trimmed implements—often considered a type fossil of Late Mesolithic activity (Woodman et al. 2006, 121)—can sometimes be found in classic Early Neolithic timber houses. At Baltyboys Upper/Boystown, Co. Wicklow, for instance, a butt-trimmed form was found in a pit forming part of the structure of a timber house (Corlett 2009). While this example may demonstrate the use of an heirloom of some kind (as argued by the excavator), it demonstrates the complexity of using small numbers of artefacts as absolute chronological indicators. There is also a frequent failure to refer to clear published standards for the comparisons being made. These problems are exacerbated by variations in practice between different lithic specialists. It is notable, for example, that Farina Sternke was the only lithic specialist who identified Early Mesolithic assemblages, often on the basis of technical characteristics of blade production. It appears that other analysts did not use the same approach. Without reanalysis of the material it is difficult to tell whether these different approaches are influencing our understanding of the distribution of Mesolithic activity. These issues surrounding the certainty of classification are reflected in variation in language between specialists and those providing overviews of material in final reports or synthetic publication, where there is frequent moderation of terminology from definite attributions to probable or possible.

In total, 18 'definite' and 17 'possible' Mesolithic sites were identified from the review (Table 2). Given that there is no reason to suppose that the sample is unrepresentative of the whole, NRA schemes will have identified 73 definite Mesolithic sites and 69 possible sites. In view of the problems with methodologies mentioned above, it is possible that these numbers are an underestimate of the true extent of Mesolithic archaeology. This is a significant contribution to our understanding of the extent of Mesolithic activity in Ireland. In 2009 Woodman argued that there were 'approximately 800 sets of artefacts or sites that may belong to the Mesolithic' (Woodman 2009b, xxxviii). It is not clear how many NRA sites were included in this total, but 73 sites (or 142 sites if all probable ones are included) is an important proportion. This is in some contrast to Woodman's assessment that 'it is remarkable how few artefacts, or sites of Mesolithic age, are turning up (on commercial excavations)' (ibid.). It is very important to note that the number of NRA sites with structural evidence from the Mesolithic period is lower (see below for discussion): only five definite structural sites were found in the sample analysed, suggesting 20 across the schemes as a whole, and three possible sites (12 across all schemes). The significance of these 20 or so NRA sites is increased by the rarity of recent excavations of Mesolithic sites in Ireland outside of the developer-funded context. Woodman argues that less than 20% of his 800 sites are excavated (i.e. less than 160 sites), and many of these are older excavations (Woodman 2009b; 2009a).

Table 2—Total number of Mesolithic sites in sample.

	Total sites	Mesolithic, definite	%	Mesolithic, possible	%
A1/N1 Newry–Dundalk	23	0	0.0%	0	0.0%
M3 Clonee–North of Kells	173	10	5.8%	9	5.2%
N5 Charlestown Bypass	42	0	0.0%	3	7.1%
N6 Kilbeggan–Athlone	57	0	0.0%	1	1.8%
N7 Nenagh–Limerick	70	3	4.3%	1	1.4%
N8 Rathcormac–Fermoy	50	1	2.0%	1	2.0%
N11 Arklow–Rathnew	66	4	6.1%	2	3.0%
Total	481	18	3.7%	17	3.5%
Sample as % of 1,957 total reports	24.6%				
Predicted total for 1,957 reports		73.2		69.1	

The NRA schemes continue a trend whereby Mesolithic evidence is being found across large parts of the country rather than being restricted to the north-east of the island (Illus. 2). The N11 Arklow–Rathnew scheme, for example, with four definite and two possible Mesolithic sites, lies in County Wicklow, which Woodman (2009b, fig. iv.2) records as one of a number of counties with only 1–10 Mesolithic groups of artefacts. Later Mesolithic sites dominate the NRA sample, with four times as many definite Later Mesolithic sites as Early Mesolithic ones (Table 3). It is not possible to comment on the significance of this distinction. It may indicate different recovery conditions, with small microliths characteristic of the Early Mesolithic being missed without sieving, or the different lengths of the Early and Later Mesolithic periods, or changing settlement strategies, changes to the structure of technology or depositional practice. Simple associations of the numbers of sites with population are highly problematic.

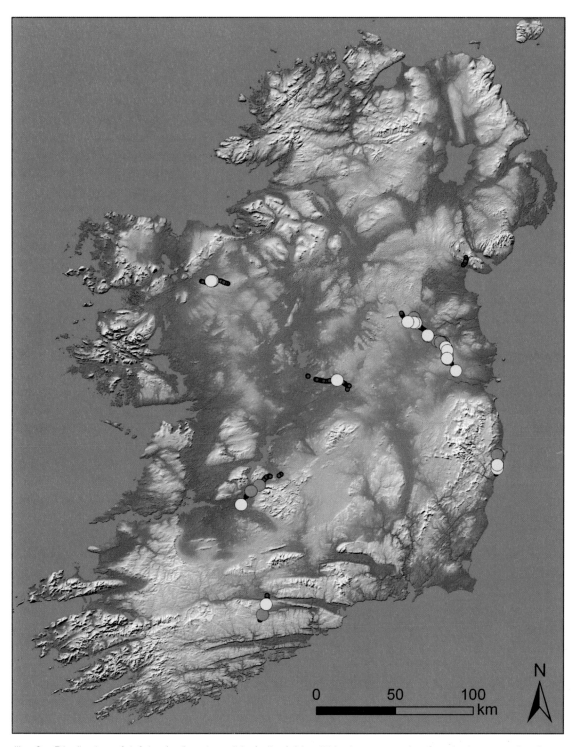

Illus. 2—Distribution of definite (red) and possible (yellow) Mesolithic sites on sample of road schemes analysed (Graeme Warren; satellite image courtesy of NASA: see http://visibleearth.nasa.gov).

Table 3—Mesolithic sites on NRA schemes by period and type of evidence recovered.

	Early Meso., definite	Early Meso., possible	Late Meso., definite	Late Meso., possible	Mesolithic structures, definite	Mesolithic structures, possible
A1/N1 Newry–Dundalk	0	0	0	0	0	0
M3 Clonee–North of Kells	3	4	8	8	2	3
N5 Charlestown Bypass	0	1	0	2	0	0
N6 Kilbeggan–Athlone	0	0	0	1	0	0
N7 Nenagh–Limerick	0	1	3	0	2	0
N8 Rathcormac–Fermoy	0	1	1	0	1	0
N11 Arklow–Rathnew	0	1	4	2	1	0
Total	3	8	16	13	6	3
Average %	0.6%	1.7%	3.3%	2.7%	1.2%	0.6%
Predicted total for 1,957	12.2	32.5	65.0	52.8	24.4	12.2

Table 4—Lithic numbers on M3 sites (possible sites with no lithics are dated to c. 4300–3800 BC).

No. lithics	No. sites, definite	No. sites, possible
0		2
1	2	3
2		3
3		1
4		
5	1	
6		
7	1	
8		
9		
10		
>10	6	

Stone tools

Many sites are characterised only by lithics, with no structural remains of the Mesolithic period. Given the often large scale of excavated areas, it is striking that many of these lithic assemblages are very small in size (Table 4). On the M3 in County Meath, for example, 40% of the definite Mesolithic sites have less than 10 lithics (some of these also have structural remains of the period). All of the 'possible' Mesolithic sites have less than five lithics. Lithics are often found in residual or derived contexts, and many of the Mesolithic 'sites' identified on NRA road schemes have been destroyed in the past and are recovered in secondary contexts. This clearly highlights the potential contribution of very small numbers of artefacts to our understanding of the distribution of Mesolithic sites across the landscape, which re-emphasises the importance of examining the topsoil and paying careful attention to the recovery and classification of lithic materials in the field.

Archaeological features and structures

Structural evidence frequently takes the form of pits and spreads of activity. It is important to note that NRA schemes have not recovered any clear evidence of Mesolithic houses. This is in some contrast to the situation in Britain and the Isle of Man, where recent infrastructural schemes have repeatedly recovered evidence of houses (e.g. Robertson et al. 2013) and very substantial areas of settlement. Given that many of these houses are described as 'Mount Sandel-type', it is somewhat ironic that the expansion of fieldwork in Ireland has not recovered more of these buildings. The contrast with the impact of developer-funded archaeology on our understanding of Neolithic houses is striking (Smyth 2014).

Our understanding of the frequency and character of pits on Mesolithic sites in Britain and Ireland has been transformed in recent years by the impact of large-scale commercial excavation (Lawton-Matthews & Warren 2015), mirroring the situation in Neolithic studies (Garrow 2012; Smyth 2012). Pits are found frequently on Mesolithic sites in Ireland, although the significance of pit-digging as a social practice remains unclear. As in Britain, some, at least, of the pits dug in the Irish Mesolithic served as formal arenas of social practice associated with clear and repeated patterns of activity surrounding the deposition of cultural material into holes in the earth (Lawton-Matthews & Warren 2015).

Spreads of activity and hearths are characteristic of the Mesolithic on NRA sites, e.g. a small complex of post-holes, a hearth and occupation soils dating from c. 4489–4356 BC at Cakestown Glebe 2, Co. Meath (P Lynch 2011). These site types are poorly understood and are often assumed to represent some form of settlement. It would appear that this kind of site is more common in the later Mesolithic, but this statement requires careful analysis to demonstrate clearly, especially given the continuity of many of these practices into the Neolithic (Smyth 2014).

Where are Mesolithic sites located?

The recovery of definite and possible Mesolithic sites on road schemes allows some consideration of the overall distribution of Mesolithic activity across the landscape. Caution is required here. NRA road schemes do not provide a random sample of the landscape as a whole. Routes are determined by a complex suite of factors—the nature of the landscape, modern settlement, protected areas and, of course, the presence of archaeology. For example, all of the road schemes analysed here run across areas of broadly defined 'lowland'. Any assessment of the distribution of material across schemes also requires control for the very real differences created by the working practices of different companies and specialists. Put simply, one person's Mesolithic is not the same

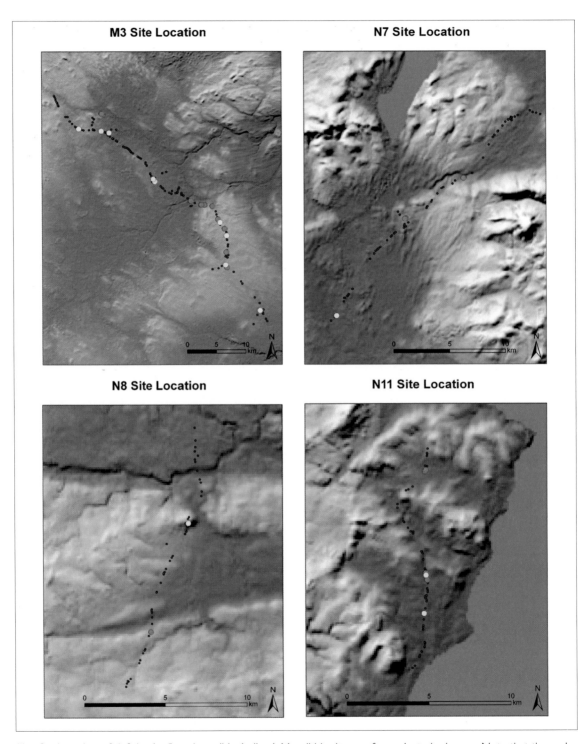

Illus. 3—Location of definite (red) and possible (yellow) Mesolithic sites on four selected schemes. Note that the scale is different for each scheme (Graeme Warren; satellite image courtesy of NASA: see http://visibleearth.nasa.gov).

as someone else's, and, given that many companies have particular specialists for particular schemes, differences between areas can easily develop. Road schemes do, however, provide transects at a unique scale and can provide useful insight. The following comparatively superficial and very large-scale observations should be seen to require further backup with detailed statistical and comparative analysis, but may provide some points for discussion.

While many sites are generally lowland, Mesolithic sites are often not found in large areas of the lowest-lying land but at the edges of these areas (Illus. 3). The N7, for example, is described as mainly running across gently 'undulating lowlands', with the exception of a peat basin on the Limerick–Tipperary county border (Taylor 2010a, 1). Sites in County Tipperary such as Gortnaskehy 1, Lackenavea and Gortybrigane lie in these undulating lowlands, often pasture today, and no sites are recorded from the large lowland peatlands. The Rathcormac–Fermoy section of the N8 'passes through undulating terrain along the lower slopes of the uplands' (Murphy 2013a). On this scheme Curraghprevin 3 lies on the gentle slopes of a prominent east–west ridge (O'Neill 2006) and Ballyoran 1 lies at the foot of a hill. Again the larger basin of lowest-lying land is avoided. The Wicklow section of the N11 mainly runs through flatter lowland areas and Mesolithic sites are found in lowland areas of this scheme.

Further detail is again available from the large sample of sites on the M3 (Illus. 4). Here, while the significant Early Mesolithic site at Dowdstown 2 is in a 'classic' location, overlooking the River

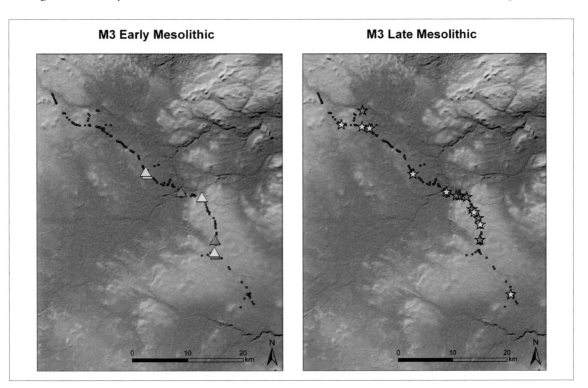

Illus. 4—Location of definite (red) and possible (yellow) Mesolithic sites of different periods on the M3 (Graeme Warren; satellite image courtesy of NASA: see http://visibleearth.nasa.gov).

Illus. 5—Word clouds for the most commonly used words from the Mesolithic chapter of the first (1998) (top) and third (2010) (bottom) editions of John Waddell's *The Prehistoric Archaeology of Ireland*, filtered for common words ('and', 'the', etc.) and for 'Mesolithic' (Graeme Warren; generated using Voyant Tools: see http://voyant-tools.org/).

Boyne, the other definite Early Mesolithic sites are not located near large rivers: Roestown 2 lies on a slight terrace in a generally waterlogged area (O'Hara 2009a) and Johnstown 1 (Elder & Ginn 2009a) at c. 100 m above sea level in 'undulating pastureland', with possible site Johnstown 4 (Elder & Ginn 2009b) in a similar setting. Later Mesolithic sites are mainly found in the same areas as Early Mesolithic ones, mainly on the stretch of the M3 south-east of the Boyne, the rolling hills east of Tara. There is a small concentration of later Mesolithic sites in the 'gently undulating lowlands' near Kells, including Cakestown Glebe 2 (Lynch 2011, 2).

The road schemes, then, provide some insight into the areas of Mesolithic activity. Accepting that road engineers preferentially select low-lying undulating or flat areas to pass through, it is notable that Mesolithic sites are often found in these locations, sometimes at their edges. Mesolithic sites are rare, but not absent, from larger lowland areas. These observations are broadly in keeping with many discussions which have stressed the importance of lowland and riverine activity in the Mesolithic. There is significant potential for a wider and more substantial analysis of site location.

Assessing the impact of the Mesolithic archaeology found on NRA schemes

The NRA schemes have thus found an important number of Mesolithic sites in Ireland and have expanded aspects of the range of evidence found—notably in the expansion of pits identified by commercial excavations. Yet beyond some of the 'super sites' such as Clowanstown, it is not clear how significant an impact this material has made. Assessing the 'impact' of archaeological research is of increasing significance, as it becomes one of the key ways of justifying the costs of research, but it is very difficult to define how best to do this. For the purposes of this paper a simple comparison was

Table 5—Top 20 most commonly used words from the Mesolithic chapter of the first (1998) and third (2010) editions of John Waddell's The Prehistoric Archaeology of Ireland. *Filtered for common words ('and', 'the', etc.) and for 'Mesolithic'. Text in grey shade relates directly to stone tools; 1998 list expanded to 25 because of the multiple words used 16 times.*

1998 First edition				2010 Third edition			
Word	No.	Word	No.	Word	No.	Word	No.
flint	42	evidence	18	stone	47	blades	26
flakes	29	fish	17	flint	43	small	26
blades	28	implement	17	BC	41	fish	25
stone	25	sites	17	flakes	35	evidence	24
site	24	various	17	remains	35	later	24
BC	23	cores	16	site	32	occupation	23
zone	23	Ireland	16	bone	31	zone	23
used	22	Mt Sandel	16	bones	31	axes	22
bone	20	produced	16	early	29	sites	22
later	20	trimmed	16	used	27	large	21
axes	19	*types*	16				
occupation	19	wild	16				
remains	19						

Illus. 6—A selection of the basket fish-traps discovered at Clowanstown (top left photo by Archaeological Consultancy Services Ltd; all other photos by John Sunderland).

made between two editions of John Waddell's *The Prehistoric Archaeology of Ireland* (1998 & 2010). The 1998 first edition effectively pre-dated the expansion of commercial archaeology in Ireland and the 2010 third edition had the opportunity to capture some, at least, of the results of that boom. Waddell's text is a standard textbook in the universities and is by far the most commonly cited authority on the Mesolithic in the NRA reports analysed. (It is worth noting that Peter Woodman's 2015 *Ireland's First Settlers: time and the Mesolithic* is the first book-length synthetic treatment of the Irish Mesolithic published since the same author's 1978 *The Mesolithic in Ireland*.)

Given the canonical status of Waddell's textbook, and the timely circumstances of the substantial revisions which comprised the third edition, a detailed textual comparison of the two editions was made (Table 5). These used basic word-counting facilities and filters provided by Voyant Tools (http://voyant-tools.org/), supplemented by simple word clouds for visualisation

(Illus. 5). Waddell's volume is not based on a systematic review of the grey literature but does include sites from a development context that have caught the archaeological imagination. Changes over this period clearly reflect broader developments in the field and not just NRA-funded excavations, but at least allow some approximation of the influence of these programmes of fieldwork. Of course, analysis of one book cannot provide an adequate reflection of changes in a discipline, and it should also be stressed that no criticism of Waddell is implied here; his textbook simply provides one way of reflecting our changing understanding of the Mesolithic.

One of the most striking features of Waddell's texts is the dominance of terms associated with stone tools. In 1998 the four most frequent terms related to stone tools, and in 2010 three of the top five still do. The increased use of 'stone' relative to 'flint' in the latter edition is notable and may reflect the increased recognition of the diversity of raw materials used in prehistoric stone tool assemblages. Bone is more frequently discussed in the more recent edition, whereas the 1998 text is dominated by functional words: 'used', 'produced', 'types'. Taken as a whole, the 2010 text is a richer account of the Mesolithic, giving more consideration to a wide range of aspects of Mesolithic life, reflecting significant changes in our approach to this period. But only one NRA site—Clowanstown—is specifically mentioned in the 2010 edition (Illus. 6). Two other key sites identified by developer-funded archaeology are included: Hermitage, Co. Limerick (Collins 2009), and North Wall Quay in Dublin (McQuade & O'Donnell 2007). As discussed above, one of the key changes in our understanding of the Mesolithic is recognition of the significance of pits, especially from developer-funded excavations. In 1998 Waddell used the word 'pit' seven times, all to discuss Mount Sandel. In 2010 he again used the word seven times, this time to discuss Hermitage. Based on the evidence of this analysis, it would seem that NRA archaeology has not yet had a significant impact on broader discussions of the Mesolithic. This is unfortunate because, as noted above, the contribution of road scheme archaeology is significant.

Conclusion

The NRA road scheme excavations have generated significant new information about the Mesolithic in Ireland. Some concern still remains about the applicability of methodologies in the field and by specialists, and the difficulties of comparative analysis arising from this. As the economy recovers and the pace of archaeological investigation increases again, it is imperative that lessons are learned from these problems. Arguably this requires the generation of wider standards of excavation, and there is much that we can learn from our European partners in this regard.

The NRA sites are a small but important proportion of all known Mesolithic sites. At present, the implications of the majority of the NRA discoveries are not widely recognised, but this situation will change over the coming years. There is a continued expansion of the scope of Mesolithic settlement, and some refinement of models of site location in the landscape. As well as noted 'super sites', there will be considerable worth in working through the mass of information available and assessing in detail how this fits in with our general models of the Mesolithic.

It would be premature to highlight new agendas or new directions for Mesolithic research based on this review. A full, systematic review of the data—and not just the excavation reports—from all Mesolithic excavations is required. At present there is sometimes a sense that the new sites are being subsumed within older stories and that truly new understandings of the Mesolithic continue to elude us.

Acknowledgements

My sincere thanks to Rónán Swan, Aidan O'Sullivan and Michael Stanley for the invitation to speak, for very useful comments on an earlier version and for patience during the production of this paper. The comments of an anonymous referee were very helpful in improving the text.

3

TRANSFORMING OUR UNDERSTANDING OF NEOLITHIC AND CHALCOLITHIC SOCIETY (4000–2200 BC) IN IRELAND

Neil Carlin & Gabriel Cooney

Introduction

The Neolithic is a transformative period marked by major cultural, social and technological change across Europe. Its global significance, its long-term social impact and its spread from several origin points continue to be widely discussed. Occurring towards the end of a process involving the spread of agriculture from the Near East around 9000 BC (Robb 2013), the Neolithic period in Ireland is commonly defined chronologically as between 4000 and 2500 BC. In this paper its final phase is considered to also include the 300 years prior to the start of the Bronze Age c. 2200 BC. The concept of transformation can be applied to this time-span from a number of perspectives, in terms not only of the establishment of agriculturally based societies on this island and the changes that ensued but also of how our knowledge has been advanced by recent discoveries.

The immediate geographic and socio-cultural context of the Neolithic in Ireland and Britain is north-west Europe, where there has been a focus on the building of monuments as a distinctive feature of Atlantic European societies (e.g. Scarre 2002). In Ireland, there are over 1,500 megalithic tombs dating from the Neolithic and into the Early Bronze Age (Cody 2002). Research on these and other related sites has long played a key role in the interpretation of the Neolithic. Taking an islandwide view and using a fairly coarse chronology, one of the current writers (Cooney 2000) presented a broad landscape-based understanding of the Neolithic that was heavily influenced by monuments, particularly megalithic tombs. While some elements of that view remain valid, the sheer volume of new evidence coming from development-led archaeology, notably the work on motorway schemes, and methodological developments have overtaken these interpretations in the last decade and a half. As Smyth (2014) has demonstrated, large-scale development-led projects, such as the linear transects provided by motorway routes, have revealed a diversity and wealth of settlement evidence. This requires a reassessment of the scale, duration and extent of Neolithic activity across the island. At the same time, the application of Bayesian statistical approaches to radiocarbon dates has enabled us to think about time-scales of generational lengths (Cooney et al. 2011; Whittle et al. 2011). Allied to interpretive perspectives aimed at providing as complex a view of the past as possible (Whittle 2003), the development and integration of a range of approaches such as environmental archaeology (archaeobotanical and zooarchaeological), isotopic analysis (data on diet and mobility) and lipid analysis (function of pottery) and their application to

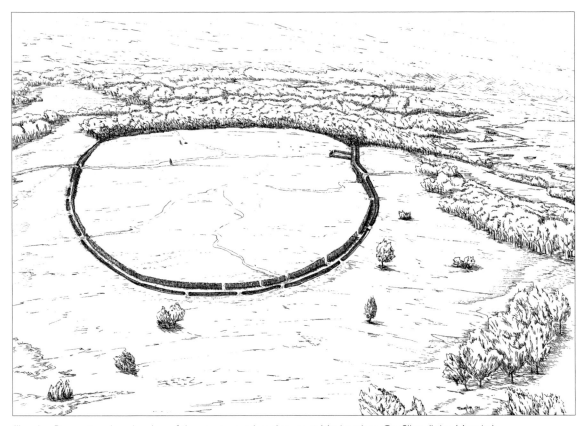

Illus. 1—Reconstruction drawing of the causewayed enclosure at Magheraboy, Co. Sligo (John Murphy).

archaeological datasets is enabling us to talk about the character of human life and activities in a way that was just not possible previously. So it is timely to examine the impact of archaeology on NRA road schemes on our understanding of the period.

Taking a broad chronological view, the discoveries from the roads schemes have been made widely accessible in several forms, including monographs on individual road schemes, thematic monographs and the NRA Archaeological Sites Database. The approach taken in this paper is to situate the results of that work for the Neolithic period in a wider context, to identify key social developments and changes over time, and to highlight major issues of debate. The archaeological record has been enriched by the work of a number of research projects which have drawn on and brought to wider attention the importance of the evidence from developer-led excavations. These notably include the Cultivating Societies project by Whitehouse and colleagues (e.g. Whitehouse et al. 2014; McClatchie, Bogaard et al. 2014; 2016; McLaughlin et al. 2016), which is a multi-disciplinary study assessing the evidence for agriculture in Neolithic Ireland from 375 excavated sites and its wider social implications. Similarly, the work of Smyth (e.g. 2012; 2014), mentioned above, has focused on the wealth of evidence for settlement and houses from over 270 sites throughout the Irish Neolithic. In addition, the publication of excavations at key Neolithic sites such as the causewayed enclosure of Donegore Hill, Co. Antrim (Mallory et al. 2011), and the portal tomb at Poulnabrone, Co. Clare (A Lynch 2014), provides another important source of data to inform discussion.

The chronological categories used by the Cultivating Societies project are employed here to provide a framework (Table 1), while key sites are used as foci to highlight the important implications of the Neolithic evidence from motorway routes. The emphasis of the discussion below is to consider the archaeological record as resulting from the activities of people who could have utilised a range of places or structures and worked materials at a range of scales, from implements held in the hand to the monumental, to create the distinctive and challenging character of the Irish Neolithic (see Smyth 2014, 150), and to see the material world of this period as an entangled ensemble which people created through their myriad and linked interactions with things and their surroundings (Hodder 2012; Lemonnier 2012).

Table 1—Chronological categories.

Period	Date range
Early Neolithic I	4000–3750 BC
Early Neolithic II	3750–3600 BC
Middle Neolithic I	3600–3400 BC
Middle Neolithic II	3400–3100 BC
Late Neolithic	3100–2500 BC
Chalcolithic (Copper Age)	2500–2200 BC

Uncertain beginnings (Early Neolithic I)

While the beginnings of the Neolithic have generally been set around 4000 BC, the number of sites from this period that can be securely dated to before 3750 BC is in reality very small. As will be discussed, there is currently insufficient evidence available to incontrovertibly support Early Neolithic beginnings before 3800 BC.

In recent years a site that has become prominent in the discussion of the earliest evidence for the Neolithic is the causewayed enclosure at Magheraboy, Co. Sligo, which produced controversially early radiocarbon dates (Danaher 2007) (Illus. 1). Located about 50 m above sea level off the summit of a ridge, excavation of over 1 ha of the eastern portion of the site within the road corridor of the N4 Sligo Inner Relief Road revealed an enclosure of irregular shape with a maximum dimension of 150 m and an estimated total area of 2.02 ha. A single segmented ditch circuit was generally accompanied by an internal palisade. There was a possible entrance on the southern side. Adjacent to this, a 14-m-long rectangular timber structure was built at right angles to and continuous with the palisade on its inner side. Fifty-five pits were identified in the interior of the enclosure. The material from the ditches, palisade and pits—at least some of which was carefully deposited—included Carinated Bowl pottery, leaf-shaped arrowheads, scrapers and blades and a couple of polished stone axeheads. These are all highly characteristic of Early Neolithic sites dating from the period 3750–3600 BC (see Early Neolithic II below). Radiocarbon dates from carefully selected charcoal samples suggested, however, a construction date of 4065–3945 BC for the site (Cooney et al. 2011, 584). Whitehouse et al. (2014, 187) provide two additional dates on short-lived material (a cereal grain and a hazelnut) which would place the use and possibly also the construction of the site to the period after 3750 BC.

Unsurprisingly, much of the discussion about this site has focused on its dating (e.g. Cooney et al. 2011; Whitehouse et al. 2014). In Ireland, the most closely comparable site is the other known causewayed enclosure at Donegore Hill, whose construction has been dated imprecisely to sometime between 3855 and 3665 BC (Mallory et al. 2011; Cooney et al. 2011, 584). More broadly, both Donegore Hill and Magheraboy can be situated within the tradition of causewayed enclosures, which are a central feature of the Neolithic of southern Britain. The Gathering Time project—a major dating programme on the Early Neolithic of Britain—has shown that the construction of those causewayed enclosures largely dates from just before 3700–3500 BC. The radiocarbon dates from Donegore are broadly compatible with the time when these enclosures first appeared in Britain, but those from Magheraboy are significantly earlier (Bayliss et al. 2011).

This created a key dilemma for Neolithic studies. Arising from Gathering Time, Whittle et al. (2011, 863–4) proposed that the Neolithic first appeared in south-east England by 4000 BC, before spreading across the rest of Britain and Ireland through the acculturation of local people, as well as small-scale colonisation over the next 200 years. Assessing the range of Irish evidence as part of this project, Cooney et al. (2011, 663) modelled the start of the Neolithic as being either between 3815 and 3769 BC (Model 3) or between 3750 and 3680 BC (Model 2).[1] Clearly, then, if the early date of Magheraboy is correct, it has major implications for our understanding of how and when the Neolithic began, not just in Ireland but also across Britain.

The initial dates from Magheraboy remain incompletely explained and at odds with existing knowledge of the period because they remain one or two centuries earlier than any other unequivocal evidence for the Neolithic. Whitehouse et al. (2014) point out that the situation at Magheraboy whereby pre-3750 BC dates were obtained from charcoal samples which potentially suffer from 'old wood' effects but post-3750 BC dates were obtained from short-life samples from the same features is an issue at several other of the earliest Neolithic sites (McLaughlin et al. 2016, 141).

If the early dates and material culture are accepted as genuine indicators that farming communities had constructed a causewayed enclosure there during the 40th and 39th centuries BC, then it becomes necessary to explain why an assemblage of characteristically Early Neolithic objects including a porcellanite axe from Antrim was deposited in Sligo 200 years before anywhere else on this island (see below and Cooney et al. 2011, 665–8). Equally, this scenario also demands

---

[1] Model 1 was rejected outright.

that we explain how a contemporary Neolithic presence remains so unidentifiable elsewhere on this island. Such explanations are difficult to support and it remains the case that the activities and materials present at Magheraboy accord much better with a date of 3750–3600 BC.

Much more robust evidence for Early Neolithic beginnings before 3750 BC is provided by the recent dating of the unburnt human remains from the portal tomb of Poulnabrone (A Lynch 2014; Schulting 2014). Modelling of these dates suggests that this monument was in use from 3820 to 3745 BC, with burial activity continuing over the next 200–300 years (Schulting 2014). This is based on the convincing argument that these human remains represent successive primary inhumations (Beckett 2014; O'Donnabhain & Tesorieri 2014). This tells us that people on the Burren had built a megalithic monument and were placing selected individuals in it from the end of the 39th century BC. Interestingly, the isotopic evidence from the earliest dated individuals at Poulnabrone suggests that these people lived locally and relied on a wholly terrestrial diet based on plant foods, with limited consumption of animal protein. While this is directly comparable to other Neolithic human assemblages (Ditchfield 2014; Schulting, Murphy et al. 2012), it is significant to note that it is not distinctively different from that for some later Mesolithic people (Warren 2015a, 5–8; Woodman 2015).

So, apart from Poulnabrone, there is currently little clear-cut evidence for a Neolithic presence on this island dating from 4000–3800 BC. Significantly, there is also a paucity of obviously Late Mesolithic sites from these two centuries. It remains the case that after the boom in excavation during the 1990s/2000s we still have few definitive archaeological traces for interactions between farming groups and indigenous inhabitants on this island other than the early domestic cattle bones from Ferriter's Cove, Co. Kerry, and possibly also at Kilgreany Cave, Co. Waterford (Woodman et al. 1999; Meiklejohn & Woodman 2012; Woodman 2015, 330–2). Clearly, our ability to identify and interpret archaeological evidence from the early fourth millennium BC (and probably also the very late fifth millennium BC) is quite limited, and consequently there is a considerable gap in our understanding about what was happening across these centuries.

Pursuing this vein of thought, it should be noted that there is evidence for continuity of place and practice from the Mesolithic into the Neolithic. For example, at Clowanstown, Co. Meath, excavations in a wetland area on the route of the M3 revealed a long sequence of activity from the Later Mesolithic into the Early Neolithic (Mossop & Mossop 2009). Basket fish-traps of late sixth/early fifth-millennium BC date were followed by Late Mesolithic platforms dating from 4250–4000 BC. At least 200 years later, low mounds with alternating layers of burnt stone, charcoal-rich soil and white clay were constructed (Murphy & Ginn 2013; Warren & Kador 2013). These produced sherds from Early Neolithic Carinated Bowls, burnt and unburnt animal bone and charred cereals dating from 3800–3700 BC (Whitehouse et al. 2014). The Clowanstown mounds are closely paralleled at Cherryville (7), Co. Kildare (Breen 2009), excavated on the route of the Kildare town bypass. There are hints, then, of a sense of continuity; while the process of Neolithicisation in Ireland is likely to have been the result of the input of both new people and new ideas, there was also interaction with people who had a long history of knowledge and inhabitation of the island.

The house horizon (Early Neolithic II)

In contrast to the limited evidence for the earliest Neolithic, the impact of newly established ways of life, traditions of practice and use of novel resources including settlement, monument-building and farming are most evident in the period 3750–3600 BC. McClatchie, Bogaard et al. (2014; 2016) have demonstrated that the earliest known evidence for cereals dates from the period following 3750 BC. This is widespread and dominated by emmer wheat, but a number of other species also occur. Critically, it appears that, as in other parts of north-west Europe (Bogaard 2004; Bogaard & Jones 2007), early farmers in Ireland were not shifting cultivators but practised longer-term fixed-plot agriculture. This was complemented by the use of domesticates—cattle, sheep/goat and pig—whose remains dominate the limited available evidence for the Early Neolithic faunal record (F McCormick 2007; Schulting 2013). Alongside these introduced resources, which probably included red deer (Carden et al. 2012; Bergh & Hensey 2013), a range of other wild mammals and gathered plant foods, including hazelnuts and fruits, were also used (F McCormick 2007; McClatchie, Bogaard et al. 2014). Smyth and Evershed (2015a; 2015b) have established, using organic residue analysis of Carinated Bowls, that the consumption of milk and dairying was practised, as was the use of pottery for the processing of meat products from the 38th century BC onwards. A model of a subsistence system focused on a mix of domesticated plant and animal products seems appropriate. As McClatchie, Bogaard et al. (2014, 214) point out, it is probable that the range of activities associated with this lifestyle must have created a specific sense of place and 'ownership' associated, for example, with fixed cereal plots and herds of animals, especially cattle. The creation of a sense of place would have been amplified by the transformation of the landscape, opening the woodland cover for agricultural clearances and other activities (Whitehouse et al. 2014, 185–90).

The most dramatic illustration of this sense of place, which has largely been brought to our attention through development-led archaeology since the 1990s, is the Early Neolithic rectangular house tradition. There are now over 100 of these timber-built structures known and their ongoing publication (e.g. McGonigle 2013) continues. A dating programme focused on these sites and critical analyses of their dates strongly indicate that these houses were only built and used over a period of up to 100 years from 3720 to 3620 BC (McSparron 2008; Cooney et al. 2011; Smyth 2014; Whitehouse et al. 2014). As Smyth (2014, 23) points out, the significance of these houses is that they represent a distinctive and novel settlement form and appear (and disappear) across the island at roughly the same time. The relatively substantial nature of these timber buildings makes analysis of their construction and use meaningful. Their striking homogeneity suggests that they represent a distinctive form of cultural and material engagement at a specific time in the early fourth millennium BC. They share features with, but are different in detail from, rectangular houses in Scotland (Sheridan 2013). They provide an important focus for an examination of the Early Neolithic. A key issue is how these houses fit with the other evidence of Early Neolithic activity.

A good place to understand the importance of this house tradition is at Monanny 1, Co. Monaghan. Here a cluster of these houses (single houses also occur) was discovered on the route

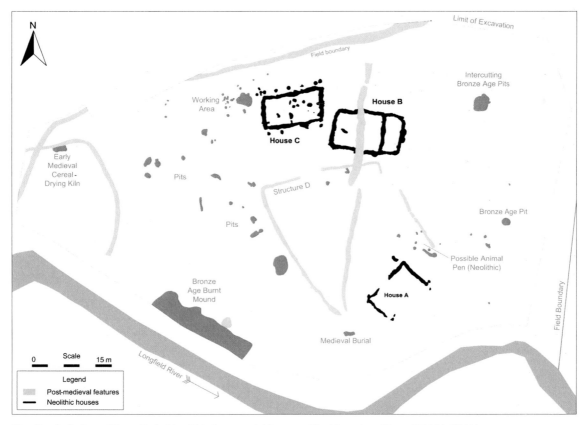

Illus. 2—A cluster of three Early Neolithic houses at Monanny, Co. Monaghan (from F Walsh 2011).

of the N2 Carrickmacross Bypass (F Walsh 2006; 2009; Smyth 2014) (Illus. 2). The site was located at the base of the south-facing slope of a drumlin, with a small river to the south. Three Neolithic structures were uncovered, all defined by foundation trenches, associated with a number of pits and gullies. House A measured 10 m by 7 m, with post-holes in key structural positions. About 20 m to the north, Houses B and C were located close to each other. House B was 13.5 m by 8 m and divided into two rooms, with post-holes again in key positions. House C measured 12 m by 7 m and had evidence of additional external supporting posts. The internal features suggest that this house may have been divided into two equal-sized rooms. The walls of all three structures appear to have been constructed of oak planks, the roof was supported by the corner posts and there was evidence for an entrance area in each case.

The location of Monanny represents a typical choice for such settlements, and Smyth (2014, 22–5), following up on earlier discussion by Cooney (2000) and Ó Drisceoil (2007a), suggests that the pattern seen at Monanny may represent a fixed or ideal unit of settlement or household size in the Early Neolithic. The range of objects—dominated by Carinated Bowl sherds and lithic tools—recovered from the houses and the exterior features gives indications of activities carried out in different areas. This pottery was among the assemblage examined by Smyth and Evershed

(2015a; 2015b) for organic residue analysis, producing evidence for dairying and also for the consumption of meat products. The construction of House B appears to have been celebrated by the deposition of a stone axehead in the foundation trench (F Walsh 2009, 63; Smyth 2014, fig. 4.5). At the end of their use, Houses A and B appear to have been dismantled and the posts and planks removed. The end of the use-life of House C was marked by the structure being completely burnt down.

What we see at settlements such as Monanny is a widely shared practice of life that, as documented by Smyth (2014), was conducted in a particular way by the people who lived there. Moving out from the detail of a particular site, we can begin to think more broadly about Early Neolithic lifestyles, including the ways in which the dead were treated. Schulting, Murphy et al. (2012) have demonstrated that the date range of 3700–3570 BC is currently the most probable time-frame for the initial use of court tombs. The similarity of this date to that of the house horizon is notable. While recognising that there were other ways of treating the selected remains of particular individuals in the Early Neolithic (Sheridan 2006), it still strengthens the evidence for the arguments that these rectilinear timber and stone structures can be seen respectively as Early Neolithic houses for the living and the dead (Cooney 2000).

The debate continues about the exact beginnings of the passage tomb tradition (Whittle et al. 2011, 848–53; Sheridan 2010; Bergh & Hensey 2013; Hensey 2015), but there is agreement that the intensive period of activity that included the construction of developed passage tombs at Brú na Bóinne, Co. Meath, and other cemetery complexes, such as Carrowkeel, Co. Sligo, peaked in the centuries between 3300 and 3000 BC (Whittle et al. 2011; Bayliss & O'Sullivan 2013; Hensey et al. 2013; Kador et al. 2015; Schulting, Bronk Ramsey et al., forthcoming). This is a point which warrants further discussion and to which we will later return. There is also agreement that simple passage tombs were definitely in use at the same time as the earliest use of court tombs and Early Neolithic houses. Bergh and Hensey's (2013) dating of 25 bone and antler pins from two of the simple passage tombs within the Carrowmore tomb complex in County Sligo indicates that deposition within these monuments was occurring from 3775 to 2950 BC. In light of this and their critical evaluation of the problematically early charcoal dates obtained by Burenhult (1984; 2001), there is now no evidence that megaliths had been built at Carrowmore before c. 3750 BC. Similarly, recent dates from the multi-phase passage tomb at Baltinglass, Co. Wicklow, also indicate that it was in use from c. 3700/3600 to 3400 BC (Schulting, McClatchie et al. 2017). An earlier date of 3946–3715 BC (UBA-14759; 5031 ± 25 BP) was also obtained from cremated human bone within the first phase of this monument, comprising a small, simple passage tomb. While hinting at the possibility that a Neolithic monument existed at Baltinglass before 3750 BC, this evidence is not sufficiently robust to be considered alongside that from Poulnabrone. What is clear is that by 3750 BC people had developed a highly structured social landscape involving the use of court tombs, portal tombs and passage tombs, very tangible traces of which are still visible today.

For those living within these landscapes, we should also envisage lives and practices that focused on intensive garden agriculture and the herding of domesticated animals, particularly cattle (Schulting 2013). The description by Whitehouse et al. (2014, 199) of a 'spatially heterogeneous landscape of varying intensity and use depending upon local circumstances and population densities' matches with the archaeological evidence from development-led projects leading to the discovery of a wide range of settlement evidence. Pits represent a particularly frequently occurring example of this. As we have seen above, these occur with structures, but also on their own or associated with ephemeral traces of settlement activity. They take the form of either clusters or single features, and their fills and contents suggest a range of roles (see below and Smyth 2012; 2014, 114).

Cultural material in pits and other Early Neolithic features provides the opportunity to show how Early Neolithic people created their material surroundings both by using local resources and by accessing materials, in some cases over considerable distances, through networks of contact and exchange. Here one might suggest that there appears to be an interesting contrast between pottery and lithics, the two materials that dominate the archaeological record. Pottery of this period took the form of Carinated Bowls, the earliest form of which is Sheridan's (1995; 2007a) Traditional Carinated Bowls. These are commonly found in court tombs and Early Neolithic houses and there is no unequivocal evidence that their use pre-dates 3750 BC. This pottery would appear to be made locally (Sheridan 1989), as perhaps occurred at Monanny (F Walsh 2009), but with techniques and forms that were widely shared across, but also far beyond, this island (Grogan & Roche 2010a; Pioffet 2014).

In relation to lithics there is a considerable variety between sites in terms of both the quantity of lithics present and the balance between finished tools and debitage (production waste). Although this may reflect variations in depositional practices, it is likely, in at least some cases, to reflect the primary working of flint and other stone resources off site, close to primary or secondary sources (see Smyth 2014, 106–7; Brady 2007). Stone axes are a good example of the potential complex web of resource use and networks of contact that underpinned Early Neolithic life in Ireland. We can document the use of widely available sources such as shale and the use of specific sources in Ireland such as porcellanite and porphyry (porphyritic andesite) as early as the 38th and 37th centuries BC, as well as noting the more limited occurrence of axeheads from non-Irish sources, particularly tuff axeheads from Great Langdale in Cumbria, western Britain (Cooney & Mandal 1998; Cooney 2000; Whittle et al. 2011; Dempsey 2013).

We can also use the contexts in which cultural materials such as pottery or lithics are found to indicate that they were in many cases placed deliberately in the ground, alongside a more casual pattern of disposal. For example, at Carrickmines Great, at the foot of the Dublin Mountains, an isolated circular pit contained nine perforated serpentine disc-beads and approximately half a Carinated Bowl (Ó Drisceoil 2006) (Illus. 3). At Newrath 35, Co. Kilkenny, on the route of the N25 Waterford City Bypass, a stone axehead was deposited in the centre of the upper fill of a small circular pit, and there were lithics and Carinated Bowl sherds in the lower fill (Hughes et al. 2011). It was argued that the artefacts had been selected for careful, structured deposition. A date of 3695–3523 BC was obtained from a charred emmer wheat grain in the pit.

Our understanding of the 150 years covered in this section has been transformed by development-led archaeology. Various elements of the lifestyle of Early Neolithic communities can

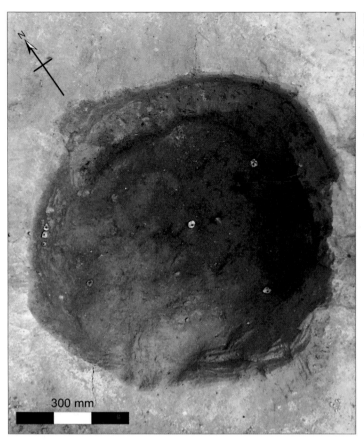

Illus. 3—The isolated circular pit at Carrickmines Great, Co. Dublin, with perforated serpentine disc-beads *in situ* (Cóilín Ó Drisceoil).

now be documented in great detail, and there is potential for our understanding of this critical time to be deepened by research. The narrative above suggests a settlement pattern comprising small-scale dispersed social units who were in contact with each other in various ways, not least through larger-scale social gatherings and activities at places like the causewayed enclosure at Donegore Hill (Mallory et al. 2011). Together with the uniformity of Early Neolithic material culture, sites like Donegore Hill hint at a level of social cohesion beyond people's immediate community.

Understanding Neolithicisation

This intensification and spread of the evidence for Neolithic activity c. 3750–3600 BC can be paralleled in Britain (Whittle et al. 2011) and it has been argued to reflect a similar boom in activity relating to the success of farming (Stevens & Fuller 2012; Whitehouse et al. 2014). This stands in strong contrast to the somewhat limited evidence for the earliest Neolithic, which equally has the potential to throw light on the processes responsible for this major social transformation, particularly in terms of when and how Neolithic things and practices began here. Thus far, there is no incontrovertible evidence for an Irish Neolithic before 3800 BC, and our knowledge of what was happening between 4000 and 3800 BC remains poor. So we are left to evaluate the two aforementioned models for the inception of the Neolithic during the earliest Neolithic period (3815–3769 BC: Model 3) or the house horizon (3750–3680 BC: Model 2) (Cooney et al. 2011, 663).

Compatible with Model 3 is the robust dating of Poulnabrone, indicating that the Neolithic (at least in the Burren) began c. 3800 BC, before the house horizon, thereby invalidating Model 2. Ann Lynch (2014) has argued with some degree of circularity that the evidence from Poulnabrone and Magheraboy appears to make the scenario of a gradual spread of the Neolithic from south-east England less likely. This argument does not, however, explain away the issues with the early dates for the Magheraboy causewayed enclosure outlined above and is reliant on the assumption that Neolithic people, domestic animals and crops must have been in the Burren for up to a century before Poulnabrone was constructed. Although the earliest dated individuals from this tomb (which undoubtedly represents a Neolithic monument) spent their early lives in the Burren and had a wholly terrestrial diet based on plant foods with only limited consumption of animal protein, it cannot be assumed that these were the descendants of Neolithic farmers. Indeed, recent work has shown that Mesolithic individuals from inland contexts also had a terrestrial diet (Warren 2015a, 5–8; Meiklejohn & Woodman 2012) and, while Poulnabrone is just 8 km from the coast, it need not be presumed that Later Mesolithic individuals (in this locale) would have had a marine-based diet. Of course, there is no trace of Later Mesolithic activity (apart from the Fanore More shell midden; see M Lynch 2013) in the surrounding area, but neither is there any evidence for Neolithic activity before 3800 BC. Furthermore, there is no other incontrovertible evidence for contemporary Neolithic activity on this island. There are other sites that have produced radiocarbon dates with estimated age ranges beginning before 3750 BC (see Schulting 2014; Schulting, McClatchie et al. 2017; Meiklejohn & Woodman 2012; Sheridan 2014), but because of the uncertainties associated with the calibration of radiocarbon ages these may not genuinely reflect Neolithic activity before the Early Neolithic house horizon and the earliest dating of crops.

Despite all this uncertainty about when or how the Neolithic began, what we can say is that the Neolithic (in some form or other) had begun in Ireland by the late 39th century BC. Poulnabrone provides us with evidence for monument use and construction before the earliest known appearance in the archaeological record of cereal cultivation, the rearing of domesticates, axe quarries, large-scale woodland clearance, the deposition of Early Neolithic Carinated Bowls, and the use of Early Neolithic houses and court tombs during the 38th century. This indicates that the various different ideas, things and farming technology which might be considered to form a Neolithic package may not all have been part of the earliest Neolithic on this island nor adopted in/introduced into Ireland at the same time. Some elements appeared earlier, potentially with various aspects appearing in different parts of Ireland c. 3800 BC before a surge in adoption and a high level of convergence across the island 50 years later. This raises the question of what exactly this earliest 'Poulnabrone Neolithic' or Mesolithic–Neolithic transition looked like and how we can recognise it within the archaeological record. This must be a priority for future research.

While the discussion revolves around a difference of only 50 years, this has important implications. It suggests that the Neolithic began gradually, not with an abrupt or sudden change, and that, contra Whittle et al. (2011), monument-building was early in this process, not a slightly later element conducted by the descendants of the first farming communities after the adoption/introduction of pottery, cereals and new domesticated animals. These novel things, practices and ideas that began to be used in Ireland c. 3800–3700 BC all arrived in Ireland by boats travelling between here and Britain and/or continental Europe. Debate continues as to how these came to be used in Ireland or Britain and from exactly where (e.g. Sheridan 2004a; 2010; Rowley-Conwy 2004; Garrow & Sturt 2011; Thomas 2013; Pioffet 2014). Clearly, there was a very significant series of changes in social practice during this transition, many of which left a far more visible imprint on the archaeological record than the Mesolithic traditions that they replaced. This must be partly due to the influence of the incoming farmers who almost certainly arrived here (probably from France or Britain), but the nature of the Irish Early Neolithic suggests that the pre-existing population of Ireland played a key role in the adoption of Neolithic lifeways from beyond these shores and in their transmission across the island. This is supported by recent aDNA (ancient DNA) analysis of a Neolithic individual from Ballynahatty, Co. Down, dating from the end of the fourth millennium BC, which revealed a combination of genes commonly seen in Early and Middle Neolithic Germany and France associated with migrating Near Eastern agriculturists, as well as an elevated 'western hunter-gatherer' component compared to other European regions (Cassidy et al. 2016, 369). This suggests interactions between earlier Neolithic and Mesolithic populations, though, given that this is based on just one individual who may or may not have resided on this island for any considerable length of time, we must be careful not to make too much of these data.

Nevertheless, both the Irish and the British Early Neolithic evidence shows significant similarities to the Continental comparanda, as well as key differences (e.g. Hensey 2015, 7–9, 24–6). This suggests that there has been a certain level of adaptation from the very beginning, presumably to enable these novelties to fit better within pre-existing traditions. It is also worth highlighting that the particular range of Early Neolithic practices and material culture found in Ireland cannot be traced back to any single region in Britain or the Continent (see Thomas 2004; Pioffet 2014; Anderson-Whymark & Garrow 2015). Whatever was happening at this time was complex in a way that defies simplistic explanations, but would almost certainly have involved repeated interactions between Neolithic and Mesolithic people at multiple locations within and beyond this island (Anderson-Whymark et al. 2015). There is increasing recognition that a network of coastal and maritime contacts is likely to have underpinned contact between areas of Ireland, Britain and north-west Europe in the late Mesolithic and early Neolithic (ibid.; Garrow & Sturt 2011; Warren 2015b). This is supported by the evidence for the bones of a domesticated cow from Ferriter's Cove dating from before 4000 BC (Woodman et al. 1999; Tresset 2003) and from Kilgreany Cave pre-dating 3820 BC (Meiklejohn & Woodman 2012), which provide a tantalising glimpse of early interactions. Pioffet (2014), on the basis of a stylistic and technological analysis of Irish and British pottery, has argued that there were distinct pathways of contact that differentiate an eastern and a western zone of Early Neolithic interactions. The western zone (comprising western Britain and probably also Ireland) seems to have had strong links with Brittany and Lower Normandy c. 3800 BC. This makes the concept of a number of ongoing points of contact between France and Ireland or Britain and stages of Neolithicisation, as proposed by Sheridan (e.g. 2010), more likely, though robust evidence to indicate that many of these occurred in Ireland before 3800 BC is largely lacking.

The Middle Neolithic conundrum

While development-led archaeology has clearly transformed our understanding of the Early Neolithic, its impact on our established or traditional understanding of the Middle Neolithic is much harder to gauge. Whitehouse et al. (2014) in their major review of Neolithic agriculture suggested that the end of the Early Neolithic (Early Neolithic II) and the first phase of the Middle Neolithic (Middle Neolithic I, 3600–3400 BC) saw major changes in the environmental and archaeological records and that these changes continued into the second phase of the Middle Neolithic (Middle Neolithic II, 3400–3100 BC). They commented that 'the period c. 3600–3000 BC was one of considerable environmental, landscape, settlement and economic change' (ibid., 200). Thus, in reviewing our current understanding of the Middle Neolithic, it seems appropriate to consider this phase of the Irish Neolithic as a unit (Middle Neolithic I and II).

The process that Whitehouse et al. see behind these major changes is a 'boom', brought about by the establishment of farming in the early Neolithic, followed by a 'bust', with associated population decrease. This is based on the decreasing evidence for Middle Neolithic settlement activity from development-led archaeological projects and specifically sites where cereals were recorded, leading them to conclude that 'there is a marked lull in settlement activity . . . from around 3400 BC to just after 3000 BC when the archaeological record is almost completely dominated by burials of the developed passage tomb tradition' (ibid., 193, fig. 12). Combining these particular aspects of the archaeological record, including the decreased evidence for cereal production, with that for re-afforestation, worsening climatic conditions and the wider north-west European picture of changes at this time, they suggest that in Ireland communities had to adjust their agricultural practices and lifestyle in the light of climatic uncertainties and potential difficulties in crop production (McLaughlin et al. 2016, 144; Whitehouse et al. 2014, 190, 199, figs 12 and 20). On an initial reading, Smyth's (2014, 81) view of the settlement evidence might seem equally stark, indicating that the nature of settlement and domestic architecture is difficult to identify and interpret after 3500 BC.

So we are left with a conundrum: in grappling with the context for the emergence of the developed Irish passage tomb tradition of the Middle Neolithic, while recognising the diversity of interpretive stances on this issue (see discussion in Cooney 2000, 112–19; Hensey 2015), it seems difficult to reconcile the scale of, for example, the three mega-passage tombs in Brú na Bóinne, the clustering of passage tombs in major complexes and the complexity of the architecture and practices at the sites with a picture of settlement decrease (and associated population decline) at this time. It is hard to square this evidence with the 'boom and bust' model. To take one example, the small passage tomb at Tara, Co. Meath, dating from the period c. 3300–3000 BC (Bayliss & O'Sullivan 2013), produced the remains of over 200 people (Kuijt & Quinn 2013), and there are strong indications that this represents the particular treatment of selected individuals over several generations rather than all the members of the living population who were connected with the construction and use of the tomb. So can we resolve this conundrum? In the context of the discussion here, the approach taken is to review the additional archaeological evidence that has emerged from development-led archaeology over the last decade or so, to compare that with other evidence for activity in Ireland during the Middle Neolithic and then to return to this intriguing issue.

In summary, the number of dated Middle Neolithic sites that have produced evidence for cereal production is over 50% less than for the Early Neolithic (McClatchie, Bogaard et al. 2014, table 2), and the range of wheat and barley types appears to be more restricted, with naked and emmer wheat the most common forms (McClatchie, Bogaard et al. 2016, fig. 7). In particular, very few cereals have been found at sites dating from 3400–3100 BC. McClatchie, Bogaard et al. (2016) and McLaughlin et al. (2016) present more nuanced interpretations of the 'boom and bust' scenario. They relate this (to varying degrees) to changes in the practices of people in the past and the activities of archaeologists in the present, thereby recognising the high level of bias created in the archaeological record by the nature of the archaeological features recovered in development-led contexts and the approaches taken to these. There remains the question, however, of whether these factors are being fully considered in terms of understanding the notion of a Middle Neolithic gap.

The paucity of faunal assemblages continues to be a problem in assessing the extent and significance of this component of agricultural activity, but an important site in this context is the enclosure at Kilshane, Co. Meath, found on the route of the N2 road. The enclosure is defined by a ditch measuring 45 m by 34 m which had been dug in a series of segments. In the base of the ditch were the articulated and disarticulated remains of a minimum of 58 cattle (Illus. 4). These deposits varied in different segments, and the patterning suggested that they had been placed from both the exterior and the interior of the enclosure. A Middle Neolithic broad-rimmed vessel deliberately placed on top of the bone was associated with a radiocarbon date of 3645–3390 BC (Moore 2007; Finola O'Carroll, pers. comm.). The deliberate placement of the cattle bone might be read as indicating an increase in the economic importance of cattle compared to the Early Neolithic and, linked to this, an enhancement of the symbolic role of cattle. Along with the increase in some wild resources seen in the archaeobotanical record (Whitehouse et al. 2014) and the decrease in cereals, this could be seen as representing a shift in the subsistence strategy, but this remains somewhat unclear (McClatchie, Bogaard et al. 2016, 315).

The evidence for settlement also changes. As Smyth (2014, 83) and Whitehouse et al. (2014, 199) note, a significant amount of settlement activity is represented by pits, post-holes, spreads of occupation material, occasional hearths and areas of burning, though McLaughlin et al. (2016, 128,

Illus. 4—An elevated view of the enclosure at Kilshane, Co. Meath (top), and the articulated and disarticulated remains of cattle from the base of the ditch (Hawkeye).

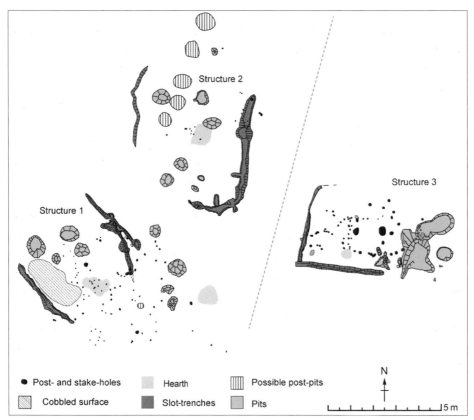

Illus. 5—Pits, stake-holes, hearths and Middle Neolithic rectangular houses were uncovered under deposits of occupational debris in an area partially enclosed by a palisade at Tullahedy, Co. Tipperary (left: after Cleary & Kelleher 2011 and Smyth 2014; bottom: from Sternke 2010).

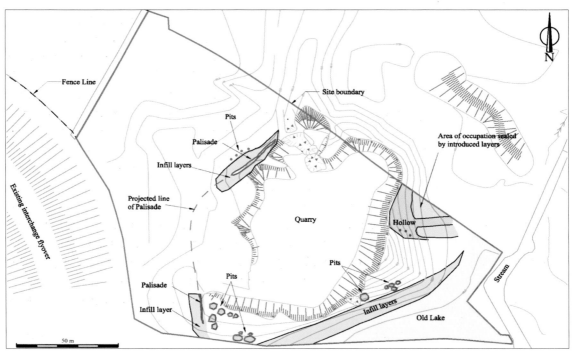

136) observe that this becomes scarcer c. 3300 BC. In trying to make sense of the more ephemeral evidence for houses, Smyth suggests two trends: (1) the continuity of broadly rectangular houses into the earlier Middle Neolithic (3640–3400 BC) represents a move away from the rigidity of the Early Neolithic tradition towards more varied forms; and (2) the buildings of the later part of the Middle Neolithic (3400–3000 BC) seem to have been stake-built and oval or circular in shape. They appear to have been rebuilt on occasions, with the central hearth as a focus (Smyth 2014, 80–1, 83). The best example of the earlier Middle Neolithic style of rectangular house comes from the enclosed settlement at Tullahedy, Co. Tipperary, on the route of the M7 (Cleary & Kelleher 2011), which dates from the cusp of the end of the Early Neolithic and the beginning of the Middle Neolithic (Schulting 2011). Here (Illus. 5), within an area at least 100 m by 120 m in extent and partly enclosed by a palisade, there was intensive activity indicated by pits, stake-holes and hearths, with three structures defined by irregular slot-trenches and post-holes. After use, the houses appear to have been deliberately covered with occupation material rich in artefacts, and at the southern end this spread was in turn covered by redeposited glacial till. Tellingly, only one of the sites discussed by Smyth in the oval or circular group of Middle Neolithic houses comes from a development-led archaeological context, and that is a curving trench with sherds from two Middle Neolithic Impressed Ware broad-rimmed vessels at Newrath 35, Co. Kilkenny, a site mentioned above. The excavators, however, describe this as a ring-ditch (compare Hughes et al. 2011, 131, and Smyth 2014, 81).

The real issue that must be confronted is that the traces of settlement and subsistence have to be considered within the broader context of a wider diversity of evidence for activity in the Middle Neolithic period. For example, in reviewing the evidence for the treatment of the dead in this period, the point is made that mortuary practice becomes increasingly varied (Cooney 2014). As Schulting, Murphy et al. (2012) note, at least some portal and court tombs continued in use. Passage tombs continued to be built and used into the Middle Neolithic, reaching a peak with the construction of developed passage tombs around 3000 BC (Whittle et al. 2011; Bayliss & O'Sullivan 2013; Kador et al. 2015; Hensey et al. 2013; Schulting, Bronk Ramsey et al., forthcoming). Linkardstown burials—a monument type with affinities to passage tombs occurring mainly in the central southern area of Ireland—appear to be communal memorials to leading individuals which were constructed and used from before 3600 to 3300 BC (Cooney et al. 2011, 637). There are also Middle Neolithic pits/graves, as at Martinstown, Co. Meath (Hartnett 1951), and Site C, Lough Gur, Co. Limerick (Ó Ríordáin 1954), linked to Linkardstown burials by the similar deposition of decorated bipartite bowls. Indeed, these bowls appear in other contexts, such as court and portal tombs (see Sheridan 1995; Cooney 2000), and also with the burials of male adults in the cave at Annagh, Co. Limerick (Ó Floinn 2011), thereby indicating a further link to the Linkardstown tradition. As Dowd (2008; 2015) has shown, the Annagh burials can be put into the wider context of the use of caves for mortuary practices during the period 3600–3400 BC.

All of this Middle Neolithic evidence for the treatment of the dead by the living is very pertinent to the discussion of the extent of activity in this phase of the Neolithic. In tandem, it also has to be acknowledged that because of the fragile nature of their archaeological signature most of our understanding of the character of Middle Neolithic settlements has come from research-led excavations, particularly of protected Middle Neolithic surfaces. The best examples of this are the 10 Middle Neolithic structures identified at the Knowth complex in County Meath (Eogan & Roche 1997, 51–2; Smyth 2014, 81–5), representing the places where at least some of the people who were building passage tombs lived for at least some of their time.

The reality is that the specific character of the archaeological record and the approaches taken to its dating and interpretation are also responsible for creating the perception of a Middle Neolithic gap. As recognised by McClatchie, Bogaard et al. (2016), the Early Neolithic houses provide a highly identifiable focus for detailed analysis and dating, for example in projects along road schemes, such as the M3 and the M1. In contrast, the probability is that there are more Middle Neolithic sites in the archive but fewer of them have been dated, hence we have fewer Middle Neolithic archaeobotanical remains. As we have seen above, these sites are less tangible and therefore harder to recognise, a characteristic that seems to strongly influence the extent to which they are selected for radiocarbon dating or other specialist analyses (see McLaughlin et al. 2016, 139). This is especially the case where they occur so characteristically on multi-period sites alongside more obvious features of 'higher potential'. When data with these fundamental problems (reflective of archaeological choices in the recent past and Neolithic choices in the distant past) are being used as the basis for an interpretation of major changes in Neolithic agriculture and for a population decrease, questions must be asked as to whether we have really advanced our knowledge of the Middle Neolithic. Are we in danger of engaging in a circular argument, pulling in as part of the rationale a suite of environmental changes when the 'chronological resolution of the material remains insufficiently well-resolved to address this issue' (Whitehouse et al. 2014, 200)?

So what was actually going on during the Middle Neolithic period? There was undoubtedly social change. The increased diversity of mortuary practice points to growing regionalisation of social patterns. This can be seen, for example, in the increasing 'style drift' and range of pottery (Sheridan 2010, 95–6) alongside the use of the same ceramic style, as with the decorated bipartite bowl, in a range of contexts. It is also indicated by the use of monuments that we separate in archaeological typologies, such as on the Burren, where a Linkardstown burial (Poulawack), a portal tomb (Poulnabrone) and a court tomb (Parknabinnia), all within a few kilometres of each other, were being used at the same time (A Lynch 2014). Farming communities were living in landscapes that had been inhabited and organised with agriculture as a focus for several hundred years. The detail and complexity of these patterns of change and continuity are best followed at the regional level, as Smyth (2014, chapter 7) demonstrates in the case of east Leinster. Here she suggests that social attention and symbolism moved from houses to other realms, such as the human body or the sacred space enclosed within the kerbs of passage tombs and other monuments during the mid-fourth millennium BC (ibid., 95). Zooming in on part of this region to consider the Neolithic and Bronze Age landscape in the Tara region, Grogan (2013, 336–9) suggests that we should see in the location of and activities at passage tombs an alliance of powerful communities that exerted social authority through the control of both local and regional networks of communication. This approach allied to Smyth's seems a productive way to approach the central question of the emergence of the developed passage tomb tradition in the later Middle Neolithic, as well as the extent and nature of associated settlement.

The Late Neolithic—going round in circles

For consistency, the chronological phasing utilised by Whitehouse et al. (2014) is used here (Table 1), even though 3100 BC was probably the most intense period of activity within the developed passage tomb tradition. While this division between the Middle and Late Neolithic phases seems rather arbitrary, it importantly highlights that the passage tomb tradition continued into the Late Neolithic, though the use of these monuments may have declined after 2900 BC compared to the peak of activity seen before then. In the Middle Neolithic, direct links between Ireland and northern and western Britain (especially between the Boyne Valley area and Orkney) intensified during the floruit of passage tomb use and culminated in a partial convergence of Irish and Orcadian passage tomb practices (Sheridan 2004a; 2014; Carlin, in press). This interaction saw the sustained incorporation of Orcadian material culture within the Irish passage tomb tradition into the early part of the Late Neolithic (Sheridan 2004b; 2014). This included Grooved Ware, a flat-bottomed pottery style decorated with passage tomb motifs which originated on the Orkney Islands c. 3200 BC (Brindley 1999; Roche 1995; Schulting, Sheridan et al. 2010; MacSween et al. 2015).

The larger size of some of these pots suggests that at least in some cases they may have been used in a wider social arena than the household. This ceramic is closely associated with the emergence of distinctive forms of social practice, material culture and monumental architecture which were widely adopted and adapted across Britain and Ireland into the first half of the third millennium BC. The characteristic Irish architectural component comprises subcircular timber-built structures with central four-post settings typified by the well-known examples initially uncovered through research-led excavations at Knowth (Eogan & Roche 1997, 220–1) and Ballynahatty, Co. Down (Hartwell 1998), which have been interpreted as ceremonial timber circles. It may also possibly include embanked earthen enclosures.

Here the focus is on outlining how our understanding of this period has been affected by the results of development-led archaeology, particularly those from road schemes. These excavations have significantly increased the quantity and distribution of Late Neolithic sites across the island, while also confirming the known concentration of this activity in the wider Boyne Valley area. Many of these sites have now been discovered in much more varied and complicated contexts outside of obviously ceremonial settings. As will be discussed, this makes their interpretation difficult. It is clear from the literature that our understanding has not advanced sufficiently to take account of these discoveries. In particular, the dating of various developments during this period is much poorer than that of the Early and Middle Neolithic phases. A key cause of this scenario is that the distinctiveness of the Late Neolithic was not recognised until the late 1990s and, significantly, its recognition has continued to be too narrowly based on Grooved Ware (e.g. Whitehouse et al. 2014, 201). Consequentially, insufficient attention has been paid to well-dated activity from this phase, such as the deposition of human remains in passage tombs (Schulting, Bronk Ramsey et al., forthcoming). Equally problematic is the challenge of trying to understand the connectedness of the domestic and ritual spheres in various practices and structures at this time (Carlin, in press).

It is primarily through the (retrospective) identification of Grooved Ware that many of the Late Neolithic features discovered during development-led excavations have been recognised as such. These represent a restricted set of contexts, mainly comprising pits, spreads and timber structures with central four-post settings, all containing very similar deposits of occupational debris. Closely comparable examples are known at Newgrange, Knowth and Ballynahatty. The presence of these related features at both monumental and non-monumental sites makes it difficult to distinguish a purely domestic or ritual component to these deposits. As we will see, there are few, if any, recognisable 'domestic' buildings associated with Grooved Ware, even though this ceramic was widely used as an everyday pottery throughout Ireland.

Grooved Ware has mostly been recovered from pits, either in isolation or clustered, which in many cases appear to have been specially created to receive cultural deposits and were filled in very soon after being dug. These vary from those containing a single sherd to others containing more 'formalised' or special deposits, including very large amounts of pottery as well as other deliberately selected or arranged artefacts, such as polished stone axeheads. For example, among a larger cluster of pits at Treanbaun, Co. Galway, on the M6, *petit tranchet*-derivative arrowheads were recovered from three different Late Neolithic pits, one of which also contained Grooved Ware (McKeon & O'Sullivan 2014). Pits containing very large quantities of Grooved Ware are known from various road schemes, including Rathmullan Sites 7 and 8, Co. Meath, Lowpark, Co. Mayo, and Scart, Co. Kilkenny (Bolger 2011a; Nelis 2011; Laidlaw 2009; Gillespie 2010). At the latter site, a single pit contained as many as 935 sherds from seven Grooved Ware vessels, and 193 lithics including 19 end-scrapers (Illus. 6). It is obvious from the partial and fragmentary condition of the pottery in this pit that after their original breakage these vessels had been previously curated in larger repositories such as middens (now represented in the archaeological record by spreads). This treatment is highly characteristic of much of the material found in Late Neolithic contexts across the country. While at least some of these pits are probably the only surviving element of longer-term occupations, it is often difficult to demonstrate conclusively that their contents stemmed directly from settlement in these places. Indeed, many of these features were created during formalised versions of everyday activities that made material statements deliberately emphasising 'domestic' aspects of life.

This leads us on to perhaps the most architecturally distinctive element of the Late Neolithic, namely the subcircular timber structures with central four-post settings which seem to have been built and used in accordance with a widely shared template. This included a central axis that divided these structures in half from their entrance through to the back posts directly opposite. As many as 20 of these have been found during development-led excavations across the island (Illus.

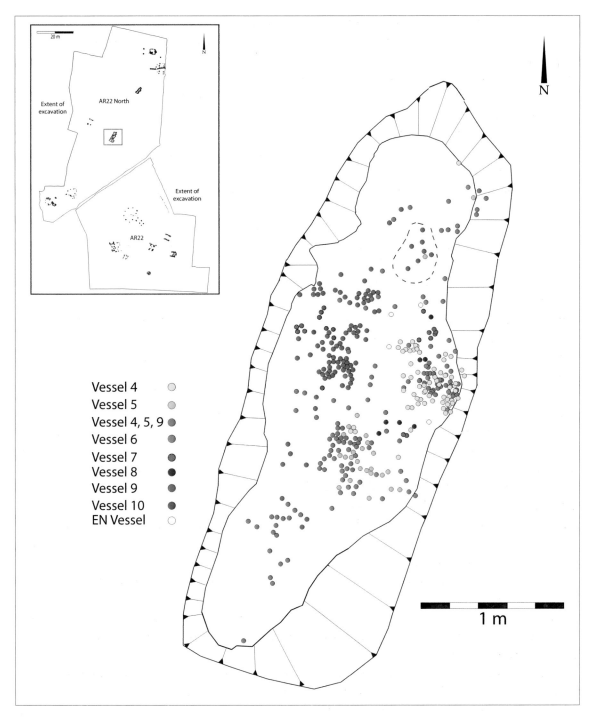

Vessel 4
Vessel 5
Vessel 4, 5, 9
Vessel 6
Vessel 7
Vessel 8
Vessel 9
Vessel 10
EN Vessel

Illus. 6—A pit containing as many as 935 sherds from seven Grooved Ware vessels and 193 lithics including 19 end-scrapers at Scart, Co. Kilkenny, which occurred on a site with extensive evidence for Late Neolithic activity, including the remains of at least four structures (after Laidlaw 2009).

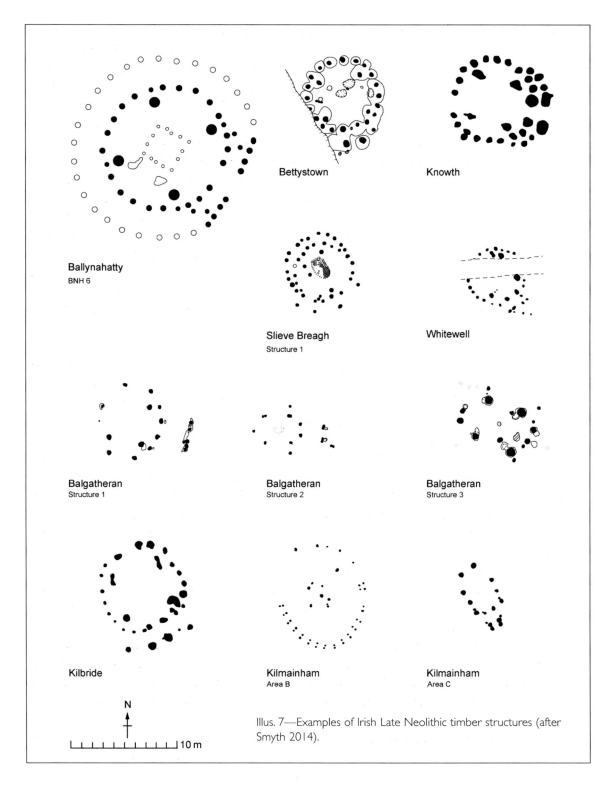

Ballynahatty
BNH 6

Bettystown

Knowth

Slieve Breagh
Structure 1

Whitewell

Balgatheran
Structure 1

Balgatheran
Structure 2

Balgatheran
Structure 3

Kilbride

Kilmainham
Area B

Kilmainham
Area C

N

10 m

Illus. 7—Examples of Irish Late Neolithic timber structures (after Smyth 2014).

7), with examples now known from Mayo, Cork, Carlow, Kildare, Kilkenny and Tyrone (Cotter 2006; Johnston & Carlin, forthcoming; Carlin, O'Connell et al. 2015; Laidlaw 2008; Monteith 2008; Dingwall 2010), though mostly they occur in the eastern half of the country, particularly in the Boyne Valley area. These occur at a range of scales, as has long been known from excavations in the vicinity of Newgrange (Sweetman 1985) and Knowth (Eogan and Roche 1997), but most of the recent discoveries occur at the smaller end of the scale (generally less than 7 m in diameter).

One such example of these highly uniform structures was excavated at Lagavoreen, Co. Meath, on the route of the M1 motorway, 7 km east of Knowth (Stafford 2012). It comprised a subcircular ring of post-holes that enclosed a central square setting of four larger post-holes symmetrically orientated with respect to a well-defined south-east-facing entrance. As is typical of these structures, finds were predominantly found within pit-like voids created in the upper part of the post-holes, post-dating their construction and primary use. At this site and elsewhere, this depositional activity mainly occurred during the dismantling of these structures, often after the timbers had rotted or been burnt as part of ritualised acts of abandonment or commemoration. This involved the deliberate placement of occupational debris, akin to that seen in pits. At Lagavoreen these deposits included sherds of Grooved Ware, large quantities of flint including debitage and scrapers, burnt animal bone and a dolerite axe (ibid.). These deposits were focused on important locations relating to the aforementioned central axis, including the four-post setting, the posts to the right-hand side, the entrance area and the corresponding back posts, in a manner highly characteristic of these structures. A good example of this spatial patterning is provided by the discovery of the polished stone axe in the front left post-hole of internal four-post settings at Lagavoreen—a scenario that is replicated exactly at Knowth and Bettystown, Co. Meath, Scart, Co. Kilkenny, and Balgatheran, Co. Louth (Eogan & Roche 1997, 105; Stafford 2012; J Eogan 1999; 2005; Monteith 2008; Ó Drisceoil 2009). Burnt fragments of animal bone from three of the post-holes at Lagavoreen produced radiocarbon dates of 2840–2470 BC (SUERC-31931, 4050 ± 30 BP), 2900–2670 BC (SUERC-31930, 4205 ± 30 BP) and 2580–2460 BC (SUERC-31935, 4005 ± 30 BP). These are compatible with ongoing analysis by one of the authors (Carlin) and Jessica Smyth which indicates that these types of structures were mainly used between 2700 and 2450 BC in Ireland.

As is well illustrated by the excavation of groups of three similar Late Neolithic structures at Ballynacarriga, Co. Cork, and Balgatheran and at least four more at Scart, it is often the case that the large four-post element and the accompanying entrance posts have been identified but some or all of the post-holes forming the outer ring have not (Carlin, O'Connell et al. 2015; Johnston & Carlin, forthcoming; Ó Drisceoil 2009; Monteith 2008; Laidlaw 2008). In such instances it has been suggested that these arrangements of posts formed a distinct stand-alone element of Late Neolithic architecture (e.g. Smyth 2014). It seems more likely, however, that the large four-post setting and associated entrance was originally encircled by a complete ring of smaller posts, of which no trace has either survived or been recognised.

Identifying which (if any) of these various Late Neolithic structures might have been domestic dwellings or ceremonial monuments is difficult. The Late Neolithic remains of architecturally similar putative houses, including stone-built versions in the Orkneys and much slighter but comparable wooden structures, such as those at Durrington Walls, have been excavated in Britain (Richards 2005, 58–60; Parker Pearson 2007; 2012). In detailed discussion, Smyth (2013; 2014, 88–95) argued that a more ephemeral domestic architecture can be identified in Ireland by the presence of a central rectangular stone-lined hearth like those found in the British examples mentioned above. Potential examples included Slieve Breagh, Co. Meath, and the circuit of rectangular hearths in front of the entrance area at Newgrange. There is a growing consensus in Britain that many of the known timber structures actually represented monumentalised versions of people's homes and, together with the more ephemeral examples, form a spectrum ranging from substantial timber circles to much less tangible constructions, all of which share some of the same basic elements (Bradley 2005, 53–6; Thomas 2007).

However, the uniformity displayed by the architecture, ceremonial deconstruction and character of deposition associated with the Irish timber structures across widely varying contexts makes any attempt to distinguish between houses and ceremonial structures highly problematic. Indeed, some of these structures may have fulfilled a range of residential and ritual functions and could even have changed from dwellings to monuments over the course of their use-lives (Thomas 2010). All of this illustrates the impossibility of identifying distinct domestic and ritual spheres during this period (e.g. Brück 1999, 325–7; Bradley 2003; 2005; 2007; Carlin & Brück 2012). What does seem clear is that people were drawing partly upon the symbolism of the home in ways that accentuated collective everyday 'domestic' activities. Ritualising the customs of daily life in these ways may have served to construct and emphasise a shared group identity, based around the idea of the household, which maintained the cohesion of the local community (see Thomas 2010; Lévi-Strauss 1983).

Another element of the Late Neolithic monumental repertoire may potentially be represented by embanked earthen enclosures or henges, which, in the Boyne Valley at least, show a close spatial relationship with passage tombs (Stout 1991; Condit & Simpson 1998; O'Sullivan et al. 2012). Important new information supporting a Late Neolithic date was revealed along the route of the M1 motorway by the excavation at Balregan 1, Co. Louth, of a site which had been placed in a very specific location at the confluence of two rivers (Illus. 8 & 9). The excavation revealed the eastern side of a large enclosure defined by a bank with an inner and outer ditch. Sealed under the bank were Middle Neolithic features and an assemblage of Impressed Ware, including unusually large vessels, while Grooved Ware was recovered from the upper fill of the outer ditch (Ó Donnchadha & Grogan 2010; Grogan & Roche 2010a). This represents the only direct association of this Late Neolithic pottery with embanked enclosures in what is the main area of the occurrence of this monument type in Ireland (Grogan 2013, 340), and it has not yet proved possible to support this attribution with radiocarbon dates. Thus this forms another of the few partly excavated and poorly dated examples of such sites in Ireland, like that at Tonafortes, Co. Sligo, which produced radiocarbon dates from apparently primary contexts ranging from 2460 to 1610 BC (Danaher 2007). Embanked or ditched circular enclosures like these seem to have been constructed in various forms throughout later prehistory in Ireland. This includes Middle–Late

Illus. 8—Aerial view of the Balregan enclosure at the confluence of the Castletown and Kilcurry rivers (Studio Lab).

Bronze Age examples like that at Grange, Co. Limerick (Roche 2004), and probably also Monknewtown, Co. Meath (Sweetman 1976; Roche & Eogan 2001, 135), as well as Iron Age examples like those at Navan Fort, Co. Armagh, Tara, Co. Meath, and Dún Ailinne, Co. Kildare (Danaher 2007, 55–6; O'Sullivan et al. 2012). This is comparable to the broad currency of similar monuments in Britain, which date from the third to the first millennium BC (Gibson 2010).

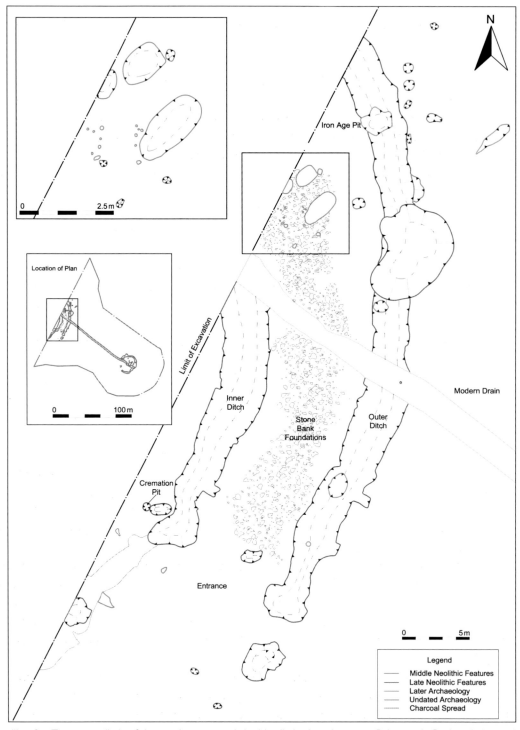

Illus. 9—The outer ditch of the partly excavated double-ditched enclosure at Balregan I, Co. Louth, located at the confluence of the Castletown and Kilcurry rivers (Irish Archaeological Consultancy Ltd).

Significantly, at both the Irish and British sites, these tend to occur in places with evidence for pre-existing Neolithic activity.

There also appears to be a pattern of continuity from the Middle Neolithic in terms of the evidence for agricultural activity (McClatchie, Bogaard et al. 2014). Unburnt animal bone has rarely been found in Late Neolithic contexts, but fragmentary burnt bone representing species such as cow, pig and goat/sheep are comparatively well known. The enduring predominance of cattle in Late Neolithic Ireland is indicated by Smyth's analysis of the lipids in Grooved Ware (Cramp et al. 2014). Development-led excavations confirm that cereal cultivation persists, but the visibility of this also remains low because of approaches taken in creating the archaeological record for this period.

A notable characteristic of development-led excavations is the persistent absence of definitive evidence for Late Neolithic human bone from any context, including timber circles or pits. Many of these features contained cremated fragments that were too small to be positively identified as human remains. This scenario appears to be paralleled in portal and court tombs, where no obviously Late Neolithic material culture has ever been found and the deposition of human bones ceases c. 3100 BC, although Parknabinnia, Co. Clare, represents a notable exception to this (Schulting, Murphy et al. 2012).

This is an appropriate place to return to a point raised at the start of this section on the continued role of passage tombs into the Late Neolithic: deposits of human bone dating from 3100–2700 BC—typical of passage tomb depositional practice—are known from these monuments (Cooney, forthcoming; Carlin, in press). This is well illustrated by Knowth Tomb 6, where the sherds of an early-style Grooved Ware pot were found at the edge of a deposit containing burnt and unburnt human bone dating from 3090–2910 BC (G Eogan 1984, 312; Eogan & Roche 1999, 103–4; Schulting, Bronk Ramsey et al., forthcoming). Grooved Ware has also been found in varying quantities inside and/or outside other developed passage tombs at Knowth, Newgrange, Loughcrew Cairn L and the Mound of the Hostages in County Meath (Roche 1995; Cleary 1983; Brindley 1999; Roche & Eogan 2001; O'Sullivan 2005). The combined evidence strongly suggests that passage tombs were still in active use in the early part of the Late Neolithic and that it is in this context that we should set the early occurrence of Grooved Ware c. 3100–2800 BC (Carlin, in press). This strongly contrasts with the Late Neolithic dataset from development-led archaeology, where the vast majority of features, including timber structures and pits, date from later in this period: 2800–2450 BC (Grogan & Roche 2010a, 34). By this time, passage tombs appear to have been superseded as ceremonial monuments by circular structures or enclosures, some of which were located close to the older centres of social and spiritual power that first emerged in the Middle Neolithic.

So, then, overall narratives for the Late Neolithic are less concrete than for the Early and Middle Neolithic phases, but a clearer picture is emerging which suggests that there is much more continuity of place and practice between the Middle and Late Neolithic than previously recognised.

The Chalcolithic decline of Neolithic practices

This strong evidence for continuity during the Middle to Late Neolithic raises important questions about how and when this period concluded. Generally, the end of the Neolithic is demarcated by the appearance of an international suite of novel practices and cultural materials that rapidly appeared across much of western Europe c. 2500 BC. These included Beaker pottery and the production and deposition of early metalwork, a co-occurrence which has resulted in these being mistakenly seen as culturally synonymous. Significantly, the transmission of these innovations to Ireland resulted from a dramatic expansion of inter-regional interactions whereby people on this island, echoing what happened earlier in the Neolithic, once again involved themselves in exchange networks with various groups across continental Europe. Contacts with Britain were also maintained, as illustrated by the prevalence of Irish copper in early British metalwork (Northover et al. 2001, 28; Needham 2004, 235; O'Brien 2004). All this activity included at least some small-scale movement of people, given the degree to which metallurgical knowledge would have been embodied, but the way metallurgy was developed and used in Ireland was strongly influenced by Neolithic traditions.

Recently, it has been advocated that this particular phase (c. 2500–2200 BC) which pre-dates the adoption of bronze technology at the start of the Early Bronze Age be termed the Chalcolithic (e.g. O'Brien 2012a; Grogan & Roche 2010a). As we will see, however, new research has highlighted the ways in which both Beaker pottery and associated objects were adopted into Neolithic contexts (Carlin 2012a; 2012b; 2013; Carlin & Brück 2012). This provides strong evidence that many pre-existing practices continued until 2200 BC and that the introduction of copper and gold metallurgy was just one of a broader range of ongoing material changes occurring during this time-frame. Thus we have decided to consider the 'Chalcolithic' discoveries from NRA road schemes here as the final phase of the Neolithic to better understand the key social developments at this time.

Most of our Chalcolithic sites have been recognised by virtue of their association with Beaker pottery (although the duration of its use extends beyond the remit of this review to 2100 BC). Prior to the 'Celtic Tiger' boom, comparatively few sites with this pottery were known. This has now been significantly altered by the widespread discovery of Beaker pottery from over 150 sites across the island, occurring in most of the areas where development-led archaeology was conducted. Importantly, it seems that, from an early stage in Ireland, this pottery was extensively used for a wide range of everyday and special purposes that was not restricted to élites (Carlin 2012a; forthcoming).

Beakers rapidly replaced and assumed many of the roles that Grooved Ware once fulfilled in similar depositional practices. This is illustrated by the deposition of Beakers into the post-holes of abandoned Late Neolithic timber circles at Paulstown 2, Co. Kilkenny, and Armalughey, Co. Tyrone, in exactly the same manner as described above for Grooved Ware (Elliot 2009; Dingwall 2010). Developed passage tombs such as Knowth and Newgrange continued to be important, as indicated by the discovery of Beaker pottery (often in association with or in deposits overlying

Grooved Ware) outside these monuments. This activity formed part of a longer sequence of ceremonial acts emphasising the exterior of these monuments dating back to their construction (Cooney 2006; Carlin 2012b; in press).

As we saw above, the dating of the construction of embanked enclosures in Ireland is very problematic and there is little recent evidence to confirm that any of these were built during the Chalcolithic (Carlin 2012b). An exponential increase is, however, seen in the evidence for a different form of monument involving the use of hot-stone technology, namely *fulachta fia*. Examples include those excavated in advance of the M4 motorway (Carlin, Clarke et al. 2008), the Bord Gáis Gas Pipeline to the West (Grogan et al. 2007) and the N4 Sligo Inner Relief Road (Danaher 2007). The construction and use of these open-air communal monuments was the product of group activity that required substantial investments of energy and time. Regardless of whether or not these sites were used for feasting or some other activity, they were almost certainly communal places and may well have had a ceremonial function.

In contrast to the Late Neolithic, we see a resurgence of interest in earlier Neolithic megalithic structures, with the placement of Beaker-associated deposits into portal and court tombs c. 2450 BC (Carlin & Brück 2012; Carlin 2012b). Much of this activity seems to have a referential character, potentially representing interactions between the communities of the living and their past ancestors. While this was certainly not exclusively funerary, recent radiocarbon dating has revealed an increased body of evidence for the deposition of human bone within these monuments, such as at Poulnabrone, where Beaker sherds were also found (A Lynch 2014). In a further departure from the Late Neolithic, c. 2450 BC people quite suddenly began building wedge tombs, in which burnt and unburnt human remains were deposited in association with Beaker pottery (Schulting, Sheridan et al. 2008; Carlin 2012b). This can be seen as a reinvention of the megalithic tradition because it occurred after a 500-year-long hiatus in tomb-building and was influenced by the architecture of pre-existing megaliths (Carlin & Brück 2012, 197).

Most of the newly discovered Beakers have been recovered in a highly fragmentary condition in pits or spreads which bear a striking resemblance in almost every regard to those containing Grooved Ware. These are typified by pit clusters containing large quantities of occupational debris or specially selected artefacts that were deliberately deposited. For example, one of several pits at Paulstown (Elliott 2009) contained 172 sherds from at least 23 Beakers, flint debitage, charred hazelnuts and cereal remains, as well as 23 stone disc-beads, representing one of the few instances of personal ornaments occurring with Beaker pottery in any context in Ireland (Illus. 10). As with the Grooved Ware pits, their contents have almost certainly been derived from what are now the poorly preserved remains of much larger heaps of deliberately accumulated occupational debris, such as the culturally rich spreads excavated in the Boyne Valley at Mell, Co. Louth, and Rathmullan 10, Co. Meath, which included numerous sherds from multiple Beakers and polypod bowls (McQuade 2005; Bolger 2012). The spread at Rathmullan also produced one of the very few provenanced examples of a wrist-bracer or bracelet in Ireland (Bolger 2001; 2012).

Significantly, these contexts provide much new information regarding diet and economy. The sherds that they contain often have carbonised residues and sooting on their interior, indicating

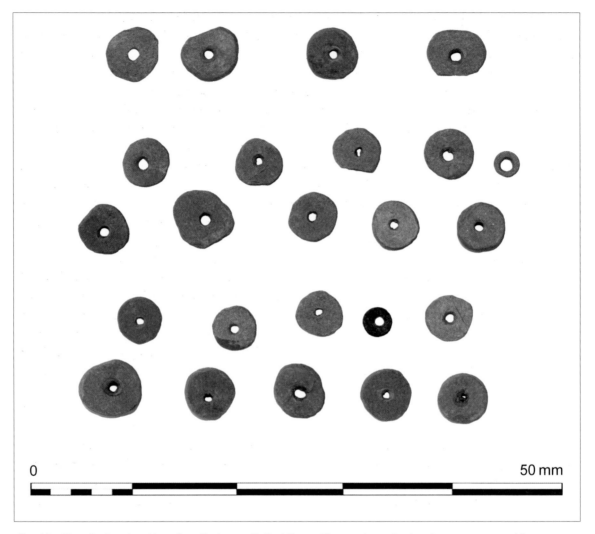

Illus. 10—The disc-bead necklace from Paulstown 2, Co. Kilkenny. Twenty-three disc-beads were recovered from a single pit, along with sherds from at least 23 Beakers, charred hazelnuts and cereal remains, as well as flint debitage (Irish Archaeological Consultancy Ltd).

that they were most probably used for cooking and serving foodstuffs. Also present are stone tools, including querns, scrapers, barbed-and-tanged and hollow-based arrowheads, polished stone axeheads and hammerstones. The discovery of burnt and unburnt animal bone from cattle, pigs, goats and sheep, as well as the charred remains of cereals (especially barley), provides evidence for animal husbandry and cultivation. The wild foods, particularly hazelnuts, and fruits found regularly in these deposits provide further evidence for food preparation and consumption. Overall, these show strong continuity with Middle and Late Neolithic agricultural activity, though the visibility of cereals in the record increases slightly (Carlin 2012b; forthcoming).

The polypods are also worthy of further comment because they have strong eastern European Bell Beaker and Corded Ware affinities and were probably used for the exchange of foods or liquids during social feasting (Hay & Carlin 2014). At least 16 of these bowls have recently been discovered along the east coast, including an intact example deposited upright in a pit at Newtownbalregan 2, Co. Louth (Bayley 2008; Grogan & Roche 2010a). The presence of two such polypods in a monumental context at Newgrange reminds us of the highly similar spreads and pits of Beaker-associated occupational debris found outside the entrances to the passage tombs at Knowth and Newgrange, which seem to reflect large-scale social gatherings that may have had a ceremonial element (Cleary 1983; Eogan & Roche 1997). This epitomises the highly intertwined nature of ritual and domestic activity at this time. The fact that houses from the mid-third millennium BC do not appear to have left a lasting trace and only a few examples such as Graigueshoneen, Co. Waterford, have been identified complicates things further (Johnston et al. 2008). So again, like the Grooved Ware deposits, we find it exceptionally difficult to assess whether these deposits are the poorly preserved remains of settlement activity in these locations.

What is clear is that middens seem to have been a resource where people stored and obtained occupational materials for deposition in a range of different settings. This is based on the presence of very similar deposits of Beaker-associated occupational debris within secondary contexts such as Late Neolithic timber circles and Early Neolithic court and portal tombs, as well as in primary contexts at wedge tombs. In all cases, people seem to have been drawing upon the symbols of everyday 'domestic' life to emphasise their shared group identity and maintain the cohesion of the local community.

As was the case for the Late Neolithic, a recurrent feature of development-led excavations has been the paucity of evidence for Chalcolithic funerary activity. This is unsurprising, given that the classic single inhumation rite practised elsewhere appears to be largely absent from Ireland until the Early Bronze Age. Indeed, with the exception of the small number of Beaker-associated inhumations and cremations known from wedge tombs, the mortuary treatments afforded to the vast majority of the population from 3000 to 2200 BC do not seem to have left a visible archaeological trace.

Highly fragmented burnt bones have been found in many pits, such as at Lismullin, Co. Meath (O'Connell 2013), but, as was the case there, these are typically too small to be definitely identified as human. In this context, two recent discoveries are noteworthy. At Mell, Co. Louth, the prone inhumation of an adult female was found within the truncated remains of a partly stone-lined subrectangular grave beside a Beaker-associated occupation spread (McQuade 2005). The body lay east–west and was accompanied by animal bone and two convex scrapers. This burial, which bears strong resemblances to Beaker burials in northern Britain, was radiocarbon-dated to 2490–2200 BC (Wk-17463; 3894 ± 50 BP). At Treanbaun 3, Co. Galway, the upper part of an inverted Beaker vessel apparently containing the cremated remains of a minimum of one individual of indeterminate age and sex was found in a highly truncated stone-lined pit (McKeon & O'Sullivan 2014, 132). It is very unusual to find an inverted Beaker and quite rare to find this pottery in association with cremated human bone, and so this seems to represent an early example of what would subsequently become a common feature of Bronze Age burial practice. A recently obtained radiocarbon date of 1886–1667 BC (UBA-29698; 3455 ± 38 BP) from a fragment of this bone (K Cleary 2016) suggests, however, that the Beaker pot may well have been an antique when it was deposited. It is also worth highlighting that this Early Bronze Age date is contemporary with that from a cremation burial in a stratigraphically later position within the same group of features. It seems that there was considerable complexity to the past activities at this site which we may not fully grasp.

The apparent lack of highly formalised burial activity during this phase can be seen as a continuation of the strong emphasis that was placed on the domestic household in Late Neolithic ceremonial activity. Both the form of ceremonial practices and their conduct in largely non-funerary settings seem to have persisted from 2700 to 2200 BC. This may partly explain the strong focus on deposition in natural places. Large numbers of objects current from 2450 to 2200 BC, such as copper axes, halberds, daggers, gold discs and lunulae, as well as stone wrist-bracers and V-perforated buttons, have been found in Ireland; they predominantly occur as stray or single finds or in one-type hoards within natural places, particularly bogs. While this patterning can be frustrating in contrast to other European regions, where many of these objects occur together with Beaker pottery and often accompanying burials, it importantly reflects the fact that the people on this island who adopted these cultural innovations consistently chose characteristic ways of depositing these artefacts which were type-, context- and place-specific (Carlin 2012b; forthcoming). In many respects, it seems that the treatment of many of these novelties echoed pre-existing traditions, such as the custom of predominantly depositing stone axeheads in wet places (Carlin & Brück 2012).

Overall, the discoveries from development-led excavations have revealed that there was a much greater degree of continuity between the Late Neolithic and the Chalcolithic than had been previously recognised. The adoption of new ideas and objects at this time forms part of a longer sequence of gradual and incremental material changes relating to identity formation strategies which fulfilled the distinctive needs of local communities dating back to the start of the Neolithic. Large-scale social changes do not appear to have occurred and there is little convincing evidence for a prestige-goods economy or any increase in social stratification. All of this seems to change c. 2200 BC with the introduction of bronze metallurgy, which coincided with an apparent decrease in Continental exchange and an increase in the regionalisation of social practices.

The future

This account focuses on the impact that archaeological investigations conducted on road schemes have had on our understanding of the Neolithic in Ireland and has used selective examples from the large number of sites that have been discovered to illustrate key points. The impact has been transformative and, while confirming some elements of previous interpretations (Cooney 2000), it has presented the basis for a new understanding of the period. The position of the Early Neolithic as a time of radical change and the establishment of a new, agriculturally based way of life has been really clarified. On the other hand, we are left with major questions about long-term social change and development after the 'house horizon' and the processes that underpinned the character of the evidence for the Middle and Late stages of the Neolithic and its final phase, the Chalcolithic. As research continues, there will undoubtedly be new answers provided, as well as questions raised. For example, there is enormous potential in studies of material culture to understand daily life in the Neolithic and longer-term cultural patterns. This is the case particularly when the detailed study of specific elements of the record is combined with an interpretive pulling together of different materials found in association, and in understanding the overall assemblages from sites as representing activities of people (see Lemonnier 2012). This, however, needs to be combined with a greater emphasis on achieving more fine-grained chronologies for sites and practices, especially those dating from 3600–2200 BC.

A theme that we tried to highlight through the different phases of the Neolithic was the occurrence of enclosures. This is to reiterate a point made in an earlier paper (Cooney 2002) that the construction of enclosures, built at different scales, was a feature of Neolithic life in Ireland. We wanted to emphasise here that the discovery of enclosures on road schemes, such as Magheraboy, Tullahedy and Balregan, is a reminder that development-led archaeology not only has enriched our understanding of daily life in the Neolithic but also has the potential to reveal monumental structures. In this sense it not only has helped to rebalance our understanding of the megalithic tombs that had dominated our view of this period but also emphasises that these stone monuments are actually only part of a wider Neolithic deployment of monumental structures built from a range of materials.

This relates to another theme that has become apparent through development-led archaeology, namely the very high frequency with which people intermittently returned to the same locales and often conducted the same sort of activities throughout the Neolithic and beyond. The phenomenon of persistent places is no longer restricted to large-scale monumental sites; instead, we see that people seem to have maintained enduring ties to many (at least) locally important places.

And as a final point, taking the Scottish Archaeological Research Framework as one potential model (Sheridan & Brophy 2012), now seems an appropriate time to identify the key research areas and questions that would allow us to address most fruitfully the data gathered through developer-funded and research excavation, to identify foci for research and to create a detailed history of the Neolithic and Neolithic society and people, from the first appearance of new lifeways in the Early Neolithic to the appearance of Food Vessels, single inhumations and bronze metallurgy around 2200 BC, marking the end of the Neolithic and the start of the Bronze Age.

Acknowledgements

Our thanks to Karen Dempsey for her comments on the text and to Jessica Smyth, Fintan Walsh, Irish Archaeological Consultancy Ltd, Cóilín Ó Drisceoil, Joanne Gaffrey, CRDS Ltd and Graeme

Laidlaw for kindly providing images. We are also grateful to the editors for their patience and comments and to Michael Stanley for his assistance with sourcing illustrations, as well as to the anonymous peer reviewer, whose helpful comments encouraged us to be more forthright about Early Neolithic chronological issues.

4

THE BRONZE AGE: A SURFEIT OF DATA?

Eoin Grogan

Introduction

Under the watch of the NRA, new data on most aspects of Bronze Age life—burials, houses, domestic space, ritual activity—have been uncovered in very significant quantities. The NRA's active programme of publication has made much of this accessible on a scheme-by-scheme basis, but the amount of new information will take some time, and significant innovation in assessment procedures, to analyse and to integrate with our existing understanding of the Bronze Age. In addition, the significantly higher-quality recording and observation of details associated with these new data pose assessment requirements well beyond simple analytical systems based on counting and quantifying. Rather like modern radiocarbon analysis, which sets very much higher requirements for the quality of evidence, new research will have to accept that many earlier discoveries and excavation results will now have to be discounted from the core analysis.

There is no doubt that this has transformed, and will continue to transform, our interpretation of this fascinating period. To date, three excellent research projects on prehistoric evidence have drawn on this large body of new data (Carlin 2012a; Carlin & Brück 2012; Ginn 2011; 2013; 2014a; 2014b; Ó Maoldúin 2014) but there remains the mammoth task of finally 'assimilating' this new information. It is also important to acknowledge the very significant contribution that environmental studies relating to both infrastructural schemes and academic research have made to our understanding of the Bronze Age (e.g. McClatchie 2014; K Molloy 2005; Molloy & O'Connell 2012; O'Donnell 2007a; O'Donnell et al. 2009; Timpany 2011). These provide an integrated context of landscape development as a result of human and natural events, and an essential backdrop to the archaeological record.

Archaeological excavations carried out through the NRA have certainly had a dramatic impact on our understanding of the Irish Bronze Age (Illus. 1). Two examples of the bounty of the road schemes should suffice. Of the 63 sites excavated on the N8 Cashel–Mitchelstown road scheme 67% dated from the Bronze Age, while 62% of the 63 sites on the N25 Waterford City Bypass were of this period (McQuade et al. 2009, table 1.1; J Eogan 2011a, tables 2–3), as were 12 of the 23 sites on the N18 Oranmore to Gort Scheme (Delaney et al. 2011, table 1.1). On the much lengthier Bord Gáis Pipeline to the West, which traversed much more varied terrain, 56% of the 245 excavations produced definite Bronze Age activity (Grogan et al. 2007, table 1.1).

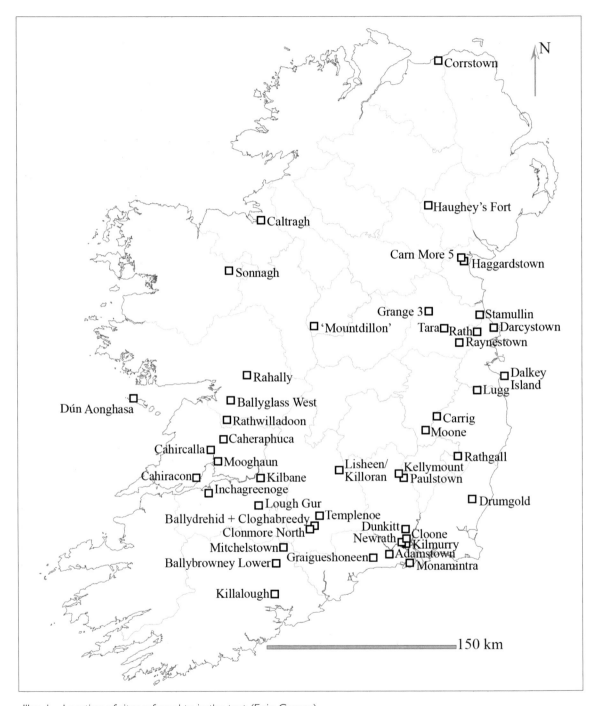

Illus. I—Location of sites referred to in the text (Eoin Grogan).

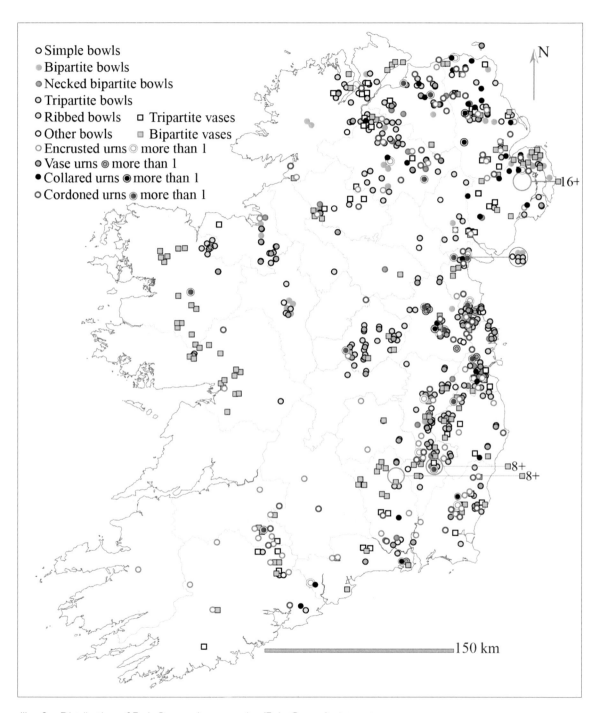

Illus. 2—Distribution of Early Bronze Age ceramics (Eoin Grogan).

Legend:
- ○ Simple bowls
- ● Bipartite bowls
- ● Necked bipartite bowls
- ○ Tripartite bowls
- ○ Ribbed bowls   □ Tripartite vases
- ○ Other bowls   ▢ Bipartite vases
- ○ Encrusted urns ◎ more than 1
- ● Vase urns ◉ more than 1
- ● Collared urns ⦿ more than 1
- ○ Cordoned urns ◉ more than 1

N

16+

8+
8+

150 km

Nevertheless, it is important to observe that road schemes provide only a narrow landscape cross-section. Furthermore, while modern roads tend to be 'terrain-oblivious', in that they smooth out the topography and often obscure the surrounding landscape, route selection is frequently 'terrain-sensitive'; elevated terrain is generally avoided—a notable exception being the M8 route across the western upland fringe of Kilworth Mountain in County Cork—and, while several important points of river crossing have been included, new roads rarely skirt river valleys, which are frequent locational preferences for both domestic and funerary sites. While, in the main, the new discoveries have confirmed, and frequently intensified, existing patterns of Bronze Age settlement, for example on the lowlands of east Carlow, north Kilkenny and north Leinster, there are also important new insights into areas such as Wexford, south Tipperary and north-east Cork (Illus. 2, 3 & 6).

It is also the case that the term 'Bronze Age' is often used as a catch-all for 'not obviously of any other period', or as a designation for sites that produce no artefactual or direct dating evidence.

The Bronze Age was a generally conservative period, rooted in tradition and in local, familial and agricultural perspectives. The pace of change was slow, as evidenced by the very gradual developments in metal technology and the gradual changes in funerary ritual. Nevertheless, the 'new' evidence has revealed subtleties that suggest that there was greater diversity and complexity in behavioural patterns, even in deeply conservative traditions such as funerary practices, than we might have suspected.

The Early Bronze Age: the age of dynastic struggle

The funerary evidence for the Early Bronze Age, which dominates our record of the period, has been accumulated over a long period and represents a very considerable dataset that has been the subject of important studies (Waddell 1990; Ó Ríordáin & Waddell 1993; Mount 1997; Brindley 2007; Grogan & Roche 2010a). The actual number of 21st-century excavations of Bronze Age burials is significant, including important cemeteries at Carn More 5, Co. Louth, Paulstown, Co. Kilkenny, and Moone, Co. Kildare (Bayley 2010; Elliot 2009; Hackett 2009), but it is dwarfed by previous discoveries (Illus. 3). The inverse is the case, however, in relation to information quality. While there are some long-identified and distinctive characteristics of Early Bronze Age burial—cremation, accompanying vessels, cists and, increasingly, pits, cemeteries—previously unsuspected complexities have been recovered and recorded in detail.

As Mount (1995; 1997) noted, most burials were placed in cemeteries rather than occurring as single, 'isolated' interments. Early Bronze Age cemeteries were established as landmarks for local communities. In addition, we can perceive an interest in lineage and genealogy as well as in physical markers of land ownership. Especially in cemeteries of considerable longevity, such as Carrig, Co. Wicklow (Grogan 1990), and the Mound of the Hostages, Tara, Co. Meath (M O'Sullivan 2005), it is clear that burials often represent episodic rather than continuous funerary activity. It appears, in some cases at least, that only from time to time, perhaps even less often than every generation, were there individuals of appropriate status for interment in familial burial grounds.

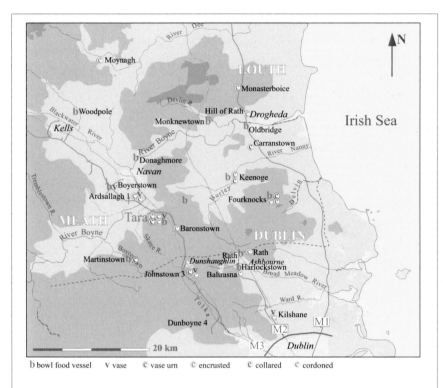

61

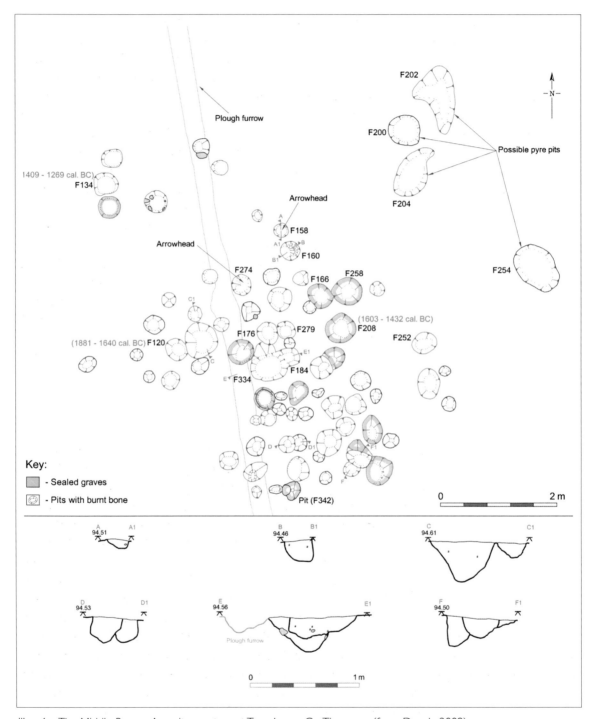

Illus. 4—The Middle Bronze Age pit cemetery at Templenoe, Co. Tipperary (from Doody 2009).

While the extensive programme of radiocarbon dating on NRA-funded sites is admirable, too little attention has been paid to ceramic grave-goods. A somewhat circular interpretation of comparative dating has developed whereby the chronology of burials is often based on ceramic typologies which are themselves reliant on the dating of associated material, most usually cremated bone. On the other hand, in some instances anticipation of radiocarbon dates ('We're waiting for the dates')—or, indeed, over-reliance on dates of limited value—can thwart or even undermine proper archaeological interpretation. The targeting of often 'incidental' site features, rather than research-based inquiry into specific aspects of site development, has created a dataset of 'floating' pits, post-holes, gullies and trenches that add little to the sum of our knowledge. This can be contrasted with, for example, the high-quality Bayesian analysis of the dates from the Early Bronze Age cemetery at the Mound of the Hostages (Bayliss & O'Sullivan 2013).

While, for example, it appears that the collared urns from Monimintra, Co. Waterford (Grogan & Roche 2010b), were buried very soon after completion, other pots, such as a vase from Carrig, an anomalous vase at Stokestown, Co. Wexford, and a vase urn from Kellymount 5, Co. Kilkenny, were clearly old and perhaps 'venerable' at the time of deposition (Grogan 1990; Patricia Long, pers. comm.; Wierbicki & Coughlan 2013; Grogan & Roche 2013a). This raises another issue, that of unaccompanied cremations, especially in simple pits. It is clear that this form of burial occurred throughout prehistory but is a feature of the Bronze Age in particular. Without specific dating of new discoveries, the prevalence of these in one period or another remains an unknown. An educated guess suggests that these became more common in the Middle and Late Bronze Age, when they may have come to dominate the funerary record.

A general sequence of the principal burial forms, and to a lesser extent their attendant rituals, can be traced from 2200 BC to the end of the Bronze Age around 800 BC. This involves gradual change that reflects burial as a deeply conservative custom that parallels a similarly gradual development in wider societal systems. At a national level, new discoveries have helped to extend the distribution of burials, although the routes of road projects have also confirmed the paucity of characteristic funerary customs in other areas. An important landmark in funerary studies is the publication of the National Museum of Ireland's 'back catalogue' of Early Bronze Age burial excavations with the attendant osteological research (Cahill & Sikora 2012). Regions with sparse settlement—on the basis of current evidence—include much of the midlands, the north–west, and substantial parts of the west and south-west. The NRA's admirable avoidance of standing monuments—and in this case the wedge tombs, with a predominantly western distribution, that were the focus for continued burial, and other ritual activity, into the Early and Middle Bronze Age (O'Brien 1999; Schulting, Sheridan et al. 2008; P Walsh 1995)—leaves us with something of an imponderable in this period. To a certain extent this evidence is augmented by that of the *fulachtaí fia* or burnt mounds (this subject is detailed later): a significant result of NRA-funded excavation is the considerably longer currency for the use of these sites than we had previously suspected, with a significant percentage dating from the Early Bronze Age. In addition, these have turned up in significant numbers in areas where there has been poor surface survival.

Nevertheless, from 2200 to 1600 BC the archaeological record is still dominated by the burial record, as is the artefact record by funerary ceramics. From the outset, however, apart from ceramics, the extensive material wealth of the Bronze Age is (with only rare exceptions) studiously excluded from the burials themselves. It is important to stress that the absence of lavish grave-goods does not imply the lack of extensive ceremony and ritual; the continuity of many funerary customs suggests that these were carefully prescribed and controlled.

But what does it represent in terms of the society that produced it? We should think here not of the myriad small pieces of evidence—the graves, funerary rite and accompanying grave-goods—but of the events, the funerals, that these represent. One plausible element of the explanation is that these are the burials of élite individuals and families who operated within a small-scale society and that they reflect ongoing efforts to establish and maintain identity and status. A funeral was an occasion to show off the rank and wealth not just of the deceased but also of their surviving family. The widespread adoption of cremation following a brief flirtation with crouched inhumation at the beginning of the period (Grogan 2004, tables 10.3–4) indicates a basic common blueprint for the treatment of the body. Compared with inhumation, cremation is a costly business but it has two major advantages: the immediate and hygienic disposal of the corpse and the planning and preparation of the final funeral arrangements. This implies, although it does not prove, that some time was required to make suitable arrangements for the funeral itself, including the all-important element of lavish hospitality, and to allow for the attendance of mourners from beyond the immediate social landscape of the deceased and their family. This may also emphasise the social significance of the event in cementing relationships and highlighting the status of the bereaved family: the recurring use of the same place—the creation of cemeteries—may reflect a concern with lineage and history, and a desire to reinforce dynastic inheritance. This extends beyond personal or familial status and privilege to the establishment of the right to pass this on to the next generation.

Within the burial record, we can occasionally discern some of the actions involved in funerary ritual. The apparently careful separation of bone from funerary pyres—and the increasing deliberate selection of bone from different parts of the body—suggests a process that chose body parts that reflected the personality, life history or perhaps lineage of the individual concerned (Lynch & O'Donnell 2007). As yet, it has not been possible to determine any pattern to the position of pots in graves or, indeed, to the placement of graves within cemeteries. What can be occasionally observed, however, is the complex treatment of some grave-goods, such as the separation of sherds from at least two cordoned urns and their disposal in different parts of a ditched funerary enclosure at Rath, Co. Dublin; similar treatment of the cremated remains may be masked by the small quantity of material, which defied closer analysis (Byrnes 2007; Brindley 2003; L Lynch 2003). To date, the episodic use of a single grave, Cist C at Carrig (Grogan 1990), for burials over a period of more than 500 years has not been replicated in the data. Nevertheless, other sites, such as the Mound of the Hostages (M O'Sullivan 2005), demonstrate considerable longevity, spanning up to 400 years. At Newrath 37, Co. Kilkenny, a ring-ditch enclosed an Early Bronze Age cist (containing an inverted vase urn); the ditch appears to have been lined with oak timbers and the site may have been further marked by a mound and two timber posts. A small cremation pit cemetery dating from the latter part of the Early Bronze Age was located 32 m to the south-west (Wren & Price 2011). The evidence from Carn More 5 (principally bowls and cordoned urns) also suggests two chronologically distinct phases (Bayley 2010).

The Middle Bronze Age: the dominance of domestic landscapes

There is a remarkable alternation in the substantive areas of evidence during the next period (c. 1600–1100 BC). Burials, of course, continue—and without doubt maintain their importance in respecting and commemorating the dead and projecting family status—but with a much simpler grave morphology. Nevertheless, the physical treatment of the dead is more complex, with a very varied process of cremation and selection of bone to include in the formal burial (Lynch & O'Donnell 2007). Typical of these burial sites, although larger than most, is the flat cemetery at Templenoe, Co. Tipperary (Doody 2009), where 74 simple pits (57 with cremated bone) were tightly clustered mainly in an area of only 30 square metres (Illus. 4).

Two other elements, however, dominate the archaeological record: houses and *fulachtaí fia* (burnt mounds). Just a brief word here on the burnt mounds. Not only are these the most common type-site of Irish prehistory, they are also the most frequently encountered sites on road projects, but they have almost become the pariahs of road archaeology. Despite the continuing difficulties of interpreting function they were, for most of the Bronze Age, a deeply significant aspect of people's lives, and this wealth of knowledge must be more fully integrated into archaeological research. There is much knowledge to be derived from their location, spatial distribution and reuse patterns. Don't let's keep leaving these little guys out in the cold!

This is not the place to rehearse in detail the several, often conflicting, interpretations of the function of these sites—for cooking meat, dying cloth, tanning leather, brewing beer or bathing. Even after hundreds of excavations the evidence is inadequate to dismiss any of these entirely (for recent discussions see S Delaney et al. 2012b; Delaney & Tierney 2011b; Grogan 2005a, 39–46; Grogan et al. 2007, 82–101; J Eogan 2011b, 264–72). Nevertheless, it is the case that the most common associated finds—from, however, no more than a sizeable minority of sites—are animal bones. Often described as the most common prehistoric sites, it is not surprising that they are most frequently subject to excavation on infrastructural and development projects. In the 15-year period from 2000 to 2014 a total of 897 previously unidentified sites have been investigated (see excavations.ie). It is, regrettably, an indictment of current strategies that this number of sites has offered little clarity on their function. Surely we require a more developed strategy, and analytical techniques, to guide future excavation and research?

What is evident is the frequency with which individual sites were used to heat water: estimates, based principally on the volumes of discarded stone, vary from several occasions to over 300 (Masterson 1999) and up to as many as 3,000 (Ó Néill 2005). Rectangular and infrequently circular or oval troughs (in which the water was heated), multiple pits and evidence for racks, water-management features (including drains and sumps), working platforms, tracks and occasionally small structures are recurrent features. In many cases a timber trough lining (to insulate, and probably to filter, the heating water) is preserved or at least indicated by supporting stakes or stake-holes. The quality of workmanship in the creation of split planks and the formation of many troughs indicates serious planning and resource commitment. Detailed environmental studies have elucidated both the contemporary local landscapes (and a very wide range of trees and other vegetation) and the preferences for some timber—oak, alder, ash and yew for trough construction, ash or alder for stakes, and a mixture of wood from both dryland and wetland woodlands (alder, ash, oak and hazel) for fuel (O'Donnell 2007a, 31–45; O'Donnell et al. 2009, fig. 8.7; Molloy & O'Connell 2012). Just as important is the revelation of the local environment: while—as is to be expected—the immediate areas were wetland dominated by alder and willow, most sites were located in close proximity to woodland dominated by dryland species such as oak, hazel and ash. Meadowland, indicated by bracken, plantain, dock, buttercup and dandelion, was also close by, as were areas of cereal cultivation. The close integration of *fulachtaí fia* in the domestic landscape is aptly highlighted by Clonmore North, Co. Tipperary, where three houses were located beside a burnt mound and trough dating from the Middle Bronze Age (B Molloy 2009a; 2009b).

Many sites demonstrate several distinct episodes of use indicated by, for example, the replacement of troughs. Occasionally, as at Inchagreenoge, Co. Limerick (Taylor 2007; Grogan et al. 2007, 92, table 4.7), Graigueshoneen, Co. Waterford (Tierney & Logan 2008), and Gortaficka 2, Co. Clare (S Delaney et al. 2012a, 90–1), these use events were separated by many decades. Shorter phases of use, abandonment and reuse were recorded at, for example, Cahiracon, Co. Clare (Dennehy 2007a), Dunkitt 8, Co. Kilkenny (Gregory & Sheehan 2011, 106–7), Ballyglass West, Co. Galway (Kerrigan 2011), Raheen, Co. Tipperary (B Molloy 2009c), and Ballykeefe 1, Co. Waterford (Bermingham 2013, 76–8).

Most of these sites still date from the Late, and especially the Middle, Bronze Age, but there is increasing evidence for their origins in the Late Neolithic, with significant numbers in the Chalcolithic (Copper Age) and particularly the Early Bronze Age (see J Eogan 2011b, illus. 178). Whatever their precise function, two aspects of *fulachtaí fia* are clear. Their use for the heating of water requires them to be located in wet places—although not so wet as to preclude control over the process—where the troughs fill naturally with water. The implication is that they were in seasonal use, probably in late summer and early autumn. It is also increasingly apparent that these sites, while located on or along the periphery of 'marginal' wetland, were an integral part of the settlement landscape, within comfortable walking distance (a few to tens of metres) of the domestic centres. Their number, and the frequency of their usage, underline their importance to Bronze Age society.

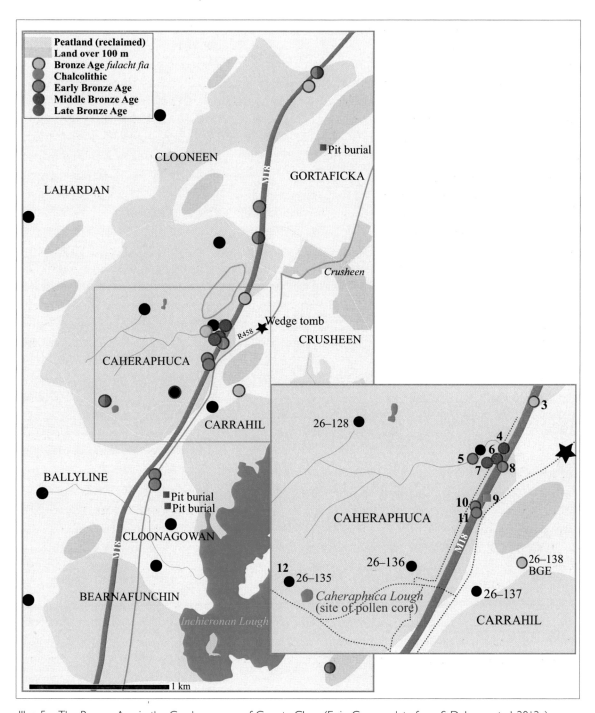

Illus. 5—The Bronze Age in the Crusheen area of County Clare (Eoin Grogan; data from S Delaney et al. 2012a).

The Bronze Age landscape of the Crusheen area of east Clare

This lowland area is dominated by low-lying, often wet terrain interspersed with low hills, peatland and rockland with frequent small or remnant lakes (such as Caheraphuca Lough) (Illus. 5). Nevertheless, there is a patchwork of good-quality agricultural land in this area and it was an attractive location for Bronze Age settlement. Archaeological investigation was associated with both the Pipeline to the West and the M18 NRA scheme (Grogan, O'Donnell et al. 2007; S Delaney et al. 2012a). Both schemes threaded their way through this landscape along what was evidently the main north–south route through Clare in the prehistoric period. For this reason it is worth detailed attention, as it draws on new information based on both pipeline and road archaeology in an area that had previously seen little research; it also produced extensive low-level evidence for everyday settlement—with little evidence for significant local social differentiation— that appears to exemplify the picture through much of the country.

It is worth noting here some differences between road and gas pipeline schemes as regards recovery processes. The larger scale of road schemes, with their necessarily much wider way-leaves, offers a greater opportunity for extensive archaeological investigation. The staged process of evaluation—geophysics, test-trenching and excavation itself—also allows for an ongoing and more prolonged process of assessment. On the other hand, the close monitoring of topsoil removal for pipelines—a requirement, since the land must be curated for return to its owners—holds greater potential for identifying all, including very small-scale, archaeological features. Further investigation, such as geophysical and LiDAR survey, beyond way-leaves has left a springboard for further excavation of important sites, including, for example, Rahally, Co. Galway (Mullins 2014), and Drumgold, Co. Wexford (Hull 2016, 81, illus. 9).

A complex of *fulachtaí fia* was identified at Caheraphuca in rocky terrain between a former lake basin to the west, already inundated by peat in the Neolithic, and Inchicronan Lough to the east (S Delaney et al. 2012a, 93–104). Ten sites were excavated, ranging from simple dumps of burnt material (Site 3) to evidence for complex and prolonged activity (such as Sites 4, 6 and 8). Further to the south of Crusheen, excavations on the Pipeline to the West scheme included a *fulacht fia* at Carrahil (Dennehy 2007b), while another was investigated in Ballyline (Flynn 2011). Other activity in this area included simple cremation pits at Cloonagowan (Sites 1 and 2; Dennehy 2007c; 2007d), Gortaficka (Dennehy & Sutton 2007) and Sranagalloon 2 (S Delaney et al. 2012a, 156).

The use of these sites began in the Chalcolithic and continued into the Early Bronze Age, which was the period of most intensive use, while there was renewed activity in the Middle to Late Bronze Age. Of particular importance in this area is the detailed analysis of the environmental evidence, not only from individual sites (O Carroll & Cobain 2012) but also the detailed analysis of the pollen record from Caheraphuca Lough (Molloy & O'Connell 2012). The palynology showed a pattern of episodic Bronze Age agricultural intensity, with peaks in the early part of the period and especially in the final stages after 1200 BC; this is a reflection of the archaeological results, although in the latter period the *fulachtaí fia* were less of a focus.

Farming made its first significant impact in the Chalcolithic and is reflected by the *fulachtaí fia* at Caheraphuca 5, 11 and an early phase at Site 8. While the palynology suggests a period of lower-level activity, the archaeological evidence indicates continuing intensity in the Early Bronze Age (Caheraphuca 1, 8, 10 and 12, Ballyline 1–3, Clooneen and Gortaficka 2). In this early phase pastoral farming dominated, with a low level of cereal production, in a landscape that continued to have extensive woodland cover. Following another period of reduced agricultural activity, the area experienced what Molloy and O'Connell (2012, 118–19, illus. 4.6) describe as a *landnam* event, with large-scale tree clearance and the expansion of pasture and especially cereal cultivation. This occurred at the start of the Late Bronze Age, c. 1200–1100 BC, and was contemporary with a renewed interest in *fulachtaí fia* (Caheraphuca 1, 4, 7 and 12, and further to the north at Sranagalloon 1). This late but dramatic expansion of farming and attendant woodland clearance is mirrored in the Mooghaun area of south Clare (K Molloy 2005; Molloy & O'Connell 2012, 120–1; Grogan 2005a) and suggests a rapid population expansion, possibly augmented by migration from the increasing landscape poverty of the Burren uplands.

This apparent ebb and flow of settlement intensity, but not ongoing activity, during the Bronze Age may indicate an element of cyclical concentration on different areas of the local landscape. Similar episodic use of *fulachtaí fia* and phases of woodland regeneration and clearance were observed, for example, in the Cahiracon area of south Clare on the River Shannon, west of the Fergus Estuary (Grogan, O'Donnell et al. 2007, 143–6, 197–201). Continuity of population is underscored by the recurrent, if episodic, use of the same sites, including Cahiracon 122a, 122c and 120, which 'shows that the locations of these sites were a fixed and permanent element in the landscape' (ibid., 146). Similar evidence came from Cloone 3, Co. Kilkenny, where the site was remodelled on at least three occasions during the Early to Middle Bronze Age (Sheehan & Leahy 2011), Cahircalla Beg and Cahircalla More, Co. Clare (Bermingham et al. 2012a, 31–6), and in the Caltragh area of County Sligo (Danaher 2007, 18–41).

The frequency with which these sites were used underscores their local familiarity; that communities, at least occasionally, had a special regard for them is indicated by the presence of votive deposits, usually as closing offerings. These include a set of graded musical yew pipes from Charlesland, Co. Wicklow (Holmes & Molloy 2006), a possible pipe from Newrath 34, Co. Kilkenny (Wilkins et al. 2009; Lyons & O'Donnell 2009), human skull fragments at Cragbrien, Co. Clare, and Inchagreenoge, Co. Limerick (Hull 2007; Taylor 2007), a gold dress-fastener at Dooras, Co. Mayo, and a flanged axe from Ballynatona, Co. Cork (Cherry 1990). A unique tin bead and another fragmentary metal bead came from the Middle Bronze Age site at Sonnagh 5, Co. Mayo (Cahill & Mullarkey 2010). Ballykeeffe 1 produced an antler pick (Bermingham 2013, 50, illus. 2.11); examples also came from Raynestown 1, Co. Meath (see below). Dugout canoes appear to have been used as troughs at Killeens, Co. Cork—which also produced a gold ring—and Teeronea, Co. Clare (O'Kelly 1954; Grogan 2005a, 43), while a hollowed-out oak log was used at Killalough 1, Co. Cork (Cotter 2013a). Beyond the meagre artefact record, the importance of *fulachtaí fia* is underscored by the frequently high level of carpentry skills evident in the construction of the troughs.

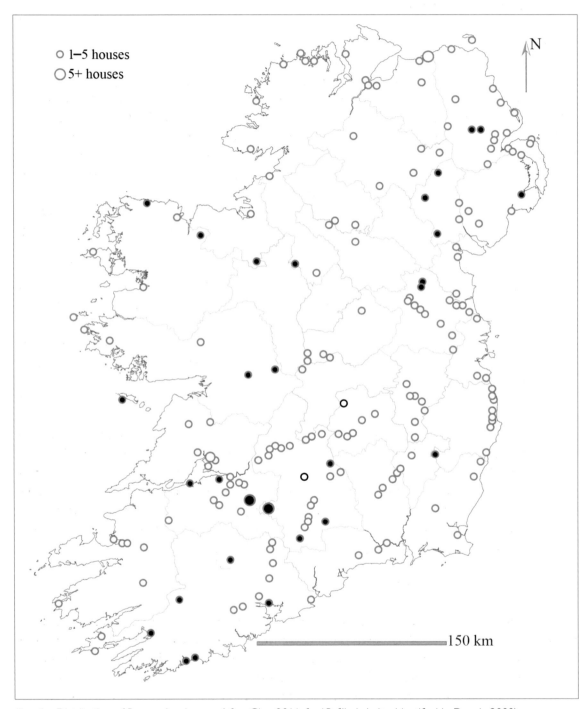

Illus. 6—Distribution of Bronze Age houses (after Ginn 2011, fig. 1B; filled circles: identified in Doody 2000).

Middle Bronze Age houses

The houses have a very extensive distribution (Illus. 6) and display a widespread blueprint that suggests a desire for uniformity and conformity. Some of these sturdy circular homes have one show-off trait: the elaborate porch (Ginn 2011; 2013, 49–51; 2014a; 2014b). They occur singly and in small groups of two to five, as at Newtown A/E and Newtown B, Co. Limerick (Bermingham 2013, 57–65), Adamstown 1 and 3, Co. Waterford, and Newrath 9, Co. Kilkenny (Russell & Ginn 2011a; 2011b; Dennehy & Halpin 2011), Cloghabreedy and Ballydrehid, Co. Tipperary (Moriarty 2009; McQuade 2009) (Illus. 7), and Ballybrowney Lower 1 and Mitchelstown 1, Co. Cork (Cotter 2005; 2013b; 2013c; 2013d), and, occasionally, in much larger numbers, as at Corrstown, Co. Derry, and Lough Gur, Co. Limerick (Ginn & Rathbone 2012; Ó Ríordáin 1954; Grogan & Eogan 1987). They represent the residences of independent farming families that appear to have enjoyed relatively comfortable and stable lives. Domestic sites are generally small, with one to three houses, reflecting family groups as the foundation of social and landscape organisation. At Grange, Co. Meath, a pair of houses with roughly cobbled yards was directly associated with field fences, cremation pits and, just 100 m to the west, a fine barrow (Kelly 2010a). Arced pits under the eaves may have been covered storage bins of a type also identified in three houses at Caltragh, Co. Sligo (Danaher 2007, 79–87).

The evidence from individual sites and house clusters indicates strong familial bonds, shared labour and comparative prosperity. There is a notable scarcity of metal artefacts, however, despite the widespread evidence for increased production of and variety in bronze tools and weapons, and the development of wider, including international, exchange systems for copper, tin, gold, amber and jet.

This paucity of metal may, of course, reflect an admirably 21st-century attitude to recycling; costly metals were certainly being reused throughout the Bronze Age. Nevertheless, this picture of restricted access to metal implements is supported by the remarkable absence of evidence for on-site production: a handful of mould fragments but no furnaces, crucibles or metal waste. This absence of evidence is a significant factor in interpreting the production, circulation and ownership of metal artefacts; what we can certainly say at the moment is that small-scale domestic production was not a feature of this period.

The Late Bronze Age: the age of avarice

As noted previously, *fulachtaí fia* continue to be used in significant, if reduced, numbers, while circular houses, although smaller and lacking the elaborate porches (Ginn 2011; 2014a), dominate the domestic landscape (Illus. 6). Up to 20 years ago the record of the final stages of the Bronze Age was dominated by artefacts. Indeed, this period witnessed something of an 'industrial revolution', with an exponential increase in the number and range of tools, weapons and personal ornaments (G Eogan 1964; 1983). These reflect impressive technological advances as well as considerable craft innovation. The evidence, such as it is, suggests a small number of large-scale

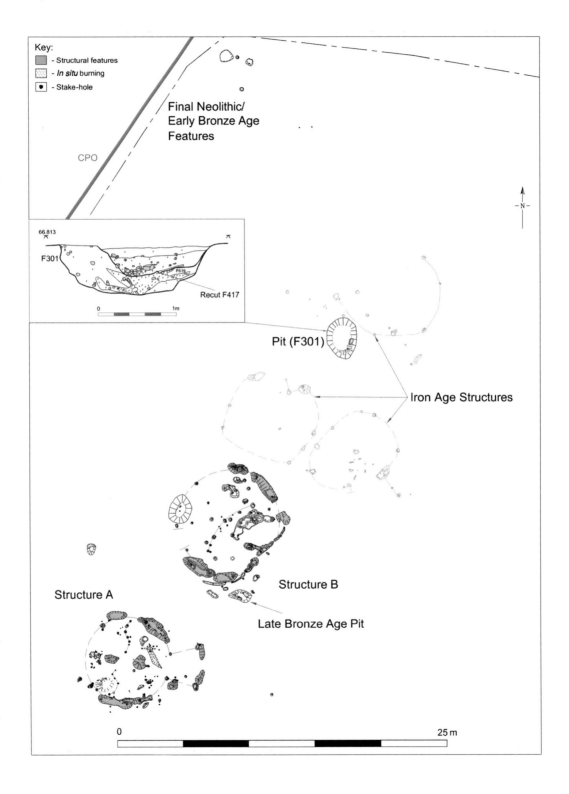

Key:
- Structural features
- *In situ* burning
- Stake-hole

Final Neolithic/
Early Bronze Age
Features

CPO

66.813

F301

F619

Recut F417

0   1m

Pit (F301)

Iron Age Structures

Structure B

Structure A

Late Bronze Age Pit

0   25 m

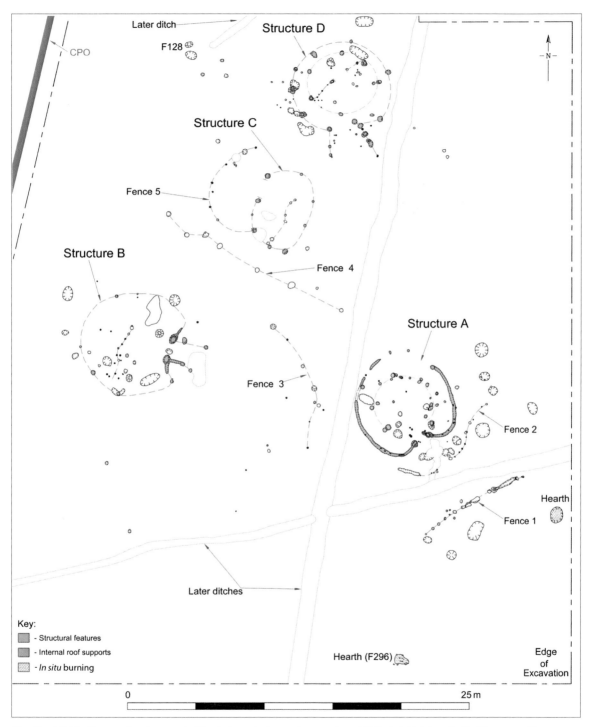

Illus. 7—Middle Bronze Age houses at Cloghabreedy (opposite page) and Ballydrehid (above), Co. Tipperary (from McQuade et al. 2009).

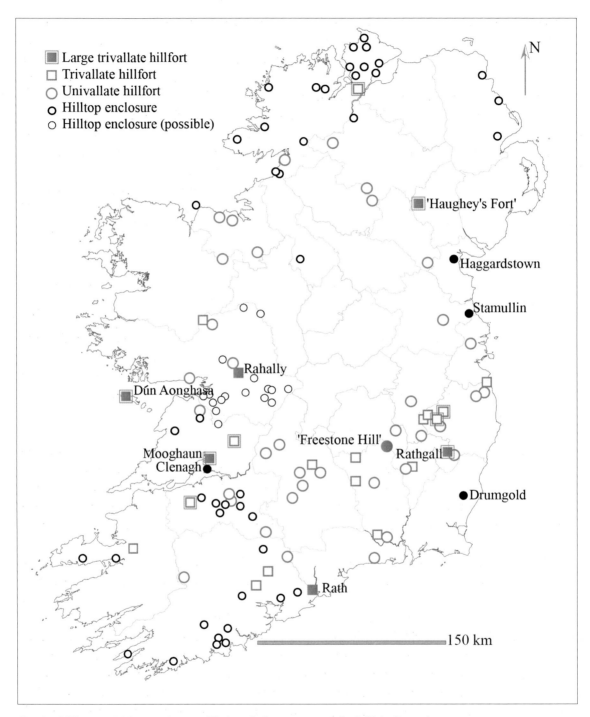

Illus. 8—Hillforts and hilltop enclosures (filled symbols = excavated sites) (Eoin Grogan).

production sites—such as Rathgall, Co. Wicklow, Lough Gur, Co. Limerick, and Dalkey Island, Co. Dublin (Raftery 1976; 1994; Ó Ríordáin 1954; Liversage 1968)—rather than widespread, small-scale, domestic manufacture of artefacts. This is in keeping with the increased technological expertise required to make these items, as well as a wider understanding of the importance of restricted control of special and costly resources and commodities. This is an area where the extensive excavations of the past 15 years have revealed virtually no evidence; despite the recovery of intensive occupation, only one site has produced anything more than the most meagre industrial activity. Even at Corrstown the Middle Bronze Age mould fragments appear not to have been in active use but had been recycled—by boring suspension holes through the matrices—as ornaments (Grogan 2012), or perhaps, given their weight, as household charms suspended at the entrances or within the houses themselves. Just a single site, Rathwilladoon 2, Co. Galway (S Delaney et al. 2012a, 43–5, illus. 2.5; Grogan & Roche 2012, 48–9), can be added to Ginn's (2011, table 2) comprehensive list of domestic sites with metal-working evidence.

Despite the significant and increasing number of Late Bronze Age settlements, these, like those of the preceding periods, show an extraordinary dearth of metal. This suggests that most people had only limited access to even basic bronze tools (Ginn 2011, 51–3). The implication is that the social, and perhaps increasingly political, élite maintained a tight control over the acquisition of the costly materials—copper, tin, gold, amber—as well as over the distribution and ownership of the artefacts themselves. It is also apparent that this group also patronised specialist craftworkers. Another feature of the material assemblage is the reduction in the number of sites associated with pottery, although some large assemblages are also recorded from this period, as at Rathgall (Raftery 1976), Raynestown 1, Co. Meath (Elder 2009), Lough Gur, Co. Limerick, and, more recently, Drumgold, Co. Wexford (Hull 2016, 81).

At least some of the resultant material wealth was accumulated into large collections, and much of this was deposited in hoards (G Eogan 1983). The depositions themselves were almost certainly public events and represented the ostentatious display of disposable wealth. They also reflect a belief system that associated access to, and appeasement of, the gods with water, as the majority of these hoards come from lakes, bogs and rivers (Bourke 2001; Cooney & Grogan 1999, 158–68).

The public display of power and influence is also reflected in the renewed construction of large-scale ritual monuments such as ceremonial enclosures and hillforts (Illus. 8). New discoveries include the trivallate hillfort at Rahally, Co. Galway (Mullins 2014), and hilltop enclosures at Haggardstown, Co. Louth (McLoughlin 2010), Stamullin, Co. Meath (Ní Lionáin 2007), and Drumgold (Hull 2016, 81). While Rahally may have been a surprise discovery, the more recent identification of another major site at Drumgold demonstrates the 'hidden' nature of even large-scale monuments and the limitations of our predictive landscape modelling. While excavated hillforts produced evidence for habitation, this is small-scale with, at most, a few houses. The function of the sites was primarily to project power—that of the local communities who built them and, at least in some areas, that of the political élite who exercised increasing authority and wealth control (Grogan 2005b, 111–32).

Substantial ceremonial enclosures were also being constructed, as at Lugg, Co. Dublin, and the Grange Stone Circle, Lough Gur, Co. Limerick (Kilbride-Jones 1950; Roche 2004; Ó Ríordáin 1951; Roche & Eogan 2007) (Illus. 9). Monuments of this type appear to have a limited distribution, although several potential sites have been identified in south-east Clare and east Limerick (Grogan 2005a, 46–54; 2005b, 47–88). While human bone was recovered from both Lugg and Grange, this did not appear to be derived from formal on-site burials. In this period, as with the preceding Middle Bronze Age, the funerary record is dominated by simple pit cremations; occasionally these contain broken pottery sherds, probably reflecting the same attitude to 'closure' as cremation and the comminution (reduction by crushing) of human bone. More elaborate burial is also recorded, however, including those contained in upright or inverted domestic pots, as at Kilbane, Co. Limerick (O'Callaghan 2012), Darcystown, Co. Dublin (Carroll et al. 2008), and Carrig. The continued use of ring-ditches is also attested. At Kellymount 5, Co. Kilkenny, a substantial ditch (external diameter 12 m) enclosed a slighter ring-ditch (diameter 5.6 m) with a central, unaccompanied, cremation pit containing a single adult or adolescent (Wierbicki & Coughlan 2013). A very similar, but much more substantial, site at Raynestown 1 was 21.5 m in external diameter, with a slighter inner ring-ditch (5.6–6.1 m in diameter) (Illus. 10). There is a striking similarity between the double barrows at Kellymount 5 and Raynestown 1 and those at Rath Grainne, Tara, Co. Meath (Newman 1997, pls 20–1). A complex sequence of events is indicated at Raynestown 1, but the first phase, possibly associated with the inner ring-ditch, dates from the Early Bronze Age, while the more monumental outer element witnessed burial and pottery deposition (a substantial quantity of domestic pottery) towards the end of the Late Bronze Age (Elder 2009). At least 37 vessels were represented; the majority of these had previously been used for cooking and some, at least, appear to have been broken immediately prior to deposition (Grogan & Roche 2009a). The reuse of domestic pottery or possibly, on occasion, the use of pottery in funerary ritual and feasting is a widespread feature of Middle to Late Bronze Age burials.

A feature of the later Bronze Age is the proliferation of small-scale monuments (stone circles and alignments, radial cairns, boulder burials, 'four-posters' and enclosures; see P Walsh 1993), and while these are concentrated in the south-west they have a much wider distribution (e.g. Grogan 2005b, 169–82, figs 10a–d, 10.2a). Few of these types of site have been excavated as part of infrastructural development programmes, but a small complex of standing stones, one of them surrounded by a small post circle (3.5 m in diameter), occurred at Kilmurry C, Co. Kilkenny, and revealed an apparently episodic sequence of construction, modification and use in the Early to Middle Bronze Age (Wren & Halpin 2011). To this can be added several small barrows and ring-ditches, such as Newrath 37, Co. Kilkenny (Wren & Price 2011) (it is necessary to insert a note of caution here, as this site type has a very long currency in prehistoric Ireland). These sites indicate an intense phase of identity and landmark creation and maintenance by local communities, and demonstrate a concern with history, land ownership and the control of local routeways (Grogan 2014). They, and the events centred on them, represent social cohesion—and the concept of community identity and social rank—at a local and familial scale similar to those of the Early and Middle Bronze Age. At many of the sites and complexes already mentioned here, such as Kilbane,

Kellymount, Raynestown, Kilmurry, Grange and Carrig, the continuity of use, however episodic, indicates a very lengthy attachment of individual families and communities to these landmark locations.

The newer, and very much more substantial, monument types, such as hillforts and large ceremonial enclosures, indicate a more extensive social scale of labour and reflect a major change in socio-economic authority. The control of these monuments and the authority to muster and direct the very significant labour input required was undoubtedly reserved to the élite, as was the power to officiate at public ceremonies and ritual occasions. The emergence of a well-defined overclass, what has been referred to as a warrior aristocracy, is heralded at the beginning of the Late Bronze Age by the development of well-defined weaponry—swords, spears, daggers and shields—as well as by an increase in tool types and numbers, and in costly ornaments of gold, bronze and amber (G Eogan 1964; 1983; 2000). It may be that the generally smaller houses of this period reflect some concomitant reduction in status for farming families, and certainly these do not, as we have seen, share in the increased material wealth of the period. As prosperity continued to be mainly derived from farming, it appears that the wealth generated from agricultural surplus was increasingly used to satisfy the desire for ostentatious display coupled with lavish deposition in hoards. It is probable, nevertheless, that the benefits derived from large-scale communal building programmes, from ritual and social ceremonial activities and from votive offerings of artefacts and hoards were seen at some level to be inclusive and of value to more than simply those with the power to control these events and projects. The Late Bronze Age witnessed the first element of regional differentiation, in both monument and artefact types (G Eogan 1974; 1993; Grogan 2005b, 169–86, figs 9.1–9.2), and in some areas the emergence of even more powerful élites capable, at least for a time, of establishing control over multiple communities and wielding very considerable economic authority (Grogan 2005a, 87–101).

Tracks and routeways

During the Bronze Age there was a network of increasingly well-established local pathways and longer regional and intra-regional routeways. These connected neighbours and neighbouring communities as well as familiar and frequently visited locales, such as *fulachtaí fia*, woodland and farmland, and ritual—including funerary—landmarks. Actual trackways of timber have been widely recognised in wetland terrain and numerous examples were investigated in the Mountdillon Bogs, Co. Longford, and in the Lisheen area of County Tipperary (Raftery 1996; Whittaker 2009; Gowen et al. 2005). At Newrath 34, Co. Kilkenny, for example, a complex of tracks and platforms and a *fulacht fia* indicated ongoing access to a small area of wetland throughout the Early to Middle Bronze Age (Wilkins et al. 2009, 116–27), while an impressive trackway (EDC 5) was identified at Edercloon, Co. Longford (Moore 2008, 2) (Illus. 11).

Proximity to these local and regional trails provided easy access to communication and resources, and settlement tended to congregate along them. Some of these are readily identifiable:

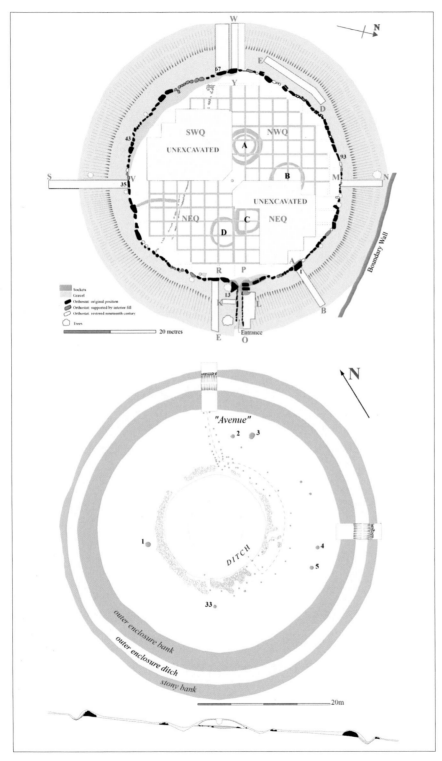

Illus. 9—The Late Bronze Age ceremonial enclosures at the Grange Stone Circle, Lough Gur, Co. Limerick, and Lugg, Co. Dublin (from Roche 2004 and Roche & Eogan 2007).

Opposite page: Illus. 10—The Late Bronze Age barrows at Kellymount 5, Co. Kilkenny, and Raynestown 1, Co. Meath (from Wierbicki & Coughlan 2013 and Elder 2009).

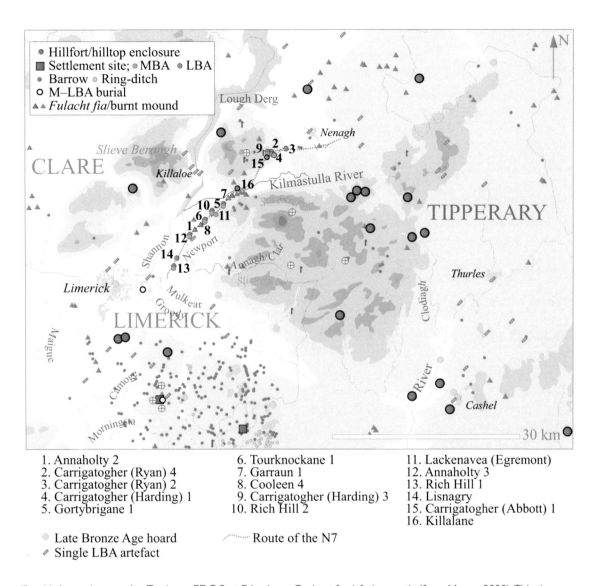

1. Annaholty 2
2. Carrigatogher (Ryan) 4
3. Carrigatogher (Ryan) 2
4. Carrigatogher (Harding) 1
5. Gortybrigane 1
6. Tourknockane 1
7. Garraun 1
8. Cooleen 4
9. Carrigatogher (Harding) 3
10. Rich Hill 2
11. Lackenavea (Egremont)
12. Annaholty 3
13. Rich Hill 1
14. Lisnagry
15. Carrigatogher (Abbott) 1
16. Killalane

Illus. 11 (opposite page)—Trackway EDC 5 at Edercloon, Co. Longford, facing south (from Moore 2008). This site dates from the Late Bronze Age (1260–970 BC, Wk-20961, 2909 ± 3900 BP) and was one of a series of trackways, extending in date from the Middle Neolithic to the medieval period, identified in the peatland of this area. Part of a timber block wheel came from the foundations of the trackway.

Illus. 12 (above)—The later prehistory of the Kilmastulla Valley, Co. Tipperary (prepared by Eoin Grogan; information from TVAS (Ireland) Ltd excavations on the N7 Nenagh to Limerick Scheme, with additions).

for example, valleys extending into, or through, upland areas such as the Boggeragh Mountains in County Kerry or the Slievefelims and Silvermines in County Tipperary (Grogan 2005b, figs 6.5, 6.7, 6.9, 9.6–9.8; 2006); these are the 'natural' means of accessing or passing through difficult terrain.

We can return here to our starting point: the startling increase in Bronze Age sites and the attendant multitude of new data. The North Munster region was the subject of intense research just as the NRA was being established. Many actual, and potential, Middle and Late Bronze Age sites had been identified before the impact of, for example, the construction of the N7 Nenagh to Limerick Scheme (Grogan 2005b, fig. 6.7). I just draw your attention in particular to the line of the N7 in the Kilmastulla Valley, Co. Tipperary, where existing sites suggested that this was a major routeway, leading to the main crossing point of the Lower Shannon at Killaloe, Co. Clare. What the work here has revealed is clear confirmation of that theory and, moreover, the time-depth of the route, extending from the Mesolithic into the Iron Age. These discoveries have also added to the picture of intense settlement, and significant population levels, in one of the wealthiest parts of Europe during this period (Illus. 12).

Conclusions

Throughout the period the basic social structure, embedded in familial and small-scale communities, remained unchanged. This was founded primarily on a mixed farming economy that provided, if not prosperity, a considerable measure of dietary and domestic stability. The ways in which identity and social standing were created and maintained altered, as we have seen, with differing emphasis on features such as burial ritual and house architecture. There appears to have been a steady, if not necessarily continuous, increase in population, with a perceptible, if not yet quantifiable, rise during the Middle Bronze Age. A phase of more dramatic change is evident in the Late Bronze Age, with significant increase in the production and range of metal artefacts, including weapons and costly ornaments, based on improved and more specialised technology. A side-effect of this increased output may have been large-scale bee-keeping (with a demand for wax in bronze-casting) and the availability of honey in significantly larger quantities; we can only speculate, but perhaps this also allowed for greater alcohol production and consumption! The demand for more resources, including tin and amber, and probably copper, produced a wider international framework of contact. These changes also reflect the emergence of new powerful élites who exerted considerable socio-economic authority and who also appear to have had control over ritual and ceremonial events and arenas. This centralisation of power is more apparent in some regions, mainly those with hillforts and evident disposable wealth, the accumulation of which may have put an increasingly unsustainable pressure—imports and high-status goods have to be paid for—on the agricultural economy and on social cohesion. Towards the end of the Bronze Age, after around 900 BC, there appears to be a reduction in population, with fewer recognised sites. At around this time, for example, the amount of pottery diminishes—with a few notable exceptions, such as Rathgall and Raynestown 1—and, after what may be a brief revival in

Illus. 13—The 'face-mask' cup from Mitchelstown 2, Co. Cork (John Sunderland).

the Hallstatt C period of the Early Iron Age, represented principally by bronze swords and chapes imitating Continental trends, pottery production in Ireland inexplicably ceases until after the middle of the first millennium AD.

A final word …

The new discoveries over the past 15 years or so have been astonishing principally for the quantity, and detail, of new information. Apart from this there were few real surprises. There were some, however, and among these were the unique tin bead from Sonnagh (see above), the related necklaces of stone beads from two cremation burials at Caltragh, Co. Sligo (Sheridan 2007b), and a necklace of 25 fine ceramic beads from a cremation burial at Burtown Little, Co. Kildare (Grogan, Dunne et al. 2016; Grogan & Roche 2009b). The most startling discovery is the 'face-mask' cup from a ritual or votive deposit in a simple pit in Mitchelstown 2, Co. Cork (Sutton 2013; Grogan & Roche 2006; 2013b, 315–16) (Illus. 13). It was part of a very carefully structured deposit nestling beside a plain, tub-shaped companion. The ceramic vessel has two splayed feet, two simple circular eyes and a very prominent and carefully sculpted nose. The combination of having only two feet and an oversized nose meant that it relied on the tub-shaped pot for support. Both vessels have lugs shaped like ears and facing, in each case, in opposite directions. In their final resting place—and, presumably, while in ritual or ceremonial use—they were positioned so that the four ears faced north, south, east and west, 'listening' in every direction, while the face and, no doubt, extra-sensitive nose faced west. A ceramic spoon, for libation or sprinkling, lay inside the tub. The deposit, which contained no evidence for burial, disturbed an earlier inverted cordoned urn—itself also without human bone—that had been carefully cut to accommodate the new entrants to the pit. This is a unique artefact deposit at both an Irish and a European level.

Acknowledgements

It has been my privilege over the past 15 years to visit a great number of excavations and I would like to extend my thanks to the companies who facilitated this, especially Margaret Gowen & Co. Ltd, Irish Archaeological Consultancy Ltd, TVAS (Ireland) Ltd, Archaeological Consultancy Services Ltd and Rubicon Heritage Services Ltd (formerly Headland Archaeology (Ireland) Ltd). I am grateful for the unfailing hospitality and generous discussion of numerous site directors. My thanks to the archaeological team in TII, especially Michael Stanley, Jerry O'Sullivan, Rónán Swan, James Eogan, Mary Deevy and Bernice Kelly. My research has been enriched by discussions with many colleagues but I would like to particularly acknowledge Neil Carlin, Vicky Ginn, Helen Roche, Fintan Walsh, Melanie McQuade and Lorna O'Donnell.

5

NEW PERSPECTIVES ON THE IRISH IRON AGE: THE IMPACT OF NRA DEVELOPMENT ON OUR UNDERSTANDING OF LATER PREHISTORY

Katharina Becker, Ian Armit & Graeme T Swindles

More so, perhaps, than for other periods, development-led archaeology, and thus in particular NRA development, has had an impact on current knowledge of the Iron Age of Ireland. It is not that more sites have been found from this period than from any other—quite the contrary, in fact, when compared, for example, to the much larger numbers found from the Bronze Age (see Grogan, this volume) and early medieval period (see O'Sullivan & McCormick, this volume). It is more that the contrast with what went before is so dramatic, as previously very few sites datable to the Iron Age had been identified. This paper will outline some of this new evidence and discuss the challenges and opportunities it presents to how we think about the Iron Age, its people and their ways of life.

In addition to conventional archaeological questions about the socio-economic organisation, cosmology, religion and cultural affiliation of its 'inhabitants', the Irish Iron Age has posed even more basic questions, many of which could hardly be addressed at all owing to a simple lack of data. Such information as there was comprised little more than a small body of artefacts (Illus. 1) and a scant distribution of possible settlement sites and ritual complexes (Illus. 2), in stark contrast to the picture in the main created by the sites found in the context of 'Celtic Tiger' developments (Illus. 3). The enduring fascination of the Irish Iron Age as the traditionally understood period of the 'Irish Celts' thus stood in striking contrast to an impoverished archaeological record that did not allow us to provide fundamental understandings about the chronological and cultural definition of the period in even the broadest sense. Questions about when the Bronze Age ended and when the Iron Age began went hand in hand with a debate as to whether there was in fact an Iron Age in Ireland at all in any meaningful sense and, if so, whether it was present only in certain parts of the country. Did it reflect the activities of significant numbers of people or merely the scattered descendants of the former Bronze Age population, for some reason depopulated and diminished?

The new dataset: challenges and opportunities

The data generated by NRA-funded excavations form a significant proportion of the overall dataset now available for the Irish Iron Age (Illus. 3). Based on figures assembled in 2012, NRA projects contributed 465 sites dated to between 1200 BC and AD 400 (the majority identified through radiocarbon dating) (Illus. 4). This represents more than 50% of the overall corpus of sites

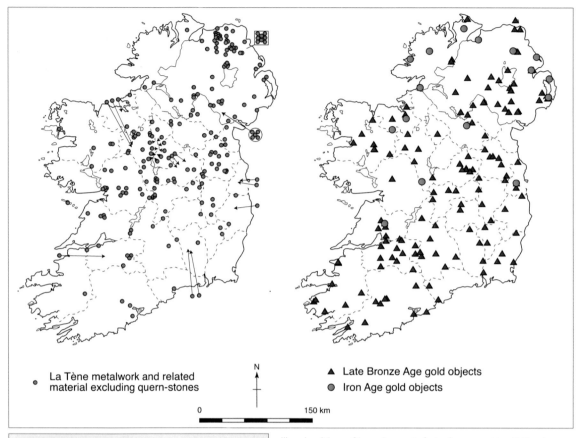

La Tène metalwork and related
material excluding quern-stones

N

▲ Late Bronze Age gold objects
⬤ Iron Age gold objects

0   150 km

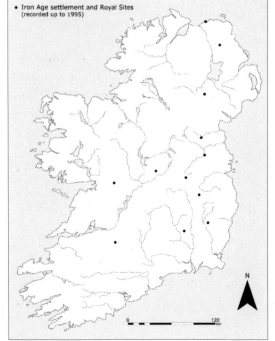

Iron Age settlement and Royal Sites
(recorded up to 1995)

N

0   120
         km

Illus. 1—Map of Iron Age artefacts (prepared by Katharina Becker, after Raftery 1983, map 23).

Illus. 2—Map of Iron Age settlement and royal sites (prepared by Katharina Becker, after Raftery 1983, map 23, and Raftery 1994).

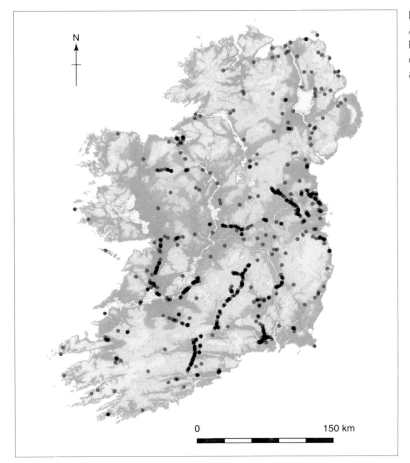

Illus. 3—Distribution of new Iron Age sites (prepared by Rachael Kershaw and Emily Fioccoprile; data collection and processing by the authors).

known from that period. The enormous role of work on road schemes in Ireland is even more striking if one also considers the contribution of 74 sites in the north of the country. Other large-scale developments have also contributed, under the auspices of, for example, Bord na Móna, Bord Gáis, the Railway Procurement Agency and numerous private developers. While we can have some confidence, based on our data collection, that these proportions of contributions from the NRA and other developers are broadly correct, the varying dissemination and publication strategies across the sector determine the numbers of sites about which information is accessible to the archaeological community and the broader public. The NRA's policy of actively making reports available and encouraging full publication has thus had a significant impact on the speed and breadth of dissemination of excavation results from Irish road schemes.

Our research has paid great attention to the particular problems and challenges inherent in datasets generated from developer-led archaeology in general and from NRA projects in particular. A number of issues that potentially affect both the generation of the dataset and its subsequent analysis have to be considered. Most of these apply to any project engaging with data generated from development-led archaeology, nationally or internationally.

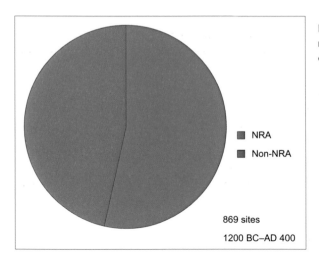

Illus. 4—Late prehistoric sites (by licence number) recorded until 2012, excavated for NRA or other developers (the authors).

■ NRA

■ Non-NRA

869 sites

1200 BC–AD 400

1. The reliance on radiocarbon-dated sites without an existing chronological framework within which to anchor them.

In the absence of typo-chronological frameworks that would provide either a relative or an absolute chronological scheme for the excavated sites, the impact of the imprecision inherent in radiocarbon dates is particularly strong. Where sequences of radiocarbon dates can be constrained by cross-reference to relative chronological frameworks such as site stratigraphies, typologies or other absolute dates, their probability can be improved. Where this is not possible, a pool of widely overlapping probability ranges obscures the true dating of the archaeology. This requires particular scrutiny in the interpretation of the dates and caution in the construction of chronological schemes (see also issue 2, below). Bayesian statistical analysis as well as the scarce traditional typo-chronological dating evidence can help to anchor and constrain sequences and sites.

2. Methodological issues for the qualitative and quantitative analysis of radiocarbon dates.

In addition to the imprecision inherent in their probability ranges, other issues also affect the validity and meaning of radiocarbon dates. Complexities surrounding the association of dates, and thus the relevance of the date for the context of interest, are crucially important. In addition, the date itself needs to be scrutinised in order to take possible own-age effects into account (i.e. the age of, for example, a piece of wood at the time of its use in an Iron Age structure). Going beyond this, the determination of quantitative trends within a dataset defined by radiocarbon dates also presents problems (e.g. Armit et al. 2013; Kerr & McCormick 2013).

3. Dominance of sites without deep stratigraphy.

The majority of sites are excavated in the context of development schemes, whose routes are heavily influenced by the systematic avoidance of visible archaeology. This in turn means that lowland locations, subject to damaging agricultural impact and unlikely to contain deep surviving stratigraphy, are over-represented. In contrast, hilltop sites, which might often have more potential for surviving stratigraphic depth, are under-represented, simply because development tends not to take place today on hilltops. Lowland sites characteristically contain clusters of cut features (i.e. the remains of pits, post-holes or ditches) and only rarely have the stratigraphic depth that would allow for the building of a site sequence, with the effect that potentially unrelated features float in chronological space and site history. Besides the impact of agricultural activities such as ploughing, detection and—particularly—excavation methods may account for the great degree of truncation frequently observed on modern Irish developer-led excavations. The mechanical stripping of topsoil, for example, even under direct archaeological supervision, has the potential to remove the remains of floor layers or upper strata of sites.

4. Interpretation of linear distribution patterns.

The map of late prehistoric sites in Ireland (Illus. 3) reveals linear distribution patterns that plainly reflect the distribution of development schemes. Similarly, clusters of sites around population centres such as Dublin reflect the higher levels of development activity there. This realisation requires a radical rethinking of the meaning of distribution patterns, as it highlights that they are not representative of real prehistoric activity but the product of modern recovery processes. Thus regional analyses that aim to work comparatively will need to rethink the traditional approach of reading distributions straight off maps.

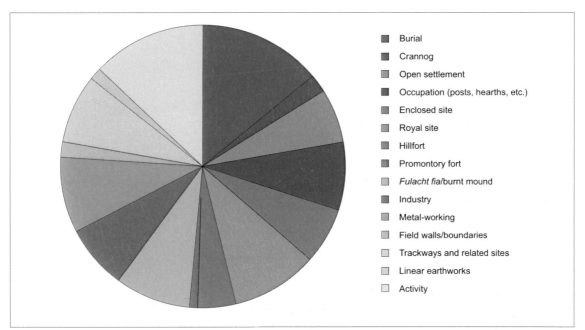

Illus. 5—Range of site types and their relative proportion in the later prehistoric dataset. A site is defined here as a functionally and chronologically discrete complex, often, but not always corresponding to an excavation licence number (the authors).

On the other hand, the new record also presents new and potentially game-changing opportunities for Irish later prehistory.

1. Undirected site selection.

The essentially random aspects of the selection of sites for excavation (at least in the sense that they are entirely independent of archaeological research agendas) through infrastructural or commercial development constitute a potential advantage over conventionally derived datasets. The linear character of schemes, cutting through different landscapes and uncovering archaeology in an *a priori* unbiased fashion, provides a relatively random and thus possibly more representative range of sites. Indeed, this aspect of recent work seems to be confirmed by the range of site types newly uncovered in addition to the well-known parts of the record (Illus. 5). An obvious caveat is the under-representation of more visible archaeological monuments or prominent locations, both avoided in development schemes.

2. Complementarity.

The new archaeological record complements high-visibility sites uncovered in research excavations, such as hillforts or royal sites. It has provided ephemeral, truncated sites, mostly without artefacts, that potentially represent the previously missing 'mundane and everyday' archaeology.

3. Critical mass

The new data provide a critical mass of well-dated sites for broad-scale analysis. This facilitates the construction of models of cultural, economic and demographic change that allow us to move beyond analyses based on anecdotal evidence.

The archaeological record of the period between 800 BC and AD 400 now encompasses a range of both secular and ritual sites, as well as a variety of craft/industrial and settlement forms. These allow us to review our fundamental vision of the period. A previously glaring gap in the record, for example, was the absence of recognisable settlements and house structures. While these are still rare, they nevertheless provide a broadly coherent picture that is beginning to suggest an essentially unbroken tradition of roundhouse-building—both plank- and post-built—from the Bronze Age through the first millennium BC. NRA schemes have revealed examples of both types, curiously appearing alongside one another at one of the earliest recent road scheme discoveries: Ballinaspig More 5, Co. Cork (Danaher & Cagney 2004) (Illus. 6). Houses can occur individually, probably representing dispersed farmsteads or smaller accumulations of up to two contemporary houses, as encountered, for example, on the N11 scheme at Site 13, Moneylawn Lower, Co. Wexford (Illus. 7 & 8). Here the road corridor captured a range of contemporary elements of the Iron Age phase of a multi-period site (McKinstry 2011). Two possible houses were accompanied by a kiln-like structure of uncertain function with a long, stone-lined flue. The site was located in a valley in a landscape characterised by lowlands and high hills. The lower parts of

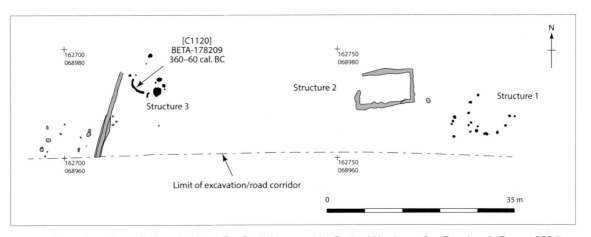

Illus. 6—Plan of the site at Ballinaspig More, Co. Cork (prepared by Rachael Kershaw, after Danaher & Cagney 2004).

the valley were rather waterlogged, but may still have been exploited for pasture and other low-intensity agriculture—field boundaries or drains in the area may be of prehistoric date. Set on sloping land, the settlement was in landscape that is today used primarily for pasture (ibid., 3). The houses, as represented in the excavation plans, can be reconstructed with a diameter of about 10 m—a very substantial size, similar to that observed, for example, at the post-built structure at Ballinaspig More. This puts Iron Age structures on a par with those of the medieval period in terms of their dimensions—the largest house of that period at Moynagh Lough, for example, measured 11.2 m in diameter (A O'Sullivan et al. 2014a, 98, fig. 3.15). While the excavated part of the site captures only one clear phase of Iron Age activity, the very early medieval date obtained from a sample of the later enclosure ditch, in the north of the site (McKinstry 2011, 23–9), suggests repeated, if not continued, use of the site for settlement.

These sites counteract to some extent the formerly prevalent idea that a dominance of impermanent, ephemeral habitation sites lay behind the apparent invisibility of Iron Age settlement (Raftery 1994, 113; but compare with Armit 2007, 135). The new impression of an established and routine roundhouse tradition is reinforced by the occurrence of a roundhouse at Site 4700.1b, Knockcommane, Co. Tipperary (Molloy 2007b), here apparently constructed to shelter an iron workshop (Illus. 9 & 10). The roundhouse, which was surrounded by a circular ditch, displayed some unusual constructional details, including a combination of post-built and slot-trench walls, although it would probably have appeared no different to any other roundhouse in the landscape. The site of Knockcommane is a further example where contemporary activity allows us to start building a more complex picture of the Iron Age use of different localities within the landscape. Here, out of the direct line of sight but only about 100 m away, was a contemporary ring-barrow (Molloy 2007a), which contained several cremation burials. It is notable that the segment of landscape captured by the stretch of road within which these sites were located is notable for a general lack of archaeological activity, only some *fulachtaí fia* having been observed in addition to the sites at Knockcommane themselves (Molloy 2007b, after Deery 2005) in a

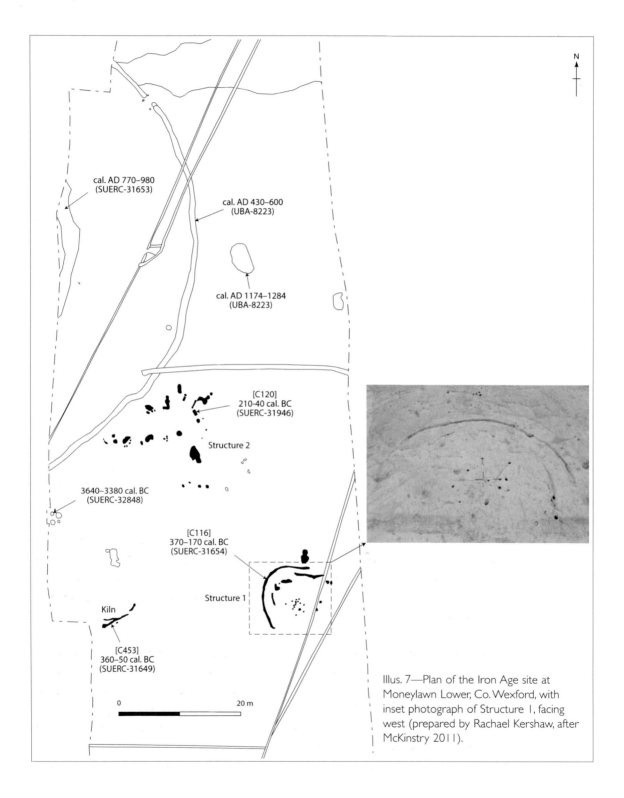

cal. AD 770–980
(SUERC-31653)

cal. AD 430–600
(UBA-8223)

cal. AD 1174–1284
(UBA-8223)

[C120]
210-40 cal. BC
(SUERC-31946)

Structure 2

3640–3380 cal. BC
(SUERC-32848)

[C116]
370–170 cal. BC
(SUERC-31654)

Structure 1

Kiln

[C453]
360–50 cal. BC
(SUERC-31649)

0   20 m

N

Illus. 7—Plan of the Iron Age site at
Moneylawn Lower, Co. Wexford, with
inset photograph of Structure 1, facing
west (prepared by Rachael Kershaw, after
McKinstry 2011).

Illus. 8—Reconstruction of the Iron Age site at Moneylawn Lower. Structure 1, in the foreground, is reconstructed as a post-ring structure with an outer wattle wall with a slight porch. We interpret the slight slot-trench as the footing for the outer wattle wall. The post-holes defining the entrance can be clearly recognised on the inset photograph opposite but not on the plan. The environmental evidence suggests a relatively open landscape (drawn by Dave Pollack and based on the authors' site interpretation).

landscape consisting of generally poor and low-lying ground that was heavily forested (ibid.). Charcoal analysis suggests a nearby supply of oak and associated hazel (O'Donnell 2007b, 34). The availability of wood, a resource used both in the fuel-intensive activities of cremation and in metal-working, as well as in water-boiling at the Bronze Age *fulachtaí fia*, may have been an important factor in choosing this location. The settlement itself, however, may have been located closer to the place of the actual subsistence activities—on cleared farmland or pasture.

The accumulating evidence provided by infrastructural developments is not ground-breaking only because it is new. Rather its impact also lies in the fact that it helps to correct potential misinterpretations of known sites. One example is the ringfort containing three houses at Lislackagh, Co. Mayo (G Walsh 1995), where previously anomalous-seeming dates—the calibration range spans from 200 BC to AD 200 (ibid., 8)—had even very recently been considered to be the result of the 'old wood effect' (Kerr et al. 2009, 441), although in fact, according to the laboratory's records, the samples were derived from 1 mm flots of charred plant remains. (The old

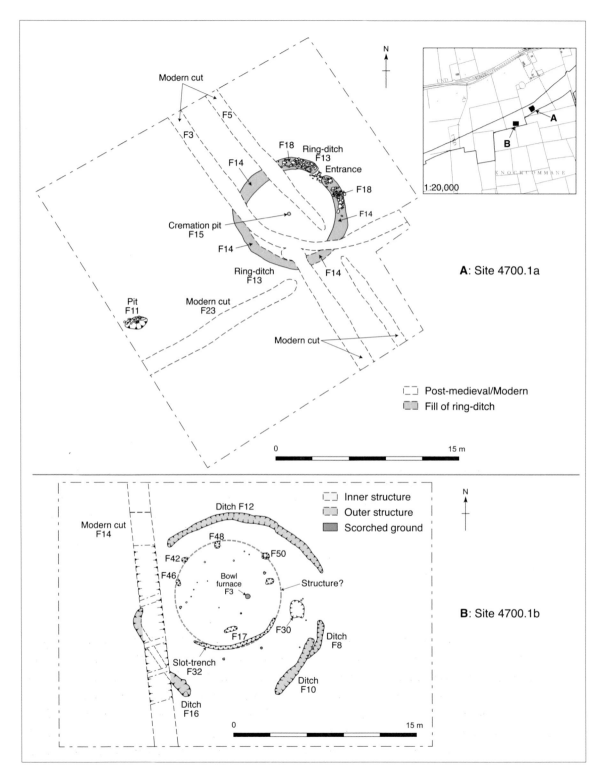

Modern cut

F5

F3

F14

F18

Ring-ditch
F13

Entrance

F18

F14

Cremation pit
F15

F14

Ring-ditch
F13

F14

Pit
F11

Modern cut
F23

Modern cut

A: Site 4700.1a

1:20,000

A

B

KNOCKOMMANE

⊏ ⊐ Post-medieval/Modern

⊏ ⊐ Fill of ring-ditch

0   15 m

N

Ditch F12

F48

Modern cut
F14

F42

F50

F46

Bowl
furnace
F3

Structure?

F17

F30

Ditch
F8

Slot-trench
F32

Ditch
F10

Ditch
F16

⊏ ⊐ Inner structure

⊏ ⊐ Outer structure

▓ Scorched ground

B: Site 4700.1b

0   15 m

N

Illus. 9 (opposite page)—Plan of Sites 4700.1a and 4700.1b at Knockcommane, Co. Limerick (prepared by Rachael Kershaw, after Molloy 2007b, combination of figs 3 & 4, and Molloy 2007a, combination of figs 4 and 5).

Illus. 10 (above)—Reconstruction of the Iron Age site at Knockcommane. We interpret the presence of both slot-trench and post-set stretches of wall as representing a functional feature of the house and suggest the use of curtains/screens as movable elements in those parts that have only post settings. This would allow the manipulation of air flow into the iron-working workshop. We have placed the bank on the outside of the ditch. This is to allow a little space around the building, which would otherwise have been immediately surrounded by the bank. While out of sight, smoke rising in the background indicates the location of the nearby ring-barrow. As our knowledge of the site is only based on the road corridor, the possibility of the existence of further houses on either side cannot, of course, be excluded (drawn by Dave Pollack and based on the authors' site interpretation).

wood effect refers to the possibility that the age of the dated wood sample may be greater than its felling date if, for example, heartwood from a long-lived tree was dated.) The association of the dates with the slot-trenches, rather than with the enclosure ditch, appears clear, and hence the occupation of the site is datable to the Iron Age. The finds assemblage from the site does, as noted elsewhere (e.g. A O'Sullivan et al. 2014a, 70), contain typologically early medieval material, but this derives mainly from topsoil contexts rather than from the houses themselves (Cleary 1993, 49). Only possibly lithics (Anderson 1993) and some small blue glass beads (Cleary 1993, no. 347) that appear to fit current understanding of Iron Age bead typologies can be demonstrated to have derived from the actual house slot-trenches. While it is not quite clear to what extent the uppermost layers of the trench fill are the result of later disturbance, two undiagnostic iron fragments (nos 141 and 144) may be either Iron Age or medieval in date (ibid.). Hence the finds do not need to raise doubts about the dating of the slot-trenches. It should be noted, however, that the dating of the enclosure itself has not been established, yet its contemporaneity with the houses appears likely, given the articulation of the buildings within its circle. Supporting this would be the fact that, according to the report (G Walsh 1993), no medieval finds came from the ditch, with only two undiagnostic iron objects associated with redeposited bank material (Cleary 1993, no. 130) representing possible medieval candidates, in contrast to views expressed elsewhere (Ó Drisceoil 2007b, 23). In fact, it would appear that the diagnostic medieval material from Lislackagh derives exclusively from topsoil contexts and may represent a later phase of use of the site.

Looking forward

The previous paradigm, which assumed the absence of a visible Iron Age settlement record, was so powerful in Ireland that newly found examples of Iron Age sites still often fell victim to the belief that 'what we know not to exist cannot exist'. This can mean in practice that radiocarbon dates that do not fit the presumed typo-chronological dating of a site are effectively discarded without any firm methodological basis—or, where the dating is accepted, that the interpretations of a site are altered to fit preconceptions of the Iron Age. The new corpus should provide us with the confidence to take sites at face value, Lislackagh being a case in point.

	1150	1100	1000	900	800	700	600	500	400	300	200	100	BC/AD	100	200	300
		Late Bronze Age			Early Iron Age/transition				Developed Iron Age				Late Iron Age			
Pottery		Coarse Ware			Aceramic											
Metalwork assemblage		Roscommon/Dowris							La Tène							
														Romanised		
Sites							Iron use				Iron production					
													Kilns			
		Hillfort construction											'Royal' sites			
										Earthworks						
								Open settlement								
	Enclosed settlement												Enclosed settlement			
							Fulachtaí fia									
						Cremation burial										
													Inhumation burial			
					Pit burial/cemeteries/ring-ditches											

Illus. 11—Chronological scheme for the Late Bronze Age and Iron Age (the authors).

Illus. 12—Post-excavation aerial view of the ringfort at Ross, Co. Meath (Studio Lab).

More importantly, however, the new corpus provides us with a critical mass of data that allows us to draw conclusions that go beyond the anecdotal and observational. Dramatic cultural and technological changes can now be traced throughout the period (Illus. 11). For example, taking houses and settlements (one of the smaller groups of sites in the dataset), some broad chronological trends can already be identified. Most clearly there appears to be a change in settlement organisation, with enclosed sites frequently occurring in the Late Bronze Age, disappearing around 800 BC and reappearing in the centuries around the turn of the millennium. This starts to provide us with answers to long-standing questions regarding the earliest beginnings of what are later known as ringforts. While still only represented by very small numbers, enclosed sites of ringfort type can be shown to emerge in the last two centuries BC (Becker et al., in prep.). One example is Ross, Co. Meath, excavated on the M3 scheme, where radiocarbon dates derived from the ditch fill (Wiggins et al. 2009, 14–17) indicate that the construction of the ditch took place not long before 60 BC–AD 80 (Illus. 12). While a ditch recut/extension produced an early medieval date, the creation of the strictly circular penannular enclosure is clearly datable to the Iron Age (ibid.). A circular house structure that would have been covered by the bank of the ditched enclosure pre-dated the enclosure and may also be datable to an earlier Iron Age phase.

Equally dramatic is the opportunity for quantitative analysis offered by the new critical mass of well-dated, radiocarbon-dated sites. Rarely are archaeologists afforded datasets that could be considered to be not only representative of past activity levels and large enough to reflect broad-

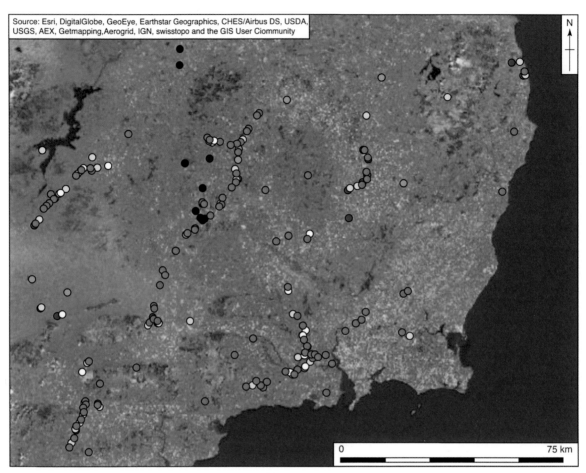

Illus. 13—Site distribution in south-east Ireland, 1200–800 BC (above) and 800–400 BC (opposite), showing a reduction in site density overall and retraction of activity inland (prepared by Rachael Kershaw, after Armit et al. 2014, fig. 3).

scale changes over time but also sufficiently well dated to be examined in quantitative terms. Previous ideas surrounding times of affluence or crisis and population levels have generally relied on relative quantities of artefacts, the emergence or disappearance of defensive features, or numbers of people visible in excavated burial sites—all features of the archaeological record that are heavily affected by cultural filters. In contrast, the new dataset can be used to infer levels of human activity through time (Armit et al. 2013), allowing, for example, the examination of changes in the archaeological record against shifts in the palaeoclimatic sequence (Armit et al. 2014). This potentially enables the correlation or disentanglement of developments in the different datasets— for example, the disassociation of the demographic collapse of Bronze Age society from an episode of rapid climate change that followed shortly afterwards (ibid.). It also allows us to trace subtle processes of change within the human past by differentiating between cultural change and shifts in activity levels, as, for example, when site activity levels fell away at around 900 BC (Armit et al.

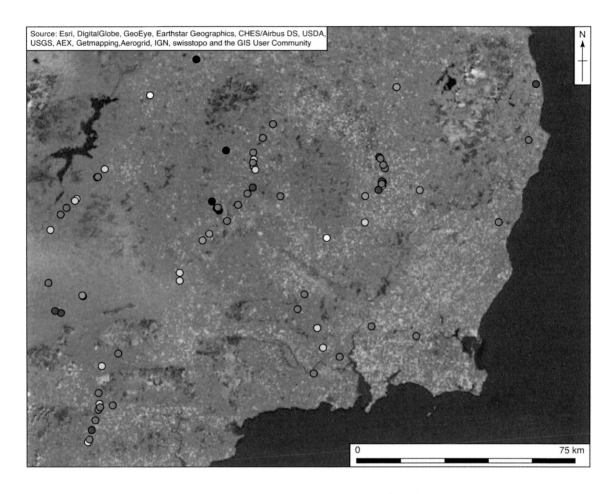

Source: Esri, DigitalGlobe, GeoEye, Earthstar Geographics, CHES/Airbus DS, USDA, USGS, AEX, Getmapping,Aerogrid, IGN, swisstopo and the GIS User Community

0   75 km

2013), whereas significant cultural markers such as pottery and Dowris-type metalwork, the characteristic form of the Late Bronze Age, only ceased to be produced at about 800 BC.

This new critical mass of data also makes our new distribution maps potentially far more meaningful than before. While the problems of linear distribution patterns have been highlighted above, when read correctly (within the confines of the margins of development schemes) they provide a potentially much more representative picture of past human activity and landscape use through time, shifts in use, and the expansion and retraction of settlement areas (Illus. 13).

The new dataset allows us finally to give substance to the Irish Iron Age. Indeed, it has opened up completely new perspectives on Irish later prehistory, importantly affording us the opportunity for significant new methodological developments. It provides, for the first time, the depth, breadth, volume and texture to form the basis for an interrogation that aims to reconstruct regional and chronological variation as well as complex processes of cultural change over time.

Acknowledgements

The research presented here forms part of the project 'Mobility, Climate and Culture: Re-modelling the Irish Iron Age', funded by the British Academy. Preliminary data collection was funded by the Irish Heritage Council. Illustrations were prepared by Rachael Kershaw and Emily Fioccoprile; Dave Pollock created the drawings of the sites at Knockcommane and Moneylawn Lower. The authors would also like to thank all individuals and organisations that facilitated access to data: Aegis Archaeology Ltd; Arch-Tech Ireland Ltd; Archaeological Consultancy Services Ltd; Theresa Bolger; Ed Bourke, Department of Arts, Heritage, Regional, Rural and Gaeltacht Affairs; Emmett Byrnes; Mary Cahill, National Museum of Ireland; Judith Carroll, Judith Carroll & Co. Ltd; Kerri Cleary, University College Cork; Rose Cleary, University College Cork; Sarah-Jane Clelland, University of Bradford; Gordon Cook, SUERC; Gabriel Cooney, UCD School of Archaeology, University College Dublin; Lisa Courtney; CRDS Ltd; Department of the Environment, Northern Ireland Environment Agency; Marion Dowd, Institute of Technology, Sligo; Eachtra Archaeological Projects; George Eogan; Vicky Ginn, Queen's University Belfast (QUB); Margaret Gowen, Margaret Gowen & Co. Ltd; Mary Henry Archaeological Services Ltd; Irish Archaeological Consultancy Ltd; Thomas Kerr, QUB; Jan Lanting, Faculteit Archeologie, Bio-Archaeology, Leiden University; Chris Lynn; Finbar McCormick, QUB; Conor McDermott, UCD School of Archaeology; James McDonald, [14]CHRONO Centre, QUB; Phil MacDonald, Centre for Archaeological Fieldwork, QUB; Tiernan McGarry; Jim Mallory; Mayo County Council; Sarah Milliken; Moore Group; Matt Mossop; Donald Murphy, Archaeological Consultancy Services Unit; Northern Archaeological Consultancy Ltd; Ellen O'Carroll, Trinity College Dublin; Aidan O'Connell, Archer Heritage; John Ó Néill; Aidan O'Sullivan, UCD School of Archaeology; Martin Reid, Department of Arts, Heritage, Regional, Rural and Gaeltacht Affairs; Paula Reimer, QUB; Rubicon Heritage Services Ltd; Matt Seaver, UCD School of Archaeology; Transport Infrastructure Ireland; TVAS (Ireland) Ltd; Hans van der Plicht, Leiden University; Fintan Walsh, Irish Archaeological Consultancy Ltd; Richard Warner; and Peter Woodman.

6

EARLY MEDIEVAL IRELAND: INVESTIGATING SOCIAL, ECONOMIC AND SETTLEMENT CHANGE, AD 400–1100

Aidan O'Sullivan & Finbar McCormick

Introduction

The early medieval period, AD 400–1100, was a time of significant social, ideological and economic transformations and innovations in Ireland. First, Ireland's early medieval archaeological evidence, in strong contrast to that of the preceding Iron Age, suggests a likely major growth in population from about the sixth century onwards, with people building and inhabiting tens of thousands of settlement enclosures—such as raths (ringforts), crannogs, churches and other dwellings—across the landscape (Illus. 1). Archaeological and palaeoenvironmental evidence suggests that the landscape was increasingly owned, appropriated and managed, and the period saw various innovations in agricultural technologies and practices, including the development of a sophisticated dairying economy, while pollen evidence and archaeobotany indicate that arable production also increased, with the use of cereal-drying kilns and horizontal-wheeled watermills to process cereals for domestic consumption and for socio-economic exchanges.

Second, the early medieval period saw the introduction of Christianity into Ireland, which also had its own impact on the settlement landscape and economy. Just as importantly, Christianity is a religion of the book and literacy, so now for the first time, from the seventh century onwards in particular, we have contemporary written documents, such as early Irish laws, saints' Lives, annals and narrative literature. These early Irish historical sources provide a new and powerful means for reconstructing an understanding of early Irish society. They provide a range of insights into early medieval Ireland's distinctive dynastic politics and its territories, as well as the character and organisation of early Irish kinship, social classes, gender roles and religious beliefs and practices.

Early medieval Ireland has long been a subject of interest, often because of its important role as the so-called 'Golden Age of Saints and Scholars' in the creation of modern Irish cultural identities. There have been numerous archaeological excavations of early medieval sites down through the years. Indeed, the landscape and settlement archaeology associated with early medieval Ireland is among the richest in Europe. It is all the more remarkable, then, that the early medieval era has been one of the chronological periods most transformed by the programme of archaeological excavations associated with the NRA's roadway developments. Indeed, it seems likely that the archaeological legacy of the NRA programme of works between c. 1997 and 2015 will require a generation of scholarship to investigate.

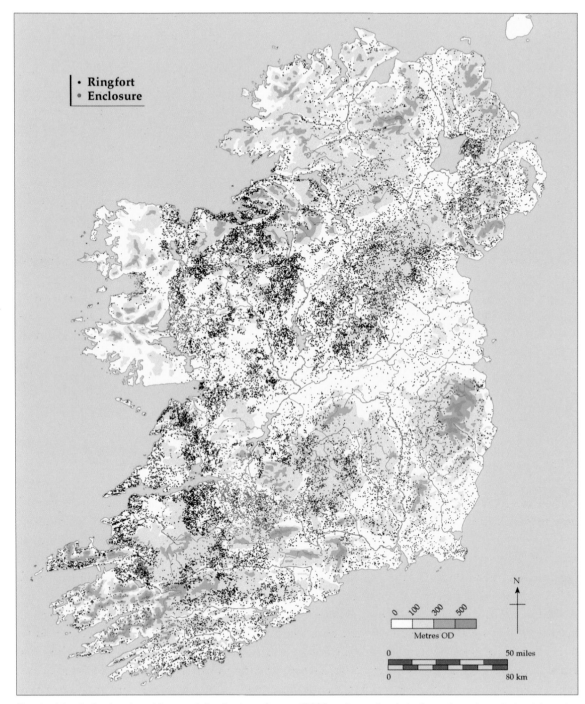

Illus. I—Map indicating the widespread distribution of over 47,000 early medieval ringforts throughout Ireland (map by, and reproduced with the permission of, Matthew Stout; from Stout & Stout 2011, fig. 42).

This work of scholarly analysis has already started, as exemplified by the various Heritage Council Irish National Strategic Archaeological Research (INSTAR) projects that have focused on the early medieval period, such as our own University College Dublin/Queen's University Belfast collaborative Early Medieval Archaeology Project (EMAP); the University College Cork-based Making Christian Landscapes Project led by Dr Tomás Ó Carragáin and colleagues; and the Mapping Death Project based in the Discovery Programme and UCD School of History and Archives, led by Dr Edel Bhreathnach and Dr Elizabeth O'Brien, which investigated early medieval burial practices in particular. In EMAP we endeavoured to characterise the results of archaeological excavations of early medieval sites from 1930 to c. 2010. The project team prepared a series of on-line reports, subsequently published as monographs, on early medieval dwellings and settlements (O'Sullivan et al. 2014b), on early medieval agriculture and food production (McCormick et al. 2014; see also McClatchie, McCormick et al. 2015), and on early medieval crafts and production (Kerr et al. 2015). Finally, EMAP also published, among many papers, a work of synthesis, *Early Medieval Ireland, AD 400–1100: the evidence from archaeological excavations* (O'Sullivan et al. 2014a).

In this paper, then, we will not describe the archaeology of early medieval Ireland again as revealed in excavations commissioned by the NRA and others, but instead will focus on one particular problem—that of identifying social and economic change across time in the centuries AD 400–1100. It is something we have attempted before in the concluding chapter of our main synthesis (O'Sullivan et al. 2014a), but we return to it here with the opportunity to offer more nuanced reflections. Before we do that, however, we will briefly consider the impact—and legacy—of the NRA programmes on our archaeological understanding of this period.

What was the impact and legacy of the NRA archaeological excavations?

Our previous EMAP publications have described the long history of archaeological excavations of early medieval sites in Ireland, and their impact and legacy (O'Sullivan et al. 2014a, and see there for a more detailed historiography). As is well known, influential early medieval archaeological excavations were carried out by the American Harvard Archaeological Expedition in the 1930s, and there were similarly important university-based digs by Seán P Ó Ríordáin and Michael O'Kelly mainly in the 1950s. There were also a series of important 'rescue'-type excavations in the 1970s and 1980s, mainly by state sector archaeologists, in the Republic of Ireland and in Northern Ireland. By the late 1990s, the newly emergent commercial archaeological consultancies started to carry out excavations in advance of such infrastructural developments as gas pipelines, housing estate developments and motorway constructions, following new environmental legislation and policy developments springing from Ireland's membership of the European Union. All this provided the major impetus to the archaeological boom that came about during the years of Ireland's so-called Celtic Tiger economy, c. 1995–2008. In particular, motorway construction continued apace throughout the late 1990s and 2000s, with the creation and expansion of an island-wide network of major roads, mostly within the Republic although there were also schemes in Northern Ireland.

Reflecting on those years, we now can see that the key, even critical, development was the agreement in 2000 of a Code of Practice in the Republic of Ireland between the then NRA (subsequently enfolded within the more recently established Transport Infrastructure Ireland, or TII) and the then Department of Arts, Heritage, Gaeltacht and the Islands. It arguably signalled a shift in terms of both policy and practice.

Experienced professional archaeologists, including several licensed site directors, were appointed as project archaeologists to the various local authority National Roads Design Offices (NRDOs). The Code, and subsequent innovations actively introduced by the NRA project archaeologists, facilitated the use of new techniques, such as more extensive geophysical surveys, as well as more comprehensive centre-line testing along the proposed road corridor. As motorways were planned, both known and previously unknown sites that could not be avoided in the pathway of new roads were to be preserved by record in advance of road construction.

This brought major changes to the practice of excavation in Irish archaeology, particularly in terms of the scale and quality of investigations. Archaeological excavations were now carried out that were much more ambitious in terms of time, area investigated and complexity. In contrast to previous generations, which tended to open trenches through banks and ditches or small areas within enclosures, NRA-funded excavations were not confined to within early medieval settlements or cemeteries themselves but included the spaces around them. NRA-funded commercial sector excavations also investigated a wide range of newly discovered early medieval sites, including new types of settlement enclosures, unenclosed habitations, burial grounds and cemeteries, agricultural field systems, horizontal watermills, cereal-drying kilns and various types of industrial or craft production sites, including features associated with charcoal production, iron-working and other craft and production activities (Kerr, Doyle et al. 2015). Moreover, these were digs that were carried out by highly accomplished and experienced archaeological site directors, supervisors and teams who were vastly more experienced in soils and their investigations than any previous generation of Irish archaeologists.

Furthermore, because of the ways that roads were generally designed to avoid previously known (and potentially costly and time-consuming) archaeology, the NRA's archaeological excavations in advance of motorway construction uncovered large numbers of previously unknown archaeological sites (see Roycroft 2005 for M1 sites, and Deevy 2005, 2006 and 2008 for M3 sites). The impact on early medieval studies of these excavations in the Republic of Ireland can quite clearly be seen by the range of publications that have emerged. Alongside traditional raths, such as at Magheraboy 2B, Co. Sligo, on the N4 (O'Neill 2007) or Leggetsrath West, Co. Kilkenny (Lennon 2006), other less typical enclosures were also uncovered. These included the early medieval settlement and burial ground at Raystown, Co. Meath (Seaver 2005; 2006; 2010), and the early medieval settlement complexes situated along the M3 scheme at Roestown 2, Co. Meath (O'Hara 2007; 2009b), and Baronstown 1, Co. Meath (Linnane & Kinsella 2009), among others, as well as sites on the M4 at Killickaweeny 1, Co. Kildare (F Walsh & Harrison 2003; F

Walsh 2008). A Viking Age *longphort* at Woodstown 6, Co. Waterford, was also discovered in advance of roadworks for the N25 Waterford City Bypass (Russell & Harrison 2011).

The first impact of these discoveries was that the archaeological classification of early medieval monuments started to change, as types of sites were identified that did not seem to fit comfortably within previous understandings of settlement morphologies. The best example of this 'new' category of sites were the early medieval sites which seemed to combine settlement and cemetery functions (variously termed as settlement-cemeteries, secular cemeteries or cemetery-settlements), such as at Balriggan 1, Co. Louth (S Delaney & Roycroft 2003; S Delaney 2010), Johnstown 1, Co. Meath (Clarke 2002; Clarke & Carlin 2008), Twomileborris, Co. Tipperary, where settlement enclosures were found with burials (Ó Droma 2008), and at Carrigatogher (Harding) Site 6, Co. Tipperary, where there was a settlement with extensive metal-working industry and burials (Taylor 2010b). It is still unclear how these sites functioned in the socio-economic landscape; they clearly had complex and changing histories and probably had no one single function. It is clear that they were centres of production, either within estates or territories, and it has since been usefully suggested that some could be early medieval assembly places associated with political territories (Gleeson 2014; 2015). In contrast to the discovery of new types of sites, there were also previously well-known categories of early medieval sites that saw little archaeological excavation. There were far less excavations in these years, for example, of early medieval churches and their associated settlements—apart from the very important work on an early medieval monastic enclosure complex and industrial activities at Clonfad 3, Co. Westmeath (Stevens 2006; 2007), or during the road development works conducted by Waterford City Council that led to excavations at Kill St Lawrence, Co. Waterford (O'Connell 2004). This, however, raises the question of what precisely we expect to find on an early medieval settlement owned by or associated with the church. At Owenbristy, Co. Galway, an early medieval cashel was the location for a possible rectangular timber building and a cemetery (F Delaney & Silke 2011). It produced a typical early medieval finds assemblage with evidence for metal-working and the butchery and cooking of cattle, sheep and pigs (Illus. 2). Was this a church and cemetery site within a settlement enclosure—how would we know?

The second impact relates closely to the fact that early medieval archaeological sites were being published promptly. Rather than focusing solely on the creation of 'grey literature' deposited in state archives (important for the preservation-by-record strategy certainly), which would effectively be inaccessible to most scholars, the NRA archaeologists established a programme of publications, including the proceedings of annual conferences, a popular magazine-type publication called *Seanda* and a series of 'scheme monograph' publications devoted to one or more major excavations along particular road schemes. In recent years, these impressive publications, well produced and lavishly illustrated, have been appearing regularly, with archaeological monographs now published for roadway schemes in Meath, Sligo, Kildare, Westmeath, Waterford, Clare, Galway, Roscommon, Mayo and Cork, and more are planned (see Danaher 2007; Johnston et al. 2008; Carlin, Clarke et al. 2008; McQuade et al. 2009; Deevy & Murphy 2009; Gillespie & Kerrigan 2010; F Delaney & Tierney 2011a; J Eogan & Shee Twohig 2011; S Delaney et al. 2012a;

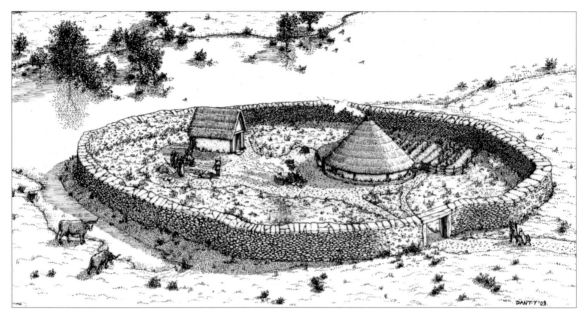

Illus. 2—The early medieval cashel and cemetery—and possible wooden church or oratory—at Owenbristy, Co. Galway, as it might have appeared in about AD 700 (Dan Tietzsch-Tyler).

Bermingham et al. 2012a; O'Connell 2013; Jackman et al. 2013, as well as Stevens & Channing 2012, which was published in conjunction with Westmeath County Council). Virtually all contain information on significant early medieval sites. These many NRA publications in themselves, as well as the vast array of data behind them in archives and collections, are likely to be the basis of a generation of research on early medieval Ireland.

How did early medieval Ireland change?

How does all this new archaeological evidence contribute to our understanding of how early medieval Ireland changed, in social, economic and landscape terms, from the fifth to the 12th century AD?

Scholars of early medieval Europe have long argued for a range of transformations in the early Middle Ages, and have suggested various models of change that would be in keeping with orthodox ideas about socio-economic change across Europe, from the decline and collapse of the Roman empire in the west, through the Age of Migrations to the development of early medieval kingdoms during the Merovingian and Carolingian periods, and ultimately the emergence of early states, many of which provided the origins for some of the European countries of today. Ireland has only rarely—or barely—been mentioned in such historical and archaeological studies of early medieval Europe (see, for example, Webster & Brown 1997; McKitterick 2001; M McCormick

2001; 2002; 2003; Wickham 2005; Smith 2005; Graham-Campbell & Valor 2007; Hamerow 2002; 2009), although Loveluck (2013) makes more use of recent discoveries.

Irish scholars, using historical sources in particular, have tended to argue for similar evolutionary social and economic changes from the fifth to the 12th century (see, for instance, Doherty 1980; 1998; 2000; Graham 1993; O'Keeffe 2000). The debate revolved essentially around ideas of emerging or 'proto-' feudalism and increased lordly power, the emergence of a 'peasant' class in the ninth and 10th centuries, and the abandonment of dispersed rural settlements like ringforts and an emergence of nucleated settlements after c. AD 800. The models also propose a transformation in agricultural and economic practices, from pastoralism, cattle-herding, gift-giving and reciprocity in the seventh and eighth centuries to a market-oriented economy based on increased cereal-growing, lordly wealth based on surpluses and a transition to a coin-based economy. It is important to recognise that some scholars have suggested opposing views, arguing that, while terminologies for social groups change, Gaelic society was essentially conservative and the same well into the later Middle Ages (Gibson 2012).

In any case, these models of socio-economic change have usually been written at the geographical scale of the island as a whole, and at the temporal scale of several centuries. Loveluck (2013, 6–7) has argued that early medieval European social evolutionary models written at such broad historical and geographical scales can be difficult to square with the evidence from archaeological excavations, which essentially concern the small-scale, local, intimate and potentially unique experiences of one particular social group across decades and centuries, all contingent on local political and economic events, or even perhaps simply the waxing and waning fortunes of one family group. In any case, it has to be said that the new Irish archaeological evidence from the last decade does not easily support these models of island-wide social and economic change, as we shall now see.

The origins of early medieval Ireland in the fifth century AD

It seems clear that the first major transformative 'event' in early medieval Ireland was the introduction of Christianity, probably in the late fourth century through a combination of missionary activities by foreign clerics and ongoing contacts with late Roman Britain and western Europe. The conversion to Christianity among some Irish communities was certainly under way by the early fifth century; for example, the Chronicle of Prosper of Aquitaine records that Pope Celestine I (422–32) sent one Palladius to be 'first bishop of the Irish believers in Christ' (de Paor 1993, 6). Famously, St Patrick himself was brought as a slave to Ireland and later escaped. On his return in the early fifth century he engaged in missionary activities, predominantly in the north and west. As a result of the efforts of Palladius, Patrick and other missionaries such as Auxilius and Secundinus, there were undoubtedly small communities of Christian believers on the island in the mid- to late fifth century. It is likely that at this time Christianity was a minority religion within a largely 'Iron Age' pagan-dominated culture, with its gods, goddesses, otherworldly forces and cult activities at watery places, mounds and standing stones (see Swift 1997, 27–48), which appear to have frequently provided a focal point for late Iron Age burials and cemeteries.

In archaeological terms, however, even after our decade of discoveries, the fifth century in Ireland is remarkably quiet. At the end of the Iron Age there are likely to have been regional political and tribal groupings throughout the island. Some of these, such as the Uí Néill, came to shape and dominate the political landscape of the sixth and seventh centuries and beyond, but there is little enough archaeological sign of them in the fifth. Several contemporary Roman authors (e.g. Pacatus, Ammianus Marcellinus and Claudian) mention an intensification of raids on Roman Britain by Irish war bands during the fourth and fifth centuries as Roman power declined (Nixon 1987; Rolfe 1950; Claudian 1956), while Irish social élites undoubtedly also desired to obtain, through trade and tribute, the prestige associated with Romano-British material culture and *Romanitas* (the traditions, power and culture that were understood to be the essence of Romanness).

The early centuries of the early medieval period are characterised by enclosure and it has been suggested that this trend may have had its origins in the Late Iron Age. Dowling (2014) has recently undertaken a review of the evidence for enclosure during the Late Iron Age and much of it tends to be rather equivocal. A palisaded enclosure around a succession of roundhouses at Baysrath, Co. Kilkenny, can be dated to the first–third centuries AD (ibid., 157) but in most cases the evidence is much less clear. Date ranges provided by radiocarbon analysis often straddle the Late Iron Age/early medieval divide and may have been affected by the 'old wood effect' (the dating of samples from timber originating from the heartwood of an oak tree that was already very old at the time). Dowling (2014, 160) suggests that the Iron Age dates from some of the palisades at Lowpark, Co. Mayo, are due to the use of oak in the radiocarbon samples and most of the other dates from the palisades are early medieval (Gillespie & Kerrigan 2010). Occasionally, a single Late Iron Age date can occur on a site that otherwise lies comfortably within the early medieval period and can lead to claims that the site had its origins in the Iron Age. An Iron Age date from the basal layers of a ditch section at Baronstown, Co. Meath, was regarded as intrusive by the excavators, as the remaining evidence from the ditches of the site indicated an early medieval date. Dowling (2014, 160–1), however, argues that the early date should not be rejected, as other features from the site produced dates that straddle the Late Iron Age/early medieval divide. A similar problem exists at Rosepark, Balrothery, Co. Dublin, where a small section of ditch produced a Late Iron Age date in a complex that is otherwise, with the exception of some probable Iron Age kilns, of early medieval date (Carroll 2008, 25–9).

The excavations of the last two decades, however, have failed to provide satisfactory evidence for actual Iron Age ringforts. The best candidate is still the Rath of the Synods at the Hill of Tara, Co. Meath. Grogan (2008, 91) notes that it displays features of earthen multivallate ringforts but that the presence of berms between the ramparts departs from the usual ringfort design. Killalane Site 2, Co. Tipperary, with its closely spaced ditches, appears on purely morphological grounds to be a bivallate ringfort (Clarke & Long 2009). Both ditches produced later Iron Age dates. The inner ditch, however, also produced a Late Bronze Age date, while the outer ditch produced a series of early medieval dates. Additionally, all the dates from features within the enclosures were early medieval. While an Iron Age date might be suggested for the site, it is more likely to be a site primarily, or even wholly, of early medieval date, with some problems of residual evidence.

In contrast to the lack of evidence for ringforts very early in the first millennium AD, there is striking evidence from the NRA's archaeological programmes that cereal-drying kilns started to be used as early as the third or fourth century, and pollen analysis from these centuries indicates that, after a period of agricultural decline in the Iron Age, woodland clearance and agricultural expansion started again during the third and fourth centuries. This early phase of land clearance clearly pre-dates the arrival of Christianity in the fifth century and may well be due to Romano-British influences in technology and agriculture. It is possible, indeed, that the fourth and fifth centuries see an increase in agricultural activity, and it is tempting to make connections between this and Ireland's trading contacts with Roman Britain. Moving on in time, in the archaeological excavations carried out on the NRA's M3 motorway in the environs of the Hill of Tara, for example, radiocarbon dating of cereal-drying kilns suggests that tillage was of increasing importance from the fifth and sixth centuries (A O'Sullivan & Kinsella 2013, 329). Kinsella (2008, 106) suggested that the early proliferation of cereal-drying kilns in the area might be related to the tribute demands of developing local élites around Tara. Monk and Power (2012, 40) suggested that the fall in the number of kilns after the eighth century may coincide with the decline in power of these dynasties.

The NRA's archaeological excavations have revealed new evidence for burial traditions in the fourth and fifth centuries that not only hearken back to the prehistoric past, as in the case of the *fertae* (ancestral burial mounds and enclosures), but also signal innovation and change, as in the case of the settlement-cemeteries (see below). Occasionally the burials were placed in sites that extended back to the distant pagan past, as in the case of the seventh–ninth-century burials at Knowth (G Eogan 2012, 45–71), but usually these burial grounds were not more than a couple of centuries old at the time of their use—that is to say, the people of early medieval Ireland were for the most part burying their dead with recent, presumably pagan, ancestors rather than with some long-dead mythical ancestors. Evidence for this can be seen at Ardsallagh 1, Co. Meath (Clarke & Carlin 2009) (Illus. 3), and Holdenstown 1, Co. Kilkenny (Whitty 2012). Archaeological excavations have also revealed that cremation, albeit on a limited scale, was still occasionally practised in the early centuries of the early medieval period in Ireland (A O'Sullivan et al. 2014a, 285–6). In contrast, burial within consecrated church grounds seems to have been reserved for clerics rather than for the population as a whole. The pagan/Christian transition remains a fascinating process, but it is probably worth remembering that people at the time probably just did what they thought was appropriate, using both traditional and changing religious practices, to bury their loved ones and repair the grief and rupture that death brought to their communities.

Early medieval Ireland in the sixth to seventh century

It now seems that the early to mid-sixth century witnessed a growth in population, climatic and environmental changes, various innovations in settlement forms, an increased sophistication in agriculture and economy, and changes in long-distance trade and exchange. It seems highly

Illus. 3—Aerial view of an early medieval penannular burial enclosure under excavation at Ardsallagh 1, Co. Meath, where 24 early medieval inhumations were found inside a ditched enclosure and beside the site of a Late Bronze Age urn burial and Iron Age cremations; six more burials were found outside the penannular ditch (Archaeological Consultancy Services Ltd).

probable that raths, traditionally *the* type-site for this period, originated in Ireland sometime in the sixth century (Kerr & McCormick 2013). Dendrochronological dates from Ulster also suggest that the building of crannogs, although they have later prehistoric origins and ancestry as a form, was particularly common over an '80-year period in the late sixth and early seventh centuries AD' (A O'Sullivan 1998, 131–3). Thus we see in the early to mid-sixth century, for whatever reason, the appearance of various settlement enclosure types, including raths, crannogs, the earliest settlement-cemeteries and some palisaded enclosures.

There is probably a range of reasons why people began to occupy such settlement enclosures in the sixth century. It is possible that plague, disease, famines and food shortages, political turmoil, migrations, a period of increased warfare and a growing perception of risk in the mid- to late sixth century were significant factors, leading an uneasy population to start living within defensible enclosures. It is, for example, in the sixth century that we see the vigorous political expansion of the Uí Néill dynasties out of their west Ulster heartlands, although it would be difficult to argue that the late sixth/early seventh century was more violent than any other period in early Irish history. It has also been suggested from tree-ring studies, ice-core studies and historical references that there was a period of global climatic deterioration for a decade beginning in 536, potentially leading to crop failure, food shortages, famine and pandemics (Baillie & Brown 2011). Büntgen et al. (2016) have recently suggested from tree-ring and other climatic studies that a series of volcanic eruptions in 536, 540 and 547 led to a synchronous cooling in the northern hemisphere, and that the period 536–660 could be termed the Late Antique Little Ice Age. They see this as contributing to the Justinian Plague, the transformation of the Eastern Roman Empire, the collapse of the Sasanian Empire, population migrations out of the Asian steppes and the Arabian peninsula, the spread of Slavic-speaking peoples and political upheavals in China. Various other environmental indicators do suggest increasingly wetter summers in Ireland in the late sixth century, so the challenge is to explore what impact this might have had on Irish society.

It may be that a key causative factor was the Justinian Plague, which had its outbreak between 541 and 543 across the Later Roman Empire. It subsequently became pandemic across Asia and Europe, potentially killing millions of people. Plague certainly appears to have been endemic in the eastern Mediterranean throughout the sixth century, moving around the ports of southern Europe until the mid-eighth century. Although it declined in virulence as it moved along the major trade routes, it ultimately reached Atlantic Europe and the British Isles too (Little 2007; M McCormick 2007; 2015). Recent aDNA (ancient DNA) studies have potentially identified the likely cause of the Justinian Plague, the pathogen genome *Yersinia pestis*, in the teeth of human skeletons found in double burials and mass graves in sixth-century cemeteries at several locations in central Europe (e.g. Wagner et al. 2014). The Justinian Plague took longer to get to Ireland but it seems to have arrived in 544 (Dooley 2007). It is difficult to determine its impact, or that of subsequent epidemics, given the relatively few references to it in Irish sources and the lack, as yet, of similar close studies of sixth-century cemeteries (aDNA analysis of the teeth of skeletons from double and other multiple burials in Ireland from NRA cemetery excavations would be interesting). Plague may have had a serious, even catastrophic, impact on Irish society, hitting both the secular and the ecclesiastical élite as well as the poor, and killing the young, the middle-aged and especially the elderly, thereby wiping out collective memories and traditions (historians use the term 'the Great Silence' to describe the impact left on Ireland by the Great Famine of the 1840s, with its countryside of empty houses and abandoned fields). It is possible, however, that the onset of endemic diseases, periodic famines or plagues might have led the surviving population of early medieval Ireland to try and somehow defend themselves and their families in this way (Lynn 2005, 16). It is also possible that Irish society was changing anyway in the sixth century; perhaps further propelled by the Justinian Plague and as part of ongoing societal changes, we see, within wider political changes, the emergence of smaller social groups based on narrower kinship ties. People may have started to define and defend their familial identities through the construction and use of settlement enclosures defined by banks, ditches and wooden palisades (A O'Sullivan & Nicholl 2011). In any case, it was not something that was happening elsewhere in north-west Europe or in Anglo-Saxon England, where settlements could involve clusters of houses but these were rarely enclosed (Hamerow 2002; 2009; 2012).

It is interesting in that regard that both early Irish secular and ecclesiastical sources define enclosures as spaces for safety, sanctuary and legal protection, possibly building on native prehistoric traditions of enclosures (e.g. ring-barrows) as signifiers of sacred space (Ó Carragáin 2010b, 59). It is also interesting that at the beginning of the early medieval period in Ireland we see burial and domestic practices together within settlement-cemeteries and some ecclesiastical sites. This was uncommon in Iron Age Ireland and would have been something totally unacceptable in the Romanised world, where burial was prohibited within towns and other settlements for fear of spreading disease (Brown 1981, 1–12). Instead, during the Merovingian and Carolingian periods in Europe, cemeteries became increasingly imbued with notions of sanctuary and were understood as appropriate public spaces for 'activities such as judicial proceedings, trade, craft and habitation' (Ó Carragáin 2009, 346). These Christian concepts of sanctuary and joining together the landscapes of the living and the dead appear to have been transferred to Ireland during the conversion period.

We can also trace various innovations in agriculture and the changing character of the environment in the sixth/seventh century. Apart from the areas of highlands and the extensive bog cover in the midlands, the pollen evidence for early medieval Ireland indicates a landscape of scrubby woodland and mixed farming, almost invariably dominated by pastureland. Dairying had been present in Ireland since the Neolithic (Smyth & Evershed 2015b), but both historical and archaeological evidence clearly shows that the management of cattle herds to maximise the production of dairy foods was now a sophisticated practice, producing a wide range of secondary produce (F McCormick 2012). Cattle dominate animal bone assemblages in Ireland for this part of the early medieval period, in contrast to England and north-west Europe (McCormick et al. 2014; Hamerow 2002). The NRA's programme has demonstrated that cereal-drying kilns, although originating earlier, also appear in their largest numbers during the sixth and seventh centuries (Monk & Power 2012, 38). Arable farming seems to have been more formalised, with the construction of some of the earliest water-powered mills in Europe at this time, such as at Nendrum, Co. Down (AD 619), and in the NRA excavations at Killoteran 9, Co. Waterford (Murphy & Rathbone 2006), and Kilbegly 2, Co. Roscommon (Jackman et al. 2013). It is also striking that most horizontal watermills can be associated with the Church, as with the above examples.

It is clear that the Church was well established in Ireland in the sixth century, and beginning to play a role in the economy and the transformation of the landscape. The documentary sources indicate that the great majority of ecclesiastical and monastic sites were founded in the middle of the sixth century (Charles-Edwards 2000, 250); there are no new Irish saints founding monasteries after AD 800. The excavated archaeological evidence indicates that these church sites were generally founded in newly settled places, with little evidence for ritual and settlement continuity with the previous Iron Age. Ó Carragáin (2010b, 70) suggests that most church or ecclesiastical sites 'were initially founded as churches with associated settlement, and that cemeteries, with their special graves, were a secondary development around these churches'. It may not be the case that churches were enclosed at the earliest stage; radiocarbon dates suggest that the vast majority of ecclesiastical enclosures were constructed between the later sixth and early eighth centuries, perhaps decades or occasionally a century or so after the foundation of many of these sites (A

O'Sullivan et al. 2014a, table 4.1, 354–7). Some early medieval ecclesiastical settlements, however, may have been laid out to a preconceived set pattern, with an innermost sacred core around the church and saints' burial/shrine, and one or two outer, concentric boundaries demarcating areas of decreasing sanctity, as most eloquently expressed in the early eighth-century *Collectio Canonum Hibernensis* (Doherty 1985, 58–9). In the Book of Mulling the depiction of a monastery comprising two concentric enclosures with crosses at the various entrances (Henry 1965, 81) provides another idealised illustration of this hierarchy of holiness, but it is likely that most ecclesiastical sites would have contained only one enclosure, which was deemed suitable to define the sacred space of the settlement. The early medieval church settlement at Clonfad, Co. Westmeath, is the best site identified by the NRA excavations to discuss in this regard, but it is striking that there was relatively little going on in terms of buildings within its large enclosures (Stevens 2006; 2007).

Although the Church had become more established by this point, it had yet to monopolise the care of the dead. Indeed, the sixth and seventh centuries witnessed the growth of settlements with associated burial grounds in Ireland, as revealed most spectacularly by NRA excavations of settlement-cemeteries at Raystown, Johnstown 1, Balriggan 1 and Parknahown 5, among others (e.g. Seaver 2006; Clarke & Carlin 2008; S Delaney 2010; O'Neill 2010). Some of these began as Iron Age/early medieval transition-era *fertae* and evolved across time into places of residence and farming activities. Some, such as Raystown, Co. Meath, also became a significant focus for intensive industrial and agricultural activity, as evidenced by features such as iron-smelting furnaces, cereal-drying kilns and, on occasion, watermills (Seaver 2010). These latter sites may well have been assembly places, but they were certainly centres of production that must have been controlled by local kings or abbots, depending on their affiliation.

Burial grounds dated to the mid- to late sixth century and the early seventh century might also be located in prehistoric barrows, natural mounds or ditched enclosures. There are some burial grounds that appear not to have been enclosed, such as Garadice, Co. Meath, where people buried their deceased in rows that referred to previous interments (Larsson 2009). Human corpses or parts of human remains were also placed in ditches, pits or in other odd contexts, suggesting the burial of individuals at the margins of the social group or who had somehow suffered a bad death through disease, murder or ill fortune. At Castlefarm 1, Co. Meath, for instance, several burials were placed in the ditches of the enclosure (O'Connell 2009, 50). The practice of digging and preparing a grave for the dead varied, from simple, earth-dug graves to stone-lined cists or lintelled graves and wood-lined graves, as can be seen at Collierstown 1, Co. Meath (Illus. 4 and 5) (O'Hara 2010). For the most part, however, people at this time at least were placing their dead on their backs, usually as unwrapped corpses, with the head typically to the west. This might be Christian burial practice, but we cannot always be sure that these people were Christian believers.

We can also trace development in long-distance trade and exchange through the sixth and into the seventh century from the increasing quantity of exotic artefacts found on excavations (Kelly 2008; 2010b; Doyle 2009; Loveluck & O'Sullivan 2016). In the later fifth century, we can trace the arrival of Phocaean Red Slipware from Turkey, as well as Late Roman Amphorae ware;

Illus. 4—Aerial view of the early medieval cemetery excavated at Collierstown 1, Co. Meath, dated to the fifth to the ninth century AD and involving a series of enclosures, monumental actions, settlement and economic activities and varying burial practices over time (Studio Lab).

Illus. 5—Early medieval burial in a lintelled grave, excavated at Collierstown (Archaeological Consultancy Services Ltd).

vessels of this type were probably for élites, who appreciated wines or exotic foodstuffs, and may also have been used for importing olive oil and wine for liturgical use by the Church. This Mediterranean trade continued up to the mid-sixth century; small amounts of Phocaean Red Slipware and possibly African Red Slipware, as well as Late Roman Amphorae (Bi and Bii), are present on Irish sites from this time.

From the mid-sixth century this Mediterranean trade ceased and the trade routes shifted to the Atlantic coast. This is demonstrated through the sixth and into the seventh century in Ireland by the importation of wheel-thrown creamware pottery vessels from western Francia, probably from ports along the Bay of Biscay, a pottery type known in Britain and Ireland as E ware (Doyle 2009; Loveluck 2013, 203; Loveluck & O'Sullivan 2016). These E ware pots and jugs probably carried foodstuffs, spices, dyes and wine. Indeed, Ireland, more than Britain, becomes the major focus of this Atlantic trade, as the sea-lanes seem to have run up the Irish east coast, and other strong connections between Ireland and the Atlantic coast of France are hinted at in the historical sources. It is assumed that prosperous secular and ecclesiastical élites were bringing in this produce, but its appearance within the early medieval Irish archaeological record could alternatively have been due to the efforts of local coastal communities operating emporia on islands and on beaches along the east coast, or of seafaring traders managing their own international trade networks. In exchange, the trading ships appear to have returned to Anglo-Saxon and Frankish ports with Irish slaves, dogs, hides and leather items, and possibly even Irish-produced foods such as butter, cheese and grain (Loveluck & O'Sullivan 2016).

Early medieval Ireland in the late seventh and eighth centuries

It is in the late seventh and eighth centuries that we can trace the emergence of the 'classic' early Irish society that we can see in the law-texts such as *Críth Gablach*, which dates from c. 700–25. Early medieval Irish society, as described in these texts, was structured around chiefdoms and local kin-based social polities; it was rural, socially hierarchical and familiar, based on kin-groups such as the *derbfine*, which consisted of all the patrilineal descendants of a four-generation group with a common great-grandfather (Charles-Edwards 2000, 86–7; A O'Sullivan & Nicholl 2011; A O'Sullivan 2011). There may have been an ongoing contraction in early medieval kinship, a process that accelerated in the eighth century and was evidenced by the change from a society based on the *derbfine* to one structured on the *gelfine*, a narrower three-generation kinship group descended from a common grandfather. This had significant implications for land ownership and partible inheritance or the redistribution of land (Charles-Edwards 2000, 86–7; Bolger 2011b).

This is the society that inhabited the tens of thousands of early medieval settlement enclosures found in the modern Irish landscape. The NRA-excavated early medieval settlement at Curraheen 1, Co. Cork, gives a reasonably good impression of what they might have looked like (Illus. 6): enclosures defined by ditches, banks and palisades, with occasional adjoining features, as well as evidence for houses and domestic and industrial activity (Danaher 2013). If we reflect on the

Illus. 6—Reconstruction drawing of Curraheen 1, Co. Cork: an artist's impression of an early medieval settlement enclosure in the seventh century (John Hodgson).

labour required to dig the ditches of these settlements (Squatriti 2002), which still exist in the Irish landscape, we gain a sense of how significant population growth may have been in this period. It is clear that early medieval raths and crannogs were at the peak of their construction and use in the mid-seventh and eighth centuries. The phenomenon and construction of raths in the early medieval settlement landscape, beginning in the sixth century, may have taken hold and developed quite quickly. Indeed, it reminds us that, far from being invisible in the archaeological record as is often thought, the slaves and the labouring poor actually created through their physical labour some of the most enduring archaeological features of the Irish landscape—the banks and ditches of early medieval raths.

Most people—from nobles to prosperous farmers to slaves—would have lived within these settlement enclosures. The Old Irish law-tracts provide us with an image of a range of early medieval Irish social grades, from kings and nobility to free commoners who owned their own land or livestock, and various semi-free grades, hereditary serfs, labourers and slaves. It was a society bound together through political and kinship affiliations and a socio-economic system revolving around the institution of clientship, whereby a lord provided a fief of land, livestock and equipment in return for *bés tige* (annual food-rent) of calves, meat, grain, dairy produce, winter hospitality, labour or military services (A O'Sullivan 2011). We can trace this social hierarchy to some extent in the settlement landscape. Some royal sites, such as Ballycatteen or Garranes, Co. Cork, may be identified by their prominent or strategic siting, by their settlement enclosure's multiple banks and ditches, or by the presence of large houses, military equipment, hostage chains, imported exotic objects or evidence of patronage of specialist crafts, particularly copper-alloy-working. Some sites might be identified by large dwelling structures. At Moynagh Lough, Co. Meath, an eighth-century crannog that was probably a noble if not a royal residence had one of the largest roundhouses known from early medieval Ireland, over 11 m in diameter (A O'Sullivan 2008; 2009; J Bradley 2011). It appears that the phenomenon of building raised raths may also have reflected lordly if not royal status, and this seemingly began in the eighth century (Kerr 2009). It is not at all definitively clear that the NRA's programme involved the investigation of an early medieval royal residence, and certainly no massive multivallate site was excavated. As Gleeson (2015) has noted, however, it may well be that the highly productive settlements with burials, the so-called settlement-cemeteries, were actually *óenaig* sites, or places of public assembly associated with the early medieval kings.

Nevertheless, in terms of early medieval raths again, site morphology is not always a reliable indicator of status. The presence of multiple banks and ditches around settlements, or even the presence of high-status objects at a site, may be the result of events and activities that we do not fully understand. It is clear from the stratigraphical and chronological evidence at sites such as Rathgurreen, Co. Galway, Roestown 2, Co. Meath, and Dowdstown 2, Co. Meath, that the multiple banks and ditches characterising these sites evolved over a period of time and may reflect changes in their use, or partible inheritance, rather than changes in social status (Comber 2002; O'Hara 2009b; Cagney & O'Hara 2009; Bolger 2011b). Indeed, this reminds us that early medieval archaeological scholars may have focused too much on social status and ranking and insufficiently on kinship, which may have been as important in the creation of the specifics of the archaeological settlement evidence.

Early medieval raths and crannogs have provided abundant evidence for the organisation and layout of settlements and the ways in which they were used (see A O'Sullivan et al. 2014a; 2014b; A O'Sullivan & Nicholl 2011 for further details). At this time they were typically the location for small roundhouses, usually built of post-and-wattle or stone and thatched with heather or oaten straw. These houses had hearths for cooking and warmth, beds and benches and a range of domestic objects such as rotary querns and pottery (in the north-east), and tools and equipment were used or stored within them. Although the enclosed farmyard could have been the place to keep cattle safe from wolves or raiders, they were generally not used as stockyards. Most raths and crannogs produce evidence for small-scale craft production, particularly and most distinctively blacksmithing and copper-alloy-working, and not always only on high-status sites. Raths were also used for the storage of food, raw materials and the discarding of waste, leading to middens building up at the edge of sites. The archetypal early medieval rath is Deer Park Farms, Co. Antrim,

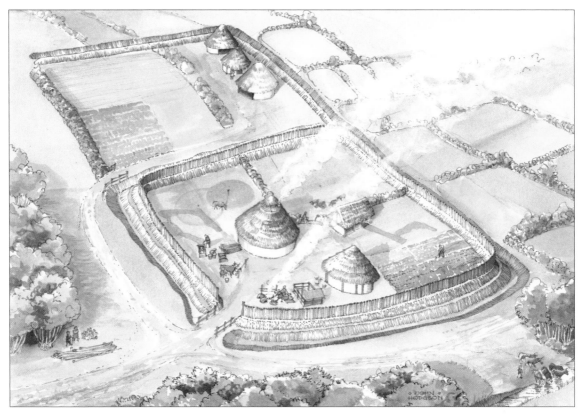

Illus. 7—Reconstruction drawing of Ballynacarriga, Co. Cork: an artist's impression of an early medieval settlement in the seventh century within a rectangular enclosure with fields of crops around it (John Hodgson).

occupied from the seventh to the 10th century (Lynn & McDowell 2011). Archaeological excavations there revealed the living practices and material goods used by early medieval families, and the evidence is similar to that from most sites, suggesting that they were occupied by farmers who enjoyed modest prosperity rather than significant wealth. The farming economy managed by these people was mostly built around cattle pastoralism, dairying and some cereal cultivation, mostly of oats, barley and some wheat. The NRA excavations have also revealed that not all early medieval settlement enclosures were round: the site at Ballynacarriga AR12, Co. Cork, was a busy seventh-century settlement with roundhouses, cereal-drying kilns, souterrains and the usual evidence for smithing and animal husbandry, but located inside a rectilinear rather than a round enclosure (Illus. 7) (Noonan 2013).

At places like Raystown, Co. Meath, however, we see something significantly different from the archetypal rath: an early medieval settlement enclosure of rather different form, with a burial ground at the heart of it (Illus. 8). Raystown was an extensive settlement occupied from the fifth to the mid-12th century, defined by a complex series of enclosures, corrals, agricultural features such as cereal-drying kilns and watermills, and its own burial ground, which may have been the

Illus. 8—Reconstruction of the early medieval settlement and burial ground, with kilns, horizontal watermills and field boundaries, at Raystown, Co. Meath (original drawn by Simon Dick, updated by Conor McDermott).

earliest feature on the site (Seaver 2010; 2016). Between the mid-seventh and late eighth centuries there were at least two horizontal watermills constructed to the south of the cemetery. Between the mid-eighth and late ninth centuries, the enclosures separating the living and the dead were filled in and at least two more watermills were constructed. Palaeobotanical remains suggest that the inhabitants at Raystown were processing large amounts of barley, oats and wheat between the seventh and 12th centuries, but were also managing cattle herds, sheep and even horses. Raystown may have been an agricultural complex or assembly site of a modestly sized community who processed and distributed food for a local king, lord or ecclesiastical authority. At Raystown we may well be looking at an early medieval community who, self-sufficient in some ways, were also carrying out work on their lord's agricultural estate.

An interesting contribution of the NRA's archaeological programme of large-scale landscape investigations is the realisation that early medieval settlement enclosures may have been largely located in open countryside. We have tended to imagine the early medieval landscape as highly apportioned and controlled, perhaps with extensive field systems. At NRA sites like Dowdstown 2, Co. Meath, however, we do get classic round raths but only some small plots and fields immediately around them; out beyond those gardens and fields (for cereals?) the wider landscape is unenclosed (Illus. 9). It conjures up an image of an open, unenclosed countryside, perhaps with scattered woodlands, where settlement enclosures would be all the more striking because of their distinctive appearance within the landscape. This evidence lets us go back to early medieval raths

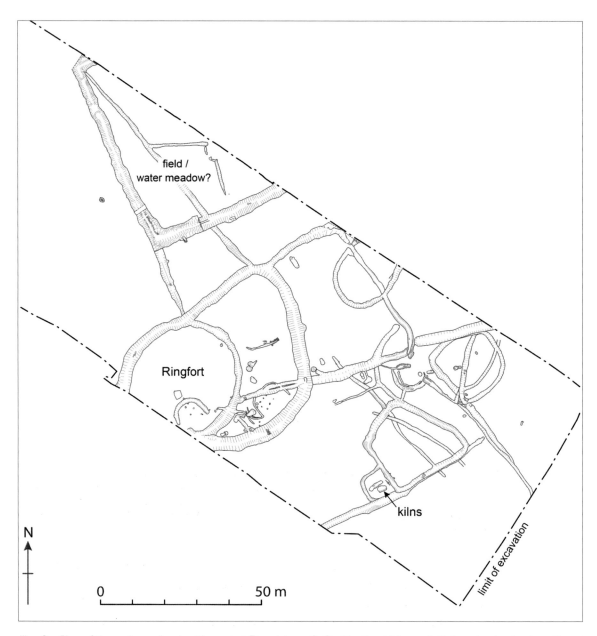

Illus. 9—Plan of the early medieval settlement at Dowdstown 2, Co. Meath, which was initially a simple, circular rath (located to the south-west) with an associated field, dated to the sixth or early seventh century, that was then replaced eastwards by a large, D-shaped enclosure with additional external enclosures, dated to the late seventh/early ninth century. Other features include cereal-drying kilns and substantial fields to the north, downslope and near the River Boyne (after Cagney & O'Hara 2009, 125).

Illus. 10—Reconstruction image of an early medieval cashel at Cahercommaun, Co. Clare, showing a likely lordly or royal site, with small gardens for vegetables and cereals immediately contiguous to it, and open countryside for cattle in its wider environs. The NRA programme has enabled us to look at previous generations of discoveries with new insights and questions (image by Conor McDermott, based on an original aerial photograph by the Photographic Unit, National Monuments Service).

and cashels excavated in previous generations, such as Cahercommaun, Co. Clare, and realise that they too may have been settlements surrounded by open country (Illus. 10).

Early medieval settlement was not only confined to enclosed sites, of course. A range of unenclosed settlements, in a variety of contexts and geographical locations around Ireland, have been dated to between the late sixth and eighth centuries (see A O'Sullivan et al. 2014a, table 3.4). These are often found on what could be considered marginal areas: in caves, coastal and dune sites, such as Doonloughan, Co. Galway (Murray & McCormick 2012), or in upland locations, such as Barrees, Co. Cork (W O'Brien 2009; 2012b). These settlements may have been occupied by people who were poor or who lived at the margins of society, but the Doonloughan example also indicates that many were occupied only for a very short period of time or were of a seasonal nature. On the other hand, the NRA's programme of excavations in advance of motorways across the island did not particularly reveal many unenclosed buildings from the early medieval period, suggesting again the dominance of settlement enclosures.

By the late seventh to eighth century the Church was becoming increasingly powerful and monasteries were long past their pioneering stage: Armagh was attempting to establish ecclesiastical primacy over the island. During the eighth century most ecclesiastical sites would have been defined by at least one, if not two, but very rarely three enclosures. Not all of these enclosures, however, were necessarily contemporary or built at the same time as each other, and there is, just as for secular raths, evidence for successive enclosures indicative of the expansion or contraction of the ecclesiastical site. This is suggested at both Tullylish, Co. Down (Ivens 1987, 112–13, 119), and Tallaght, Co. Dublin (C Walsh 1997, 8, 26), where the inner enclosure ditches were dug sometime between the sixth and early eighth centuries, before the outer enclosures were subsequently constructed between the early eighth and 10th centuries. Turf and timber were still the main building materials in monasteries during these centuries. Even on the west coast, where stone would have been more accessible and presumably less costly, churches in sites such as Illaunloughan, Co. Kerry (Marshall & Walsh 2005), were first built in turf and timber during the seventh and early eighth centuries. The earliest reference to a stone church is at Duleek, Co. Meath (688–93), which is referred to as *Domum Liac*, literally 'house of stones', but it is only from the 10th century onwards that the construction of stone churches becomes more common (Ó Carragáin 2010b).

Archaeological excavations have demonstrated that the earliest monastic burials seem to have been confined to clerics or members of the community. The early burials at Illaunloughan, for instance, are all male, and indeed this phenomenon can be observed on High Island, Co. Galway, as late as the 10th to 11th century (Marshall & Rourke 2000, 106). The documentary evidence, such as the *Collectio Canonum Hibernensis*, however, makes it clear that the laity were being encouraged to be buried within church grounds from at least the eighth century onwards (E O'Brien 2009), and the resulting burial fees must have greatly added to ecclesiastical coffers. It was during this period (c. 700–850) that the cult of relics was developed to increase the status of, and promote burial within, formal consecrated church cemeteries, a relationship highlighted by the use of the word *reliquiae* or 'remains of saint' to denote a cemetery or *reilig* (Ó Carragáin 2003, 134, 147). At some of the more important sites, this cult of the relics sometimes involved the translation of the corporeal remains of sixth/seventh-century saints and their re-interment and enshrinement in specially built shrines within the church graveyard between the early eighth and mid-ninth centuries (Ó Carragáin 2010b, 67). That said, burial still continued in so-called early medieval settlement-cemeteries, some of which were probably occupied by secular communities. There is a sense that farming groups could still bury their dead with them, on the land they occupied. There is evidence, too, that some of the larger monasteries were beginning to display some 'urban' attributes. At Clonmacnoise, Co. Offaly, the zooarchaeological material indicates that the monastery was already a consumer site, as opposed to a producer/consumer site, for some aspects of its food requirements (Soderberg 2004).

Intriguingly, the evidence for international trade declines significantly in the Ireland of the late seventh to early eighth century (Loveluck & O'Sullivan 2016). The occurrence of E ware appears to cease by the mid-eighth century. The absence of this pottery does not, however, necessarily mean a cessation of international trade; wine was vital for liturgical purposes, after all. It may well be that it was now imported in wooden barrels without accompanying ceramics (Wooding 1996). Fine metal-working on Irish sites of this period was of the highest quality, by international standards (Ryan 1983; 1988; 1989). In contrast, iron-working in Ireland, although it had developed in the sixth century, did not reach the standard of sophistication noted in Anglo-Saxon England. This implies that fine-metal craftsmen worked within an international rather than a local sphere.

Palaeoclimatic proxies for Ireland suggest that, in general terms, the early medieval climate was warm and wet. Recent palaeoenvironmental studies suggest that climatic conditions took a downturn possibly after the late eighth century (Kerr, Swindles et al. 2009). These studies combined evidence for extreme weather based on the annalistic records with testate amoebae-derived water-table reconstructions. The palaeohydrological data suggest that a date of c. 770 marks the end point of a 750-year-long dry phase and the beginning of a wetter period that culminated in the Little Ice Age of the later medieval period. The annalistic records confirm a change at this date, with the ninth-century records recording more frequent incidences of hard frosts, severe snows and heavy rains, while the summer droughts recorded in earlier centuries become rare. Reconstructing climatic change and its social consequences is complex, however, and further palaeoenvironmental and archaeological studies will be required to assess the impact of any climatic change at the end of the eighth century.

It is also true that climatic deterioration, harsh weather conditions and the consequent hunger, food shortages and more catastrophic famines caused by crop failures would have brought malnutrition, starvation and death to agricultural communities (Peters 2016). It is reckoned that food shortages and occasionally famines were regular events in early medieval Europe from c. 800 onwards, occurring regionally every few years. Both the saints' Lives and the annals often refer to harsh winters that led to slaughter of the cattle of Ireland and subsequent suffering among the community. In the late eighth century (e.g. 764–5, 780 and 789, as well as 855 and 965) there are frequent references to protracted spring snow and ice. The Annals of Ulster for 900 describe a 'rainy year . . . great scarcity amongst the cattle'. For agricultural communities, even such short snaps of poor weather such as prolonged drought, a snowstorm or rainfall could bring catastrophe, delaying the planting of crops, destroying them in the ground or lengthening the late winter, always a difficult time of the year when food stocks ran low. The early medieval tale *Erchoitmed Ingine Gulidi* describes a farm on the verge of starvation owing to such prolonged cold and the depletion of 'old food' (i.e. last year's foods) (Meyer 1894, 67–9). Difficulties of food production would also lead to disease taking hold among a weakened population. The Annals of Ulster for 764 describe heavy snowfall, drought, famine and dysentery (*riuth fola*) throughout Ireland, the clear implication being that a weakened population went down to other ailments. On the other hand, it is also important to note that there was only rarely a Europe-wide famine—that food shortages tended to be regional or local. Indeed, archaeological evidence for such local patterns of hunger and malnutrition, particularly among the young, can often be found among early medieval communities in Ireland. At Raystown (Seaver 2005, 10), or the recently published medieval cemetery at Ballyhanna, Co. Donegal (McKenzie et al. 2015), there was evidence that some people suffered from dietary deficiencies such as scurvy and rickets.

It has already been noted that the Justinian Plague that swept across Asia and Europe in the early 540s came to Ireland around 544. It is likely that this and several other pestilences and diseases struck the Irish population in the sixth and seventh centuries (Dooley 2007). Both Irish and Anglo-Saxon sources refer to 'yellow pestilence', 'mortality of children', 'great mortality' and 'pox'. It is suggested that there was an outbreak of it in England and Ireland in 664, and that it remained endemic there until 668. Bede, writing of Northumbria, states that 'this most grievous pestilence . . . brought with it destruction so severe that in some large villages and estates once crowded with inhabitants, only a small and scattered remnants, and sometimes none at all, remained' (Smith 2005, 62). Plague broke out again in 683–4, leading in particular to the death of children, who were without resistance to it. It has also been suggested that the outbreak of *lepra* in 680, 742, 769 and 779 refers to the virulent disease of smallpox. The Annals of Ulster for 709 record an outbreak of *baccach*, a disease which left people with a temporary paralysis of the limbs (not a good thing for the labouring poor) and which has since been interpreted as poliomyelitis or another viral infection (Ó Corráin 2005, 581). In the annals there are also references to an epidemic of *fluxus sanguinis* accompanied by diarrhoea between 764 and 778, which may have been dysentery or cholera. This was also occurring at the same time as smallpox, fever and rabies. Another disease, known as *scamach*, which was apparently pulmonary in character and was perhaps influenza or streptococcic pneumonia, broke out in 783, 786, 806, 814 and 825.

It is evident, then, that epidemics of disease struck the Irish population in the latter part of the seventh century, throughout the eighth and in the first quarter of the ninth century (Ó Corráin 2005, 579). Lynn (2005), as mentioned above, suggested that the construction of raths—physically bounded spaces used by small social groups—came about during the seventh and eighth centuries as a response to fear of disease and a perception that defensive measures might save the household from outside forces. It has also been suggested that the high mortality rate and the subsequent decrease in population would have contributed to the growth of monastic federations and the emergence of secular dynastic powers (Ó Corráin 2005, 579).

Early medieval Ireland in the ninth, 10th and 11th centuries

The social and economic organisation described in the early Irish law-tracts reflects the reality of the seventh and eighth centuries, or at least the reality as it was perceived by legal scholars and the educated élites. It is by no means clear that it reflects Irish society from the ninth century onwards. The laws describe a rural landscape dominated by the rath, but, as we have seen, the construction and use of raths, at least new ones, began to decline from the eighth century onwards. The ninth and 10th centuries saw the growing obsolescence of this settlement type. Interestingly, a similar situation seems to be indicated on church sites. Already by the later eighth and ninth centuries, radiocarbon dating evidence suggests that sixth-/early seventh-century church or monastic enclosure ditches were becoming obsolete at sites such as Clonfad, Co. Westmeath, and Clonmacnoise, Co. Offaly. At Clonfad, both the outer and middle enclosure ditches appear to have been deliberately backfilled as single events at roughly the same time in the later eighth or ninth century (Stevens 2010; Stevens & Channing 2012, 121–4), though excavations indicate continued industrial activity along the banks of the stream to the east of the church into the 10th century (Stevens & Channing 2012, 123). This is interesting because it implies that the infilling of these ecclesiastical enclosures should not be seen as a decline in the status of the sites but rather as indicative of the increasingly obsolete role of enclosures as symbolic boundary markers for settlements in the later centuries of the early medieval period—a pattern which is perhaps replicated with the abandonment of raths after the ninth century.

There is a general consensus among historians, historical geographers and archaeologists that there were significant political, social and kinship changes from c. 800 onwards, and particularly in the 10th and 11th centuries (e.g. Graham 1993; Ó Cróinín 1995; Doherty 1998; 2000; O'Keeffe 2000; but see Gibson 2012 for an opposing view). These putative socio-economic changes include the decline of petty kingdoms, as local kings and chieftains lose their power, and the emergence of regional polities, with much more powerful provincial kings, in the 11th and 12th centuries (Byrne 1973; Ó Cróinín 1995). Whereas the economy of the earlier periods seems to have been dominated by gift-giving, reciprocity and clientship, it has been suggested that there now emerged a system whereby a greater proportion of the population belonged to a lower social class that provided labour services to their lord by working on his land; this type of arrangement would generally be taken to be more indicative of 'feudalism' (Doherty 1998, 322–4). On the other hand, others have argued that Irish society remained essentially conservative and that, while the historical terminologies change, power relationships and social stratification remained broadly similar (Gibson 2012). In economic terms, it has also been suggested that from the ninth century onwards in Ireland there emerged a 'market economy', perhaps controlled largely by the Church. This would be taken to be accompanied by the accumulation of agricultural surplus by secular and ecclesiastical authorities, and a shift from cattle as a currency to silver bullion/coinage as items of exchange (Doherty 1980; F McCormick 2008; Sheehan 1998).

There is little enough historical documentation of settlement from the ninth and 10th centuries onwards. It has been suggested from this that a gradually transformed settlement landscape emerged, in the form of either unenclosed (Doherty 1998, 323) or nucleated village-like settlements (Doherty 2000; O'Keeffe 2000). This model proposes that raths were abandoned owing to population relocation within new territorial frameworks under lordship control (O'Keeffe 2000, 26), and that such societal reorganisation may have necessitated the emergence of the central lordly 'fortress' around which people lived (Graham 1993, 44). There are certainly many examples of raths being abandoned after the 10th century. At Deer Park Farms, Co. Antrim, a site that had been occupied since the seventh century, and built up across time into a raised or platform rath, was abandoned sometime in the 10th century (Lynn & McDowell 2011). O'Keefe (2000, 26–

9) has argued for the emergence of new types of village-like settlements (*baile*) around these 'fortress' sites. In the Gaelic historical sources as early as the 10th century these are referred to as *longphort, daingen, dúnad* or *dún*, while in the early 12th century they are referred to as *caistél* or *caislén*.

If the recent NRA-driven archaeological excavations have revealed anything, however, it is that there is little clear evidence for any such nucleated settlements within the ninth- to 10th-century landscape. We may well have had nucleated settlements at larger monastic or church establishments, the so-called 'monastic towns', though that is debatable, and we certainly have densely occupied, proto-urban settlements in the late ninth-/early 10th-century Viking towns. Nonetheless, the archaeological excavations of the last two decades, both in advance of NRA motorways and gas pipelines traversing the Irish countryside and in our smaller rural towns and villages, have failed to provide convincing evidence for any early medieval secular, nucleated, rural settlements in the ninth and 10th centuries. Archaeologists have not found anything that could be described as an early medieval 'village', although two earlier excavated sites dating from this period, Knowth, Co. Meath (G Eogan 2012), and Ballywee, Co. Antrim (Lynn 1988), do provide evidence for settlement with multiple houses, which suggests occupation by more than one family. There are also some ninth- and 10th-century settlement enclosures with houses immediately outside them, possibly the dwellings of labourers working on their lord's land, for example Carraig Aille, Co. Limerick (Ó Ríordáin 1949). These, however, are not the same thing as the nucleated settlement that scholars have imagined. There is also little evidence to show that people started to live in unenclosed dwellings as raths were abandoned.

There are some enclosed settlement types, however, that were clearly occupied during this period, namely the raised rath, the crannog and, most interestingly, the cashel. The raised rath, which emerged in the late eighth century, continued in use for some time, and many were built upon and reused as timber castles or mottes after the Anglo-Norman invasion of 1169. Comber and Hull's (2008; 2010) important archaeological excavations in the Burren, Co. Clare, are revealing that cashels may well originate at this time, i.e. after 800. In the Burren, at least, they were the residences of the Gaelic Irish in the later Middle Ages, and in terms of their construction and occupation can be regarded as medieval in date. On the other hand, the NRA site at Owenbristy, Co. Galway, is a cashel (although the enclosing element could also be described as an earthen bank with stone facing) and is substantially earlier in origin than 800 (F Delaney & Silke 2011).

The Church had certainly established itself as a significant power and influence in ninth-century Ireland, much as power was being centralised in contemporary secular society, and there is evidence for a profusion of different types of church scattered every few kilometres across the landscape. These included small local proprietary churches that had been established in earlier times to provide pastoral care to particular communities, and larger monastic settlements that the documentary evidence shows were now becoming centres of large and diverse populations. Trade and exchange may have become increasingly concentrated at these settlements. Doherty (1985) suggested that the tribal *óenach* of the earliest period may have been transferred to market-places (defined by crosses) within some of the largest ecclesiastical sites from the 10th century. During the ninth and 10th centuries there was also a general shift away from small family-run churches towards larger community-based churches; this development can be partly attributed to the centralisation of power structures during the Viking Age, as numerous petty kings and chieftains appear to have lost their noble status while the numbers of lay commoners appear to have grown (Ó Carragáin 2010a, 222–3; 2010b, 149, 227). It was at this period that burial in consecrated church graveyards tended to become the norm, and, as a result, the use of settlement-cemeteries for burial generally went into decline from this time onwards. At Faughart Lower, Co. Louth, for instance, burial ceased during the Viking Age (Buckley & Conway 2010, 54). Burial at Raystown, Co. Meath (Seaver 2010), and Camlin 3, Co. Tipperary (Flynn 2012, 43), also ceased at this time.

The NRA's excavations have also made a substantial contribution to our understanding of the Viking *longphort*, through its programme of investigation at Woodstown 6, Co. Waterford (Russell & Hurley 2014). There has been little debate as to the role of Viking *longphuirt* (plural) in the settlement economy of the ninth and 10th centuries. The tendency has been to treat these sites in isolation from wider native settlements and to view *longphuirt* simply as raiding bases. The discoveries during archaeological testing at Woodstown (Russell & Hurley 2014), the potential scale of the Dublin *longphort* (see Simpson 2012) and the recent identification of a very large *longphort* at Annagassan, Co. Louth (Clinton 2014), however, have revealed something of the enormous size of these settlements, as well as the potential industrial activities carried out within them. At Woodstown, for example, there was evidence for extensive iron-working, as well as the working of stone, bone, antler and amber, and possibly textile manufacture (Russell & Hurley 2014). *Longphuirt* were established in the 840s and they have typically been seen only as raiding bases, but some seem to have been occupied or used for decades. It is possible that these sites were centres for production and trade, established by Scandinavian population groups intent on long-term settlement, rather than simply bases for military raiding. If this is the case, it implies that these sites established relationships based on production, trade, exchange and possible intermarriage with the inhabitants of the native hinterlands prior to the establishment of formal Viking towns. We are unlikely to know much more until there is a major research excavation of an Irish *longphort*.

Perhaps the most remarkable transformation of all in this period was the emergence of Ireland's Viking towns in the 10th and 11th centuries, notably Dublin, Wexford, Waterford, Cork and Limerick. The best archaeological evidence comes from Dublin and Waterford, both of which were large, defended urban settlements, strategically situated on estuaries and rivers. Within their enclosures were tightly packed houses laid out along streets, lanes and pathways. Their populations were engaged in manufacturing and production, were undoubtedly consuming large quantities of food and raw materials brought in from the surrounding countryside, and were engaged in local, regional and international exchange within a wider Atlantic trade network (Wallace 1987; 2016). Having briefly discussed health and disease above, it is worth noting here that townspeople would have been similarly exposed to epidemics—probably more so, in fact. There were periods of disease in the 10th century, particularly in 907, when there was a year of mortality (*annus mortalitatis*), and the Vikings in Dublin experienced an epidemic in 951. Indeed, one might surmise that the close, tightly packed conditions of life in the streets of the Viking towns would have been favourable to the rapid spread of disease. It has also been noted that, historically speaking, there is evidence for epidemics in the middle of the ninth century, and again on an island-wide scale in the latter part of the 11th century. The Annals of Tigernach claim that the plague of 1084–5 killed a quarter of the population of Ireland. The NRA's excavations of 10th- and 11th-century settlements, cereal-drying kilns and industrial sites in the environs of the towns should now be analysed in detail to trace the town–countryside economic relationships, which must have been key to the towns' success and growth.

The agricultural economy in Ireland appears to have undergone significant change from the ninth century onwards. There is a concentration of dendrochronologically dated mill construction in the last quarter of the eighth century into the first quarter of the ninth century, which would seem to indicate changes in the way in which grain-processing, and potentially cereal production, was organised (Brady 2006; Rynne 2013a). This, along with the use of larger cereal-drying kilns (Monk & Power 2012), suggests a move away from subsistence farming to the production of agricultural surplus controlled by the political élite. This theory finds support from Kerr (2009), who noted that there is a tendency for the high-status raised raths of this period to be located on land that is advantageous for arable production. Elsewhere, Meriel McClatchie's analysis for EMAP noted that macro-plant assemblages are more common on post-800 sites than on earlier sites, while there is a decline in animal bone assemblages for the same period, and cattle lose their predominant role in some areas (F McCormick 2014; F McCormick et al. 2014; McClatchie, McCormick et al. 2015).

If there were changes in agricultural economies at this time in Ireland, they might seem to mirror changes noted elsewhere in north-west Europe (see Hamerow 2009; Loveluck 2013). Hamerow (2009, 69–70) concluded that the period c. 680–830 marks a time of settlement and economic change throughout Europe. In north-west Europe, settlements based on the household give way to types designed to accommodate larger, non-nuclear households. These changes suggest that there was a shift away from essentially (though never entirely) self-sufficient communities, whose economies involved reciprocal exchange and the circulation of prestigious goods, towards an economy based on the redistribution of surplus and trade of commodities via regional networks (Hamerow 2002, 139). It is argued that this change involved an intensification of agricultural production, especially arable farming, and the growth of 'consumer' communities such as towns and monasteries (ibid., 139). Yet we should still be cautious, as there seem to be significant differences between the Irish evidence and the evidence from the Continent. In north-west Europe, for instance, the intensification in crop production is often accompanied by species specialisation (ibid., 135), while, as Meriel McClatchie has noted, in Ireland it is diversification of crop production that seems to have been the trend (F McCormick et al. 2014; McClatchie, McCormick et al. 2015).

The emergence of the Viking towns must also have had an impact on crafts and production, both because of the markets they provided and their ability to support communities rather than just individuals. It has been proposed that there was a migration of craftworking from rural to urban areas in Anglo-Saxon England during these centuries (G Thomas 2011, 412–14). In Ireland, during the seventh and eighth centuries fine craftwork appears to have been concentrated in high-status secular and monastic sites (Ryan 1988; 1989; 2002). The possibility of a concentration of craftworking in urban areas in later centuries is more difficult to address, but it is clear that there was substantial craft production in the Viking towns (e.g. see Wallace 2016). Few 10th- to 12th-century high-status rural sites in Ireland have been excavated, though at places like Knowth there were probably craftsmen working to the demands of their kings (G Eogan 2012). It is possible, however, that craftworking had migrated to urban settlements at places like Dublin, Waterford, Cork and so on, thus mirroring trends in contemporary Anglo-Saxon England. In fact, the whole topic of crafts and production in early medieval Ireland needs much more close analysis now that such vastly increased material culture assemblages have been recovered from settlement sites.

The end of early medieval Ireland in the 12th century

Although the NRA's excavations have enhanced our knowledge of late medieval settlement (see Gardiner & O'Conor, this volume), there is relatively little archaeological evidence for secular rural settlement in the twelfth century. It would seem from radiocarbon dates that certainly raths and crannogs were not being constructed at this time, although, as we have seen, cashels in the west were certainly being occupied (A O'Sullivan et al. 2014b). We would need closer analysis of other evidence, however, particularly the diagnostically late artefact assemblages recovered from many sites. Even so, there are only a few early medieval settlements in the east of the country that have evidence for continued occupation into the 12th century. These include Castlefarm 1, Co. Meath, excavated in advance of the M3 motorway, where there was substantial late medieval activity (O'Connell 2006; 2009), and Johnstown 1, Co. Meath, where settlement and industry continued into the 14th and 15th centuries (Clarke & Carlin 2008). Some raised raths in the north-east and east were used by Anglo-Norman colonists as the location for defended mottes in the late 12th and early 13th centuries, perhaps for symbolic as well as practical reasons (O'Keeffe 2000; Ó Drisceoil 2002). It is difficult, however, to demonstrate a direct continuity in settlement between early medieval and Anglo-Norman times, as opposed to the reuse of previously abandoned sites that had not seen occupation for decades, if not centuries.

If raths were being abandoned in the south and east, it seems, in contrast, that raths, cashels and crannogs in the west and north-west continued in use as settlements or were actually being built anew (A O'Sullivan 2001; Comber & Hull 2008; 2010; FitzPatrick 2009). We may have distinct regional differences in both settlement and practice, and perhaps even in the social order, so that in the regions that were to become 'Gaelic Ireland' people held on to their traditions and dwelling practices. We should be careful, however, of thinking that any one region, north, south, east or west, can stand for the whole island, and regional comparative studies will be required to identify regional and local traditions and practices across the entire period.

It is also clearly apparent that some of the most significant monastic settlements, such as Clonmacnoise, Glendalough and Armagh, were places where there was a growing clerical and lay population in the early 12th century. In contrast, there was no such development at places like Clonfad (Illus. 11), which remained relatively quiet. Some monastic or ecclesiastical settlements were centres of political power and patronage, education and agricultural wealth, supporting a range of clerics, scholars, craftspeople and agricultural labourers and tenants on their extensive estates, while others were not. This century also marks the demise of the old monastic *paruchiae* system of ecclesiastical governance and the establishment of the diocesan system, with the development of new urban centres associated with this reorganisation. The Viking or Hiberno-Norse towns of Dublin, Waterford, Limerick and Cork were now fully formed urban settlements with enclosing walls, and they functioned as centres of manufacturing production that traded with ports across Atlantic Europe and beyond, as what we term early medieval Ireland came to an end.

Conclusions

We have only begun to tell the stories that it is now possible to relate about the lives of the peoples of Ireland from the fifth to the 12th century AD. The NRA archaeological excavations have produced a remarkable body of evidence for the early medieval period, and we have been able to go from description to debate as we are confronted with an archaeological landscape that is much more complex than we thought. Secular settlement has been expanded from the certainties and comfort zone of the ringfort/rath/crannog to a situation that is more difficult to interpret, as we are presented with dwelling and settlement types which were not clearly described in the rich documentary sources of the period. The archaeology of death and burial has likewise been transformed, and this process will continue as osteological and aDNA studies start to focus on the realities of people's lives in the past.

In this study we have tried to untangle the chronology of the period, but it is clear that we should expect regional and local complexity. Amidst the stories of long continuity through the centuries, we might start to look for ruptures and discontinuities, whether due to politics or plagues. We still do not understand the latter centuries, the 10th, 11th and 12th centuries. There are phases of occupation dating from this period at places like Dowdstown, Raystown and Castlefarm, all in County Meath, and there is an emerging sense of the construction of cashels and crannogs in the west and north-west at this time, but the situation in much of the remainder of the country needs to be established.

How should we go on? Answers to some of these empirical questions are likely to be found in the further analysis and interpretation of the massive body of evidence amassed from the NRA excavations, as well as from other important excavations such as Knowth and Deer Park Farms. While excavations have been admirably published in summary form in the NRA Scheme

Illus. 11 (opposite page)—Vertical aerial view of Clonfad, Co. Westmeath, incorporating a schematic plan of the excavated features and a pre-excavation topographical survey by Valerie J Keeley Ltd, and the interpretive results of geophysical surveys by Target Archaeological Geophysics Ltd and IGAS Ltd (after Stevens 2010).

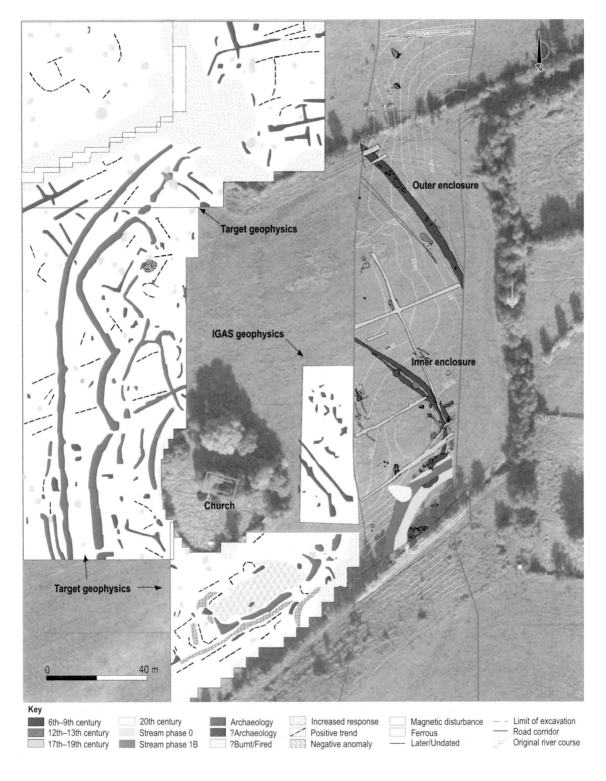

Key

■ 6th–9th century	□ 20th century	▦ Archaeology	▦ Increased response	□ Magnetic disturbance	--- Limit of excavation
■ 12th–13th century	□ Stream phase 0	▦ ?Archaeology	⟋ Positive trend	□ Ferrous	— Road corridor
▦ 17th–19th century	▦ Stream phase 1B	▦ ?Burnt/Fired	▦ Negative anomaly	— Later/Undated	⬓ Original river course

Monographs series, much crucial information is also contained in the detailed stratigraphical and specialist reports, artefactual and environmental, contained in the grey literature, which has also been made available in digital form. The records of these archaeological excavations, stored in archives, and the objects and materials retained from the excavations will hopefully be the focus of both detailed and synthethic studies in years to come. The detailed analysis of this material—which will certainly take years, if not a generation—will produce crucial new information on the period. It is because of this that the curation of the actual material recovered from the excavations is of such importance, not only the artefacts but also the organic environmental material. Such material can be further analysed but will also provide samples for further radiocarbon dating and for types of archaeological scientific analyses that have not yet even been fully developed.

The information provided by the NRA campaigns has been augmented by the recent publication of some major early medieval 'old' excavations as well as other development-led excavations. The Knowth and Deer Park Farms excavation monographs are equal in stature to the Lagore and Ballinderry excavation reports of previous generations. Many of the NRA early medieval sites—not only those mentioned above—can easily take their place in that canon, especially those that are most fulsomely published, and, with the more sophisticated archaeological sciences in play, the NRA sites will probably dominate our thinking and rethinking in years to come. Other developer-led excavations have contributed significantly to urban archaeology in particular, while publications of non-NRA sites such as Rosepark and Balrothery are also major additions to rural early medieval settlement studies. There is much still to be done as regards analysing, publishing and understanding the early medieval archaeological evidence uncovered during the last 20 years or so. Finally, we have the challenges of multidisciplinary approaches to confront, and the gaps therein between texts and material culture. We also have the challenges of using theoretical approaches to continue to engage with the performed social identities—including ethnicity, politics, religious beliefs, kinship, status, gender, role—of the peoples of early medieval Ireland. In any case, it is true that the NRA's programme of archaeological investigations over the last two decades has led to a situation that can best be summarised in D A Binchy's famous words as 'the passing of the old order'.

Acknowledgements

The authors would like to thank the Heritage Council for financing EMAP as part of the INSTAR initiative. They would also like to thank TII and all those individual excavators who allowed access to their unpublished excavation reports during the project.

7

THE LATER MEDIEVAL COUNTRYSIDE LYING BENEATH

Mark Gardiner & Kieran O'Conor

Ireland is still a relatively rural country in comparison to the rest of western Europe, with few large cities. Later medieval Ireland was very definitely mainly rural in nature, with the vast majority of its people, whatever their ethnic origins, living in the countryside and with agriculture the predominant economic activity by far (O'Conor 1998, ix). The later medieval period is taken in this paper to mean the period between the early 12th century and c. 1600, incorporating what scholars term the 'high medieval' and 'late medieval' periods, although it must be noted that some archaeologists feel that the events of the mid-17th century, such as the Cromwellian Wars and Settlement, marked the real end of the medieval period in Ireland (O'Conor 1998, ix; 2014, 342; McNeill 2007). About 200 sites with later medieval remains (which include sites of earlier date on which the last phases of activity belong to this era) have been excavated since the 1990s by archaeologists working on 59 road schemes on behalf of the NRA and the relevant local authorities. In all, about 10% of the total number of NRA-funded excavations produced evidence for activity of this period. Sites investigated include manorial centres, moated sites, farmsteads, nucleated settlements, cemeteries, fields, ringforts, cereal-drying kilns, refuse pits, iron-working sites, charcoal-production sites and limekilns. The majority of these excavations have taken place in the parts of Ireland that were under the control of the Anglo-Normans in the period from the late 12th century until the 14th century and by their descendants after that date (Illus. 1). Areas that continued to be dominated by Irish princes and lords during the later medieval period have not seen the same amount of excavation, simply because these regions are relatively remote from the infrastructural work that has been undertaken in recent years by the NRA. Also, many later medieval Irish-dominated areas lay west of the River Bann within the bounds of Northern Ireland, and hence beyond the NRA's area of responsibility. As a result, the information generated by these NRA-funded excavations tells us more about life, settlement, society and landscape in the areas under Anglo-Norman control, particularly eastern and south-eastern parts of the island, and less about the regions of medieval Ireland that were dominated by Gaelic lords.

Archaeological and historical research on the later medieval period in Ireland to date has tended to concentrate on the sites of the élite in society or on urban centres. Much work has been carried out on castles, abbeys, priories and manorial centres, as well as on cities and towns. The road schemes undertaken by or on behalf of the NRA have mostly avoided these sorts of sites—places where known archaeological complexes exist or that remain centres of population today.

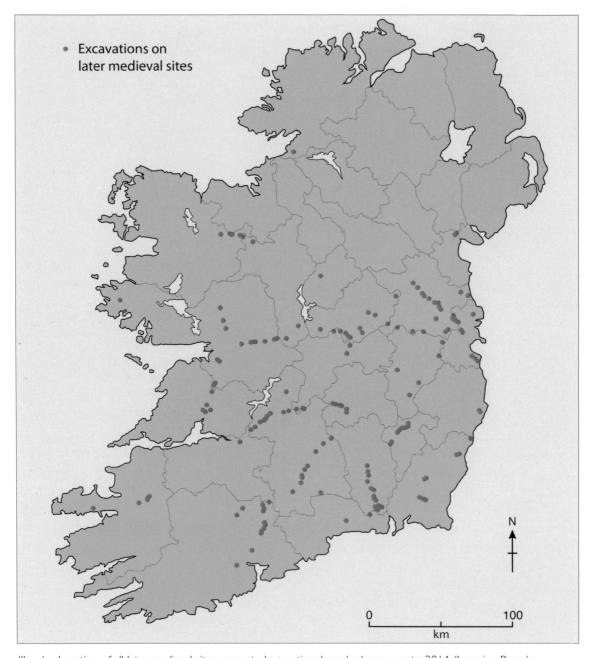

Illus. I—Location of all later medieval sites excavated on national road schemes up to 2014 (Lorraine Barry).

These excavations have occurred in more peripheral areas away from such 'central' places, in parts of the landscape that have not been examined in any detail before. In fact, this is the great strength of the work carried out by archaeologists and archaeological consultancies working on national road schemes. The road excavations have opened up to scholarship an entirely different view of

Irish archaeology. They have lifted the sod and exposed a cross-section of the later medieval landscape. The picture that emerges from these excavations of sites that were located in what might be termed the 'deep' countryside of later medieval Ireland is one of an organised, agricultural landscape of fields, farms and productive woodlands.

Manorial centres

The documentary evidence for manorial centres has been discussed in recent summaries, but until now it has been possible to add very little detail from excavation (O'Conor 1998, 26–33; 2002b; Murphy & Potterton 2010, 169–79). The link road at Twomileborris, Co. Tipperary, passed close to the site of the village of *Burgaslethe*, which had the status of a borough in the later medieval period. Close by was a ringwork, church and 16th-century tower-house. The conjunction of these suggests that there may have been a manorial centre adjoining the village, located initially at the ringwork and later at the tower-house. Excavation in the townlands of Blackcastle and Borris revealed a watermill with stone footings and a probable timber superstructure. It could only be dated broadly to the 12th century. A second mill lying to the north was constructed of masonry to eaves height and had a possible slate roof (Illus. 2). This was an unusually elaborate method of construction for such a building. The mill was dated by dendrochronology to the last decade or so of the 12th century or the first decade of the 13th century, suggesting that it was built by the Anglo-Norman lord of this manor. Some 50 m to the east of the second mill was a cereal-drying kiln, probably of similar date. There were a series of iron-smithing hearths, some certainly dating from the 13th century. On the opposite side of the stream from the mills and the kiln was a substantial square clay-walled (cob) structure, measuring about 6 m^2 and built in the 13th century. It seems to have had a number of uses, including serving as a forge for iron-working in one of its later phases. It is not clear whether these crop-processing and industrial activities were associated with the manorial farmstead, but it is likely. In the same area was a sump or well, backfilled in the 14th century, with a coin hoard concealed in its deposits. Hoards were typically buried just beyond the periphery of settlements, so that the owners would not be seen hiding their coins by their neighbours but close enough that an eye could be kept on the spot. Coin hoards are generally associated with peasants, and the modest value of this cache—54½d—does not imply lordly riches (see Dyer 1997, 38). In the 15th or 16th century two ditched stands were dug in the same area for ricks (stacks) for crop storage. These lie some distance south of the tower-house, but again we cannot know whether they were associated with it.

A major excavation of an important, originally Anglo-Norman manorial centre took place at Carrickmines Great, Co. Dublin, in advance of the construction of the south-eastern part of the M50 motorway. The original castle here seems to have been a well-defended ringwork which evolved over time (after a period of abandonment in the first half of the 14th century) into a masonry castle protecting the southern borders of the Pale but also acting as the seat of the Gaelicised Walsh family. The castle was finally abandoned in the 1640s after a siege (O'Byrne

Illus. 2—Elevated view of the late 12th-/early13th-century watermill at Blackcastle and Borris, Twomileborris, Co. Tipperary (Hawkeye).

2002). Evidence was also found for agricultural activities at the site throughout the later medieval period, starting in the 12th and 13th centuries, reminding us that castles had residential, administrative and agricultural functions too and were not just fortresses. The site and its environs produced evidence for cereal-drying kilns, wells, fields, furrows and mill-races (Breen 2012). As already stated, however, by far the great majority of the excavations carried out in advance of road construction took place away from such manorial centres.

Moated sites

Moated sites mainly appear in the landscape today as rectangular earthworks bounded by internal banks and external ditches which are often water-filled, being fed from adjacent streams or springs by artificial channels known as leats. Wedge-shaped and, far less commonly, circular moated sites also exist (O'Conor 1998, 58). The overwhelming majority of moated sites in Ireland were in some way semi-defended farm centres, whether built and occupied by prosperous peasants of mainly English origin, minor Anglo-Norman lords or important Gaelic dynasts. Some may also have marked the centres of monastic granges, while a few others may have been hunting lodges associated with the highest echelons of Anglo-Norman society. Wooden palisades (or perhaps thick hedges in some cases) would have surmounted the banks of these moated sites, and timber (and sometimes cob) domestic and agricultural buildings, which were built in a variety of ways, occurred within their interiors. Moated sites in Ireland are dated to the 13th and 14th centuries, with research over the last 40 years or so suggesting that their construction and occupation centred on the second half of the former century and the earlier part of the latter one. In eastern and south-eastern Ireland, at least, they seem to represent a secondary movement out from the initial areas of Anglo-Norman settlement into more marginal areas of agricultural land, and in some cases their construction was linked to assarting (land clearance for agriculture) (Glasscock 1970; Barry 1977; 1987, 84–95; Empey 1982, 332; McNeill 1997, 148–9; O'Conor 1998, 58–69, 87–9; 2000; O'Keeffe 2000, 73–80; Finan & O'Conor 2002; Murphy & Potterton 2010, 202–7). Many moated sites in Ireland also occurred in what were often turbulent, *de facto* frontier areas on the march (border) between lands heavily settled by the Anglo-Normans and those dominated by Gaelic Irish lords. The occupants of the moated sites in these districts felt that they needed the defences of these sites as a form of protection against the general lawlessness of these frontier areas (Barry 1977, 176; 1981; 1987, 84–7).

Excavations linked to the road-building work of the NRA have clearly deepened our knowledge of moated sites. Only four definite moated sites had been excavated on the island of Ireland prior to 2000 (see O'Conor 1998, 58–69), but a further four moated sites have been excavated since then during the course of NRA-funded road-building schemes. These are Coolamurry (Illus. 3; Fegan 2009) and Camaross (not Carrowreagh, as previously reported) (Tierney 2009), Co. Wexford, Busherstown, Co. Offaly (Chrobak et al. 2012), and Ballinvinny South, Co. Cork (Cotter 2009), meaning that this work has doubled the number of excavated moated sites in the country. In dating terms, the results of these new excavations have confirmed that most moated sites in this country were built and occupied from c. 1250 into the 14th century at least (see, for example, O'Conor 1998, 59–69; O'Keeffe 2000, 73–7, for our knowledge about the dating of moated sites in Ireland prior to the NRA excavations). Calibrated radiocarbon dates from organic materials found in secure, apparently primary contexts at Coolamurry and Busherstown seem to suggest that these sites post-date c. 1250 and were occupied into the 14th century (Table 1; Fegan 2009, 91; Chrobak et al. 2012, 55, 67, 72). Furthermore, the pottery assemblage at Coolamurry, where datable, also suggests a date for the construction and occupation of the site after the mid-13th century (Fegan 2009, 101; McCutcheon 2009, 106). The excavator of the moated site of Camaross dated the construction of this site to the 'early 13th century' (Tierney 2009, 192), but a calibrated radiocarbon date from organic material in the basal fill of the ditch points to a very late 13th- or 14th-century date for the primary occupation of the enclosure (ibid., 195; Table 1). The suggestion that the great majority of moated sites in Ireland were built after the mid-13th century is further supported by evidence from Cloonfree, Co. Roscommon.

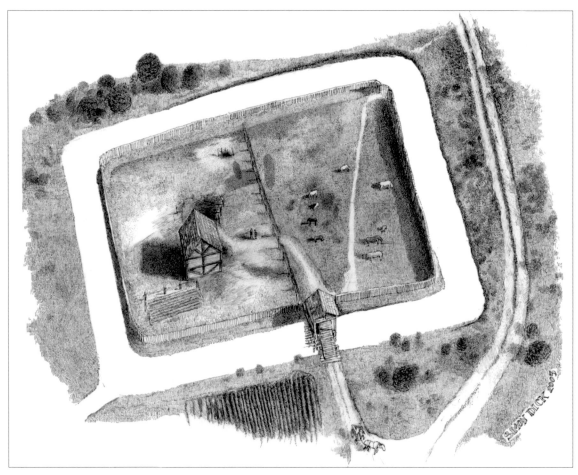

Illus. 3—Reconstruction of Coolamurry moated site, Co. Wexford (Simon Dick).

Literary and historical evidence suggests that this site was built around the year 1300 by Aodh O'Conor (Finan & O'Conor 2002, 78–9). Furthermore, annalistic references produced evidence for the 14th-century occupation of moated sites in the same general area (O'Conor 2001, 338–40). Interestingly, evidence from the Camaross moated site indicates that it continued to be occupied up to possibly as late as the mid-15th century (Tierney 2009, 195).

The moated sites at Camaross, Coolamurry, Ballinvinny South and Busherstown are located away from historically attested manorial centres (see Chrobak et al. 2012, 10–11, for a discussion of the latter site's location within the manor of Castle Philip). Again, the placing of these sites in seemingly non-lordly locations away from manorial centres may suggest that they were the homes of prosperous peasants who farmed quite large holdings in the vicinity, rather than members of the minor élite. The inhabitants were probably (but not definitely) free tenants of English origin, either recent immigrants (O'Keeffe 2000, 75–80) or, just as likely, descended from colonists who first came to Ireland in the late 12th or very early 13th century, enticed over to provide labour and

Illus. 4—Reconstruction of the gatehouse and drawbridge of Coolamurry moated site (Simon Dick).

extra tenantry on newly created Anglo-Norman manors (O'Conor 1998, 41–3). Copper-alloy dividers from the Coolamurry moated site appear to have belonged to either a stonemason or stonecutter (Fegan 2009, 98, 100; Carroll & Quinn 2009). This evidence suggests what we would now call a dual income for at least one of the occupants of this moated site. A recent reinterpretation of some of the excavated evidence from just outside the ditch at Camaross has suggested that perhaps two cereal-drying kilns existed here when this moated site was in use (J Eogan & Kelly 2016). The existence of these two features, in turn, hints at quite large-scale cereal production at these sites that went beyond just subsistence agriculture. Again, this is all further evidence to suggest that moated sites in eastern and south-eastern Ireland were often the homes of prosperous members of the peasant class—the rural equivalent of urban artisans and merchants. Such people, entrepreneurial in spirit but not members of the local élite, would have done well in the economic climate of later 13th- and early 14th-century Ireland, selling their agricultural produce for good prices in the regional market towns (O'Keeffe 2000, 75–80). They could perhaps have employed servants and labourers and, because of their wealth, had access to certain luxuries. The rather complex entranceway at Coolamurry, with its drawbridge, effectively a small timber gatehouse (Illus. 4), adds to this picture of prosperity—such a structure took resources to build (Fegan 2009, 95). It was also, perhaps, a statement of aspiration for a member of an increasingly prosperous element at that time in rural Ireland. The 'strong farmer' class of 19th- and 20th-century Ireland might be a good modern analogy for the type of men who built and occupied many moated sites in south-east Ireland.

How defensive were moated sites? This is a difficult question to answer, owing to the nature of the excavated evidence and, more importantly, how their excavators chose to interpret this evidence. The complex entranceway feature at Coolamurry, with its drawbridge, clearly represented quite a serious barrier and encourages us to look at the evidence from earlier moated site excavations. There is a distinct possibility that the moated sites at both Kilmagoura and Rigsdale in County Cork also had quite serious entrance features in the form of timber-framed gatehouses, although there was little attempt to argue this in their original excavation reports (Glasscock 1968; Sweetman 1981; Barry 1987, 89–91; O'Conor 1998, 63, 66). Little is said, however, by the excavator of Coolamurry about the original palisade that would once have surmounted the bank of the moated site, most of which was levelled in the early 1950s. The excavator only commented that its original palisade was probably built of earthfast posts and stakes, although it was stated that bits of palisade may have been found in the ditch during the course of the excavation (Fegan 2009, 92). In this respect, it is noteworthy that no evidence for a palisade was found on the bank defining the moated site at Rigsdale and, indeed, its excavator suggested that this lack of a palisade was evidence that this site was never fully finished or properly occupied (Sweetman 1981, 204). It seems odd for the builders of the moated site at Coolamurry (and, indeed, Rigsdale) to have constructed what was effectively a small gatehouse and drawbridge, dig quite a deep and wide ditch, and just erect a relatively flimsy palisade on its bank. Research in Britain, however, has indicated that there was a movement away from the use of earthfast posts in house—or, for that matter, palisade—construction during the late 12th and 13th centuries (e.g. Higham & Barker 1992, 326–47). An alternative to setting vertical posts into the ground to construct a palisade was to lay large sill beams directly onto the flat top of a bank, into which upright timbers could be fitted to provide quite a formidable barrier, especially if braced at the rear. Such a palisade would leave little or no archaeological trace (O'Conor 1998, 66; 1999, 201). It is quite possible that a palisade of this type existed at Coolamurry. If this was the case, Coolamurry, if defended resolutely by its owners and farm servants, could have seen off more than just a few thieves, perhaps even a small raiding party. Its entranceway, wet ditch, bank and palisade would at least make the latter think twice about attacking it, realising that, while they could force an entry into the moated site, their gains would not compensate for their potential losses.

On the other hand, the excavation of the Ballinvinny South moated site near Cork City showed it to have had extremely light defences. The excavator suggested that these could only have acted as a security measure to prevent the nocturnal theft of livestock by a few thieves, nothing more (Cotter 2009, 50, 52, 54, 57). The moated site was apparently located in a secure area close to the urban centre of Cork, well away from frontier areas, and for this reason needed little in the way of defence. It was argued that the existence of a palisade, bank and partly wet ditch at Ballinvinny South was as much a symbol of status for the inhabitants as anything else (ibid., 57). The apparent contrast between the defences at Ballinvinny South and the seemingly more formidable defences at Coolamurry was linked to the more exposed nature of the latter site. Obviously, moated sites in quite turbulent frontier zones needed stronger defences than ones in more peaceful areas.

Glasscock (1970) was really the first scholar to recognise that moated sites existed in some numbers in the Irish countryside. He believed that about 750 of them had been built in medieval Ireland, exclusively by the Anglo-Normans (ibid., 164). O'Conor (1998, 63), however, noting the number of hitherto-unrecognised moated sites found during the 1970s, 1980s and 1990s by scholars such as Terry Barry (1977) and, more recently, by the comprehensive fieldwork of the Archaeological Survey of Ireland, suggested that the number may have been as high as 1,000. It is noteworthy that none of the four moated sites excavated by NRA-funded archaeologists had been recognised until the advent of the roads programme and its associated excavations. Therefore these sites are new to scholarship and constitute further evidence to support the view that far more moated sites were built in 13th- and early 14th-century Ireland than was believed back in the 1970s. This begs the question of whether further detailed studies of districts, such as parts of mid-Wexford, will turn up more, perhaps many more. Indeed, such studies might find that even the figure of 1,000 moated sites is itself a conservative figure. It must be remembered that numbers are important, as the recognition of new moated sites and, indeed, other types of medieval sites, such as isolated, undefended farmsteads away from manorial centres, fill out distribution maps and perhaps show us that the landscape of 13th- and early 14th-century Ireland was more managed, populous and prosperous (because it took a certain degree of wealth to build something like a moated site) than scholarship has hitherto believed.

Other farmsteads

The occupants of the 14th-century farmstead at Boyerstown, Co. Meath, were only one step down in status from those who inhabited contemporary moated sites (Martin 2009). The farmstead lay beside the road from Navan to Athboy and, although the occupants were wealthy enough to possess silver personal items, such as a ring-brooch and a crucifix pendant, the building was undefended. It was well built, with a timber frame set on drystone footings, and had a central hearth. Evidence was found for a door to the rear of the building, and it is likely that there would have been another to give access from the road (Illus. 5). A second building that adjoined the house seems to have served as an outbuilding, perhaps for food-processing, including cooking, as there was a hearth in one corner. Other buildings were situated around a yard to the rear of the farmhouse, though their plan is uncertain. Over 1,000 iron nails were found during excavation, another sign of the quality of the construction, since iron was expensive and sparingly used in

Illus. 5—Reconstruction of the farmstead at Boyerstown, Co. Meath (Libby Mulqueeny).

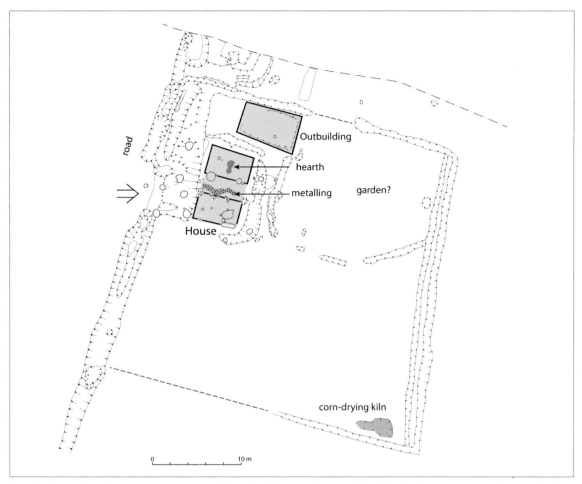

Illus. 6—Plan of the farmstead at Leggetsrath East, Co. Kilkenny (prepared by Libby Mulqueeny, adapted from a plan by Irish Archaeological Consultancy Ltd).

buildings, which were generally held together with wooden pegs. Stray losses of coins from the 14th, 15th and 16th centuries found in a programme of metal-detecting reinforce the impression of prosperity at this site.

The site at Boyerstown is particularly important because not only were the house and adjoining building excavated, but also enough of the surroundings were examined to place the whole of the toft (farmstead) in its broader setting. The farmstead was not part of a larger settlement but stood on its own, directly facing the road. The plot on which the house was situated was defined by two large ditches that ran back at right angles from the road. Behind the farmstead was a field with furrows which had been formed by ploughing or spade cultivation. The plan looks very like the pattern of toft and croft (cultivated land) that was common in northern England at

143

this period, with a building set at the front of the site and a band of land stretching away behind (Hall & Wrathmell 2012, 280–8). A similar pattern is shown in a 1765 map of Dalkey, Co. Dublin, which seems to record a pattern of tenure of later medieval origin, while geophysical work at Castlemore, Co. Carlow, and excavation at Portmarnock, Co. Dublin, have identified comparable settlements (Otway-Ruthven 1951, 7–8; Corlett 2006; Moriarty 2011, 236–7; Brady 2014, 306). Unlike Boyerstown, however, all these other examples were settlements with multiple farmsteads. It does suggest that the plan of the toft and croft was adopted widely in Anglo-Norman areas, both for isolated farmsteads and nucleated settlements.

Indeed, the plan is repeated, at least in some respects, at the later medieval farmstead at Leggetsrath East, Co. Kilkenny. Again the farmhouse stood facing a possible road, with an adjoining outbuilding to one side (Illus. 6). In this case the farmyard was surrounded by a ditch, not wide or deep enough to be called a moat, and the whole site was clearly not intended to have any seriously defensive features. The entrance to the farmstead, which was probably constructed in the later 13th century, was marked by a metalled causeway across the ditches. It led towards the front door of the house. The position of the door is suggested by an internal partition within the house and a hard surface representing a cross-passage which ran between the front and back entrances. The main room or hall lay to the north of this, with a centrally placed hearth which had a base of stone, including broken pieces of a quern-stone. Beyond the house to the north was a smaller building marked only by a depression, measuring 6 m by 3.5 m, and a small number of post-holes. There were traces of burnt clay, suggesting that there was a hearth within the building, and charcoal recovered from it gave a 14th-century date (Table 1). Behind the buildings was an enclosure, perhaps marking the position of either a garden or an animal pound. The boundaries of the toft were indicated by ditches, within which was a cereal-drying kiln at the corner furthest from the buildings. We must envisage the farmyard as filled with henhouses and ricks of wheat awaiting threshing: the archaeobotanical report shows that the vast majority of grain present on the site was wheat, the most valuable of medieval crops and a sign of the quality of the surrounding farmland.

The Boyerstown and Leggetsrath farmsteads stood in isolation, but one of the more significant discoveries from this period in the roads programme was the village of Mullamast, Co. Kildare. Such villages, which were deserted in the 15th and 16th centuries, have been found across north-western Europe, reflecting a contracting population owing to the effects of plague and other epidemics. In this case, the village seems to have been established in the late 12th century, flourished in the 13th and 14th centuries, and contracted in the late 15th and early 16th centuries. The excavators at Mullamast identified three tofts or house enclosures on the south-east of a central road and four to the north-west, although the identification of the positions of individual buildings within these was much more difficult. The sites of two buildings were well marked by drainage trenches around their periphery, and shorter lengths of other ditches almost certainly surrounded other buildings. A number of lengths of stone footings were also found. These seem too wide for sill walls for a timber frame, and stone construction for what seem to be peasant houses would be unusual. The more likely interpretation is that these stone footings were for cob structures, which were often set on such a base to reduce rising damp (Bolger, forthcoming).

Other cob buildings were found at Monadreela, to the north-east of Cashel, Co. Tipperary, where just two structures were identified, though there may have been others set in the series of plots alongside a ditched road. The hamlet was first occupied in the 1220s with a single cob building, and the second identified example was built later in the 13th century. The excavator suggests that the houses accommodated both animals and people under one roof, a type of building known as a 'longhouse', but in fact the evidence for this is fairly slight: a series of post-holes set against the wall that could have been used for tethering livestock. The settlement did not last long and was abandoned in the early 14th century (Hughes & Ó Droma 2011, 21–8).

Later medieval buildings

Before the start of the roads programme scarcely more than 10 rural houses of 13th- and 14th-century date had been excavated (summarised in O'Conor 1998, 48–57), but the new discoveries have cast further light on the character of later medieval buildings and allow us to talk more confidently about the nature and character of peasant housing. The key to interpreting these later medieval buildings is an appreciation that the ditches, which are often the only indication of their position, do not mark the position of the walls but of a trench dug around the outside. Many of the trenches are somewhat irregular in shape and have rounded corners. They were intended to catch water running off a thatched roof, but were quite unsuitable for holding timbers for the structure of a building, which has been the interpretation offered in a number of site reports. For example, work in Waterford City has shown that by the 13th century most buildings there were timber-framed rather than constructed with posts set into the ground (as partly noted above in the moated site section). This allowed the timbers to be kept drier and to last longer (Scully 1997, 38–9).

The ditches around these rural buildings served to channel the water away from the timbers (which were placed on the surface of the ground) and kept the interior dry. The evidence for interpreting the trenches as eaves-drip ditches rather than as part of the structure of the building is particularly clear from the excavations at Mondaniel, Co. Cork (Illus. 7). The edge of the floor on the interior of the house is marked by a sharp drop in the surface produced by both wear underfoot and regular cleaning, and also by stone surfacing which must have been added to counter this wear. The edge of the building interior was set 1.4 m away from the trench, suggesting that it had either a substantial cob wall or a thick layer of thatch that cast the rainwater well away from the walls. Similar evidence was found at the moated site at Ballinvinny South, where a stone chimney with clay bonding was set inside and beyond the trench, almost certainly in line with the wall of the building marked by two post-holes to the west (Cotter 2009, 50, 53). Most 13th- and 14th-century buildings, however, have left no direct trace of the position of the walls below ground. They were very probably timber-framed structures with the sill beams set directly on the ground surface inside these shallow trenches, a method of building also found at the same period in England (Gardiner 2014, 18–20).

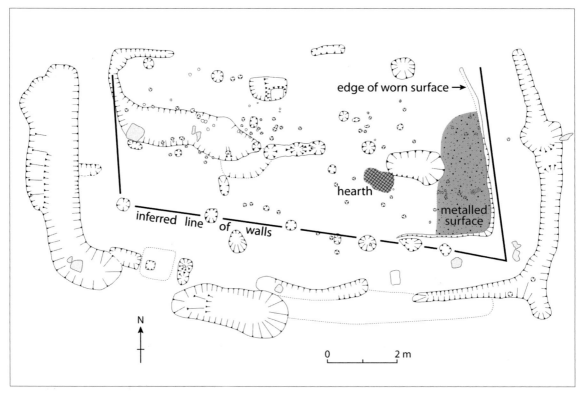

Illus. 7—Plan of the medieval house at Mondaniel, Co. Cork (prepared by Libby Mulqueeny, adapted from a plan by Archaeological Consultancy Services Ltd).

With this understanding, we can now reinterpret another of the buildings found on a national road scheme. The excavator realised that the number of finds in the trench at Moneycross Upper, Co. Wexford, indicated that it must have been open at the time the building was occupied. The trench therefore could not be interpreted as marking the line of the walls, but instead was identified as a ditch running around the interior of the building (Schweitzer 2009, 178–9). This seems most unlikely, since it suggests that the building was hardly weatherproof. If we regard the ditch as lying on the exterior, then it implies a rather narrower building, which is altogether more credible than the house as reconstructed.

Gaelic settlement

It was noted above that most of the excavations funded by the NRA were not located in the parts of Ireland that remained in some way under the control of Gaelic lords during the later medieval period. This is not to say, however, that NRA-funded excavations have told us nothing about the

Illus. 8—Elevated view of the ringfort at Mackney, Co. Galway (Hawkeye).

way of life of the Gaelic Irish during the period. For example, we know that a large proportion, even a majority at times, of the population on Anglo-Norman manors were Irish tenants or betaghs, even in eastern Ireland. It is probable that many of the sites excavated throughout these manorialised areas were the homesteads of Irish-speaking tenants. The difficulty lies in deciding what is the archaeological signature for a farmstead inhabited by an Irish tenant rather than an English-speaking peasant. A brave attempt was made to do this by the director of the excavation of the nucleated settlement at Attyflin, Co. Limerick. It was argued that the lack of cooking ware found in the ceramic assemblage was linked to the Irish tendency across large parts of the medieval island not to use pottery in the preparation of food. This point, taken with Attyflin's location away from its manorial centre, was used to argue that this site possibly represented the remains of a Gaelic settlement, whose inhabitants were tenants of the local Anglo-Norman lord (J Eogan 2009, 75–7).

Three excavated ringforts indicated continued occupation into the later medieval period. Indeed, the ringfort at Mackney, Co. Galway, showed quite substantial evidence for continued occupation into the later medieval period, possibly associated with a branch of the O'Kellys (Illus. 8; F Delaney 2014, 194–5, 199–200). This mirrors work in the Burren area of County Clare, which has found substantial evidence for members of the minor élite, service families and cadet branches of ruling dynasties occupying cashels throughout the later medieval period (FitzPatrick 2009). Excavation at Caherconnell, Co. Clare, for example, has indicated that this cashel was constructed in the late 10th century and was occupied continuously down to c. 1600 (Michelle Comber, pers.

comm.; https://caherconnell.com). The picture emerging from all this work is that a considerable number of ringforts continued to be occupied into later medieval times.

Timber-framed buildings from the south and east of Ireland can be contrasted with a quite different tradition of construction found in the north and west, one example of which is the oval building found in the west of County Galway at Derrylea in Connemara. This building, which was only partly excavated, had walls constructed of sod up to 1 m high, but perhaps were originally higher since much of the material had tumbled down. The entrance was tucked in next to a rock outcrop so that it was well protected from the weather, but it was situated in a rather wet place in which rushes were growing at the time of construction. Radiocarbon dating of that rushy material found beneath the sod walls suggests that the building belongs to the period 1220–1410 (Table 1). Oval buildings of this sort in the uplands are often referred to as booley huts, which implies that they were used only on a seasonal basis (Horning 2012, 181). The example at Derrylea is not in the uplands, and the size of the building—over 5 m on the long axis—is a good deal larger than the buildings occupied by cattle-herders in the summer months, and so it may have been lived in throughout the year. The existence of this house is yet another indication that oval and, indeed, circular houses and buildings continued to be built and occupied long after the 11th century, especially in parts of the west of Ireland (O'Conor 2002a, 201–4). One reason why such houses continued to be built into the later medieval period may have been that their shape made them very stable in high winds, and so their continued existence in some areas was to a certain extent determined by the local environment (ibid., 201–2).

The wider landscape

The archaeology of the road schemes is particularly valuable because it not only focused on 'sites' (i.e. the centres of past activity) but also provided a view of the wider landscape and included those minor features which are so important in understanding the broader context of settlement. Discussion of the later medieval landscape in the past has had to rely on the evidence from documentary and cartographic sources, since so many upstanding features of the later medieval countryside have been swept away in the agricultural improvements of the last 250 years. Although improvement has led to the restructuring of many features, work on the road schemes showed that earlier features do still survive and indicated the ways in which these might be identified. For example, a study of the field patterns and cartographic evidence undertaken in advance of the proposed M20 Cork to Limerick road located traces of the medieval open fields in the present land boundaries (Hanley 2011, 42–7). Excavation on many road sites demonstrated, however, that few later medieval boundaries could be traced in the present-day pattern of hedges and ditches. Yet the traces of the earlier boundaries have not been entirely eradicated. Laser scanning and detailed GPS surveys of the surface of the fields were able to identify the very slight earthworks of later medieval field boundaries which have survived ploughing. Excavation identified a later medieval curving field boundary at Rahally, Co. Galway, which cut across a prehistoric hillfort and early medieval enclosure, and a combination of aerial and ground survey then allowed it to be traced beyond the road corridor into the land on either side. At Laughanstown, Co. Dublin, field ditches were identified but surface survey also found the associated field bank, and the excavators at Knockmoylan, Co. Kilkenny, noted a faint ridge before the topsoil was stripped, which they concluded was the bank that had stood next to a medieval ditch. This showed that slight traces of former field boundaries survive in a number of places, even after they have been ploughed over for a number of centuries (see also Hall et al. 1985). It also raised questions about the view that the Irish countryside was largely open and unfenced (Nicholls 1987, 411).

Ridge-and-furrow was one of the few methods used in the later medieval period throughout north-west Europe to drain fields and prevent waterlogging. It allowed water to drain off the ridges where the crops were grown and into the furrows, where it could run away to ditches at the edge of fields, and it was particularly important on heavy soils in wet climates. It is rather surprising, then, that the extensive excavations on the roads programme produced so little evidence of the parallel system of ditches between the cultivation ridges. Deep drainage ditches found at the margins of fields were a common discovery, but lines of cultivation furrows between the field boundaries were comparatively rare, possibly because they were not deep enough to cut the subsoil. One problem that has dogged the study of the remains of cultivation in Ireland is that of distinguishing the ploughed later medieval ridges from the spade-dug ridges of later date. It has been suggested that medieval cultivation ridges can be distinguished by their width—between 4 m and 10 m (M O'Sullivan & Downey 2007, 36–7)—which was somewhat wider than the spade-dug potato beds, but the evidence from road schemes suggests that it is by no means so clear. The excavations at Rahally, mentioned above, found two sets of ridges. The first set, later medieval in date, were between 2.4 m and 6.8 m wide, while the later ones, at right angles, were not narrower, measuring between 3.3 m and 4.2 m in breadth. Extensive ridging was found at Bricketstown, Co. Wexford, where a much larger area stretching over a distance of more than 100 m was found lying parallel to a field bank. The date of this area of cultivation is not certain, though it seems to lie in the 15th or 16th century. The ridges were 3.9 m apart.

The arrival of the Anglo-Normans in Ireland brought a change in both settlement and agricultural practice. Villages were formed, some of which had the status of boroughs, and we have already noted an excavated example. The consolidation of settlement may have been connected with the adoption of open-field agriculture in which land was cultivated in strips managed communally (Otway-Ruthven 1951). The production of arable crops was intensified to provide for the growing population of towns and for export. One of the few datable archaeological manifestations of this increase in arable farming are plough pebbles, the stones inserted in the sole beam of a wheel-less plough to reduce the wear on the timber. Brady (1988; 2009) suggests that these can be dated in Ireland to the 13th century and has catalogued all the examples known to him. Not surprisingly, they have been found predominantly in the east and south-east, the main arable areas of Ireland, but, as he notes, the finds of plough pebbles are almost certainly connected with the work of those who are interested and aware of them. The discovery of 25 plough pebbles in the excavation at Laughanstown does not so much mark an area of intense 13th-century cultivation as a site where the archaeologists were assiduous in their collection (Seaver & Keeley

2007, 96). Nevertheless, that site shows the considerable number of pebbles that almost certainly remain in any area that was ploughed extensively in the 13th century.

The growing population of the 13th century, the commercialisation of agriculture and the increased market provided by closer ties with England encouraged the expansion of farmland. Much of the moated site series in south-east Ireland and the foundation of the hamlet at Monadreela outside Cashel in the 1220s, mentioned above, may be connected with that, and so may the woodland clearance at Newrath, Co. Kilkenny, which produced two almost identical radiocarbon dates, one of which was 1184–1276 (Table 1). On the other hand, the almost total lack of later medieval settlement sites along the 18-km-long N5 Charlestown Bypass in counties Mayo and Roscommon is interesting. The only real evidence for activity dating from this period along this stretch of country consisted of charcoal-production pits. It was argued that this was an indication of woodland clearance (Kerrigan & Gillespie 2010a, 20–1), but the evidence for charcoal production and a lack of settlement in the form of habitation sites suggests large tracts of managed woodland across this region.

Conclusions

Our understanding of medieval rural settlement in Ireland before the excavations on NRA road schemes was summarised by O'Conor in *The Archaeology of Medieval Rural Settlement in Ireland* (1998), which was commissioned by the Discovery Programme. It is clear from the present review that our knowledge of this subject has been both widened and deepened by the new discoveries along the line of these roads. The picture that emerges from these excavations is that the rural landscape of 13th- and early 14th-century Ireland was a more managed, populous and wealthier place than was thought back in 1998. The results of these investigations indicate a productive, organised agricultural landscape of fields and farmsteads (some of which were defended, while others were not) during this period, particularly in the manorialised landscape of eastern and south-eastern Ireland, not just in the immediate vicinities of manorial centres but in peripheral parts of the manors as well. Again, it was suggested that many of the tenants on these Anglo-Norman manors, whether Irish or English in origin, partook in the economic boom seen in 13th-century Ireland, which seems to have continued into the early 14th century. Indeed, such prosperity persisted into the 15th century, as the extraordinary boom in the construction of tower-houses and the work on friaries imply. It was argued that this evidence from this review of road-scheme excavations suggests that a class of prosperous peasants existed in the countryside of Anglo-Norman Ireland. This indicates that not all wealth was concentrated in the hands of the landowning élite and that ordinary people were permitted, even encouraged, to prosper during this time. The evidence from the four moated sites excavated in advance of road construction hints strongly that Anglo-Norman Ireland was at its wealthiest in the second half of the 13th century, a point argued for by O'Keeffe (2000, 77–80).

We have suggested that the results indicate that the number of moated sites has been underestimated and that many more remain to be found, especially in south-eastern Ireland, where the landscape has been intensively farmed in post-medieval times. How would such a study to find more moated sites be carried out? The answer to this question lies in the stratigraphic reports of these four moated sites excavated with NRA funding and in the subsequent articles published on them (see Cotter 2009; Fegan 2009; Tierney 2009). For example, the moated site at Busherstown was visible from the air as a cropmark (Chrobak et al. 2012). There was local knowledge at Camaross, Coolamurry and Ballinvinny South that sites of archaeological potential existed at these places (Tierney 2009, 190). The field in which the levelled moated site at Camaross was located was traditionally known as the 'Raa' (rath) field, and the landowner remembered that various earthworks in this particular field were levelled about 20 years prior to the excavation (ibid.). Something similar happened at Coolamurry, as the landowner here knew that various earthworks at the site had been levelled c. 1950 (Fegan 2009, 91). The farmer at Ballinvinny South stated that there was a local tradition of a fort being located at the site (Cotter 2009, 49). Furthermore, O'Keeffe (2000, 75) has noted that it is likely that many extant moated sites throughout Ireland have not been identified as archaeological monuments because their mostly rectangular shape meant that they were easily incorporated into the modern field system. In turn, this means that at times the 19th-century Ordnance Survey did not recognise these sites for what they were and marked them on the six-inch maps as modern fields. For example, the moated site at Ogulla, Co. Roscommon, is marked as a small field on the relevant Ordnance Survey six-inch map for the area, but fieldwork in the mid-1990s by the Archaeological Survey of Ireland showed it to be a fine bivallate moated site (O'Conor 2001, 340–3). This evidence suggests that the way to identify hitherto unrecognised moated sites in any given area is to visit literally every small rectangular or wedge-shaped field within it, to talk to and engage meaningfully with landowners to tap into their unrivalled knowledge of the landscape of their farms, and to carry out regular aerial surveys at different times of the year.

While we of course welcome the information that this extraordinary programme of archaeological work in advance of the construction of the road schemes has delivered, we are also aware in retrospect of some of the opportunities that were missed. The work showed that, even in heavily ploughed fields, earthworks marking former field boundaries might survive and might be revealed by laser scanning. The systematic study of the ploughsoil at Boyerstown and Laughanstown demonstrated the richness of material which was present but which elsewhere was often removed without examination. Phosphate sampling, which can illuminate where animals were stalled and where human and animal waste was collected, was rarely employed systematically on these road-scheme excavations. Should the opportunity arise in the future to undertake similar excavations, these methods should be employed.

Excavators should also take better note of the fact that methods of building adopted from the late 12th century often leave little archaeological trace, and this includes structures that were two or even three storeys in height. As stated in this review, there was a movement at this time away from the use of earthfast posts in house construction towards timber framing. The foundations of these timber-framed houses were often laid directly on the ground surface, meaning that at times they can be difficult to recognise during excavation. In other instances, however, shallow trenches were dug around such buildings. Many excavators have wrongly interpreted these as marking the slots into which the foundation beams of timber-framed buildings were placed. It was argued in this paper, however, that this was not the case and that these shallow ditches were, in fact, dug to catch and carry away water running off roofs, thus allowing these buildings to be kept drier and therefore to last longer. Furthermore, palisades were often pegged into sill beams that were laid horizontally on the flattened top of the earthen banks of timber castles or moated sites—again a method of construction that is difficult to trace archaeologically.

Overall, however, these excavations undertaken in advance of road construction have greatly added to our understanding of the later medieval period in Ireland, particularly of rural ways of life during Anglo-Norman times. This extensive archive of about 200 excavation reports will, with further study, continue to yield new insights about Ireland's later medieval past.

Acknowledgements

We are grateful to Lorraine Barry for assistance with Illus. 1 and to Libby Mulqueeny for preparing Illus. 5–7.

Table 1—Radiocarbon dates.

Lab code	Site	Sample/context	Yrs BP	$\delta^{13}C$ ‰	Calibrated date ranges
UB-15049	Busherstown, Co. Offaly	Wheat (*Triticum*) and Cerealia from base of moat ditch	627 ± 17	−24.2	AD 1299–1389 (1σ) AD 1292–1394 (2σ)
Beta-219126	Camaross, Co. Wexford	Mixed charcoal from fill of moat ditch	630 ± 40	−25.8	AD 1300–1400 (1σ) AD 1290–1410 (2σ)
UB-7685	Coolamurry, Co. Wexford	Oak (*Quercus* sp.) from base of moat ditch	707 ± 31	−28.0	AD 1269–1295 (1σ) AD 1257–1386 (2σ)
Beta-210097	Derrylea, Co. Galway	Reeds and moss beneath bank	690 ± 70	−26.0	AD 1270–1390 (1σ) AD 1220–1410 (2σ)
UB-15447	Leggetsrath East, Co. Kilkenny	Fruitwood (*Prunus* sp.) from fill of hearth	587 ± 24	−25.5	AD 1317–1403 (1σ) AD 1303–1411 (2σ)
UB-6647	Newrath, Co. Kilkenny	Oak (*Quercus* sp.) charcoal spread by ring-ditch	799 ± 31	−26.3	AD 1220–1261 (1σ) AD 1184–1276 (2σ)
UB-6648	Newrath, Co. Kilkenny	Oak (*Quercus* sp.) charcoal from upper fill of ring-ditch	791 ± 30	−26.7	AD 1223–1263 (1σ) AD 1191–1278 (2σ)

8

ROUTES ACROSS THE FAMILIAR PAST: REFLECTIONS ON NRA-FUNDED EXCAVATIONS AND THE CHALLENGE FACING THE 'POST-MEDIEVAL' ARCHAEOLOGY OF RURAL IRELAND

Tadhg O'Keeffe

Unnamed journalist: 'Why did you want to climb Everest?'
George Leigh Mallory: 'Because it's there.'
—*The New York Times* (18 March 1923)

Experienced archaeologists will know that some papers almost write themselves, especially when they are concerned with putting new finds into context and, as the next step, evaluating the significance of those finds in terms of advancing our common understanding of a period or a phenomenon. It was with envy—an envy that will be explained below, along with the opening quotation—that I followed the papers of colleagues at the symposium on which this book is based and thought about the tasks facing them for publication. Yes, there is probably less consensus in the interpretation of different pre-AD 1000 pasts than I, as a non-specialist, could detect by eavesdropping on their post-lecture conversations, but there is evidently a lot of common ground too. First, there are sites that need no introduction to the conversationalists because they belong in the canon; there are, for example, certain excavated Neolithic houses that are known to all the Neolithic specialists, and no introductions to them, or even images of them, are needed. Second, particular views are closely associated with particular scholars whose names do not require highlighting. Third, the excitement of new discoveries is self-evident to people who know all of the old discoveries. In each case, of course, such familiarity with the archaeological resource and with the interpretations made of it is possible because decades of previous research have left deep sediments of 'things to know'.

One could not claim, however, that the area assigned to me at the symposium, 'Post-Medieval Archaeology' (I will drop the inverted commas hereafter but will retain the upper-case letters to distinguish the praxis from the subject-matter), has been subjected to comparable research over a comparably long period. Important archaeological work, complementing the longer tradition of architectural-historical work, was carried out by archaeologists in the 1980s on Plantation-era Ulster (as noted in Donnelly & Horning 2002), and there is also an established tradition in the same province of industrial archaeology (see especially McCutcheon 1980). Relatively little work, however, was done on the archaeologies of the 18th, 19th and 20th centuries until the 1990s and 2000s, particularly in the Republic of Ireland. The context in which much of the new work was undertaken in those two decades was Contract Archaeology (the capitalisation of which here follows Gnecco & Schmidt Dias 2015). Although one is naturally mindful of the seminal contributions of Chuck Orser and Audrey Horning, Colin Rynne (on later Industrial Archaeology), and some others, one could even say that Post-Medieval Archaeology is unique among the branches of the discipline on the island of Ireland by virtue of the fact that it developed principally among archaeologists at the data-coalface of Contract Archaeology rather than among archaeologists working within the research-led culture of the academy. By extension, one could also say that Post-Medieval Archaeology is unique in having in its formative phase a disproportionately huge volume of information from excavations. It is unique in other respects, too, the principal one being that it deals with a period that is very comprehensively documented.

The most obvious impact of NRA-funded excavations (and associated surveys) on the archaeologist's particular understanding of rural Ireland since the Middle Ages is a quantitative one. I stress *rural* Ireland here because the excavations being reviewed were in rural settings, although that designation is slightly misleading in the case of, say, the fascinating brick-making site at Coonagh West 1, Co. Limerick (Reilly 2013, 132–8), and the brick-kilns at Ballynora 1, Co. Cork (Murphy 2013b). We now have more information with which to fill out a cultural-historical narrative of rural Ireland that, especially once we move past the era of the plantations, owes an enormous debt to the work of historical geographers, social-economic historians and folklorists, like Estyn Evans, Louis Cullen and Caoimhín Ó Danachair respectively. Any archaeologist who queries this dependence on non-archaeologists should reflect on how often he or she has opened the *Atlas of the Irish Rural Landscape* (Aalen et al. 2012) for guidance on the history of Ireland's rural landscapes and settlements. But is this quantitative enrichment enough? Is it the sum total of what Post-Medieval Archaeology offers?

In asking that question, I am not looking back with a critical eye at what has been done already in terms of excavations of post-medieval sites, a lot of it under the auspices of the NRA. Rather, I am looking forward and asking the profession to reflect now on (a) the purpose of pursuing an archaeology of the modern and contemporary pasts when so much information is available through the documentary record, and (b) how that archaeology—Post-Medieval Archaeology, if one insists on calling it that—might achieve its goals.

I am, in a sense, rejecting here the challenge given to me of reviewing how the results of NRA-sponsored work on post-medieval sites fit into, or significantly change, the state of our knowledge of Ireland over recent centuries. The main reason is, quite simply, that the excavations seem to me to have produced no great surprises, no sudden jolts to force a radical rethinking of any part of that narrative of rural Ireland and its post-medieval spatial/material histories that is accessible in the *Atlas of the Irish Rural Landscape*.

This is not to say that this work produced no interesting results (and it is certainly not to suggest that anything was lacking in any technical or recording sense). I will highlight here just three of the many interesting outcomes. First, we are reminded by the NRA's programme of work of the extent of small-scale rural industry. We are reminded especially of the importance of limekilns (see, for example, Kerrigan & Gillespie 2010b, 359–62; McQuade et al. 2009, 206–7; Bermingham et al. 2012b, 96–100; Reilly 2013, 129–31). These monuments developed not just

Illus. 1—A reconstruction of a 19th-century limekiln based on the example excavated at Keelty, Co. Clare, on the N85 Western Relief Road section of the M18 Ennis Bypass (Tadhg O'Keeffe).

morphologically but also functionally, having been used mainly for mortar (for the possible example of a kiln for mortar-lime see F Delaney & Tierney 2011a, 159–60) prior to the age of Improvement in the 18th and 19th centuries, the period in which lime began to be burned for use as fertiliser (Illus. 1). Second, the excavations have revealed sites—none more interesting than Ballinvinny South AR16, Co. Cork (Cotter 2013e)—at which attested continuity of settlement reminds us that our division of historical time into medieval and post-medieval is close to meaningless in analysing how space was used and place created. Third, excavations of individual sites have yielded material culture that might prompt future research. For example, from the 19th-century farmstead at Lavally, Co. Galway (F Delaney & Tierney 2011a, 166–71), came items like locks and keys, which make us reflect on the ownership and safe keeping of certain objects (Illus.

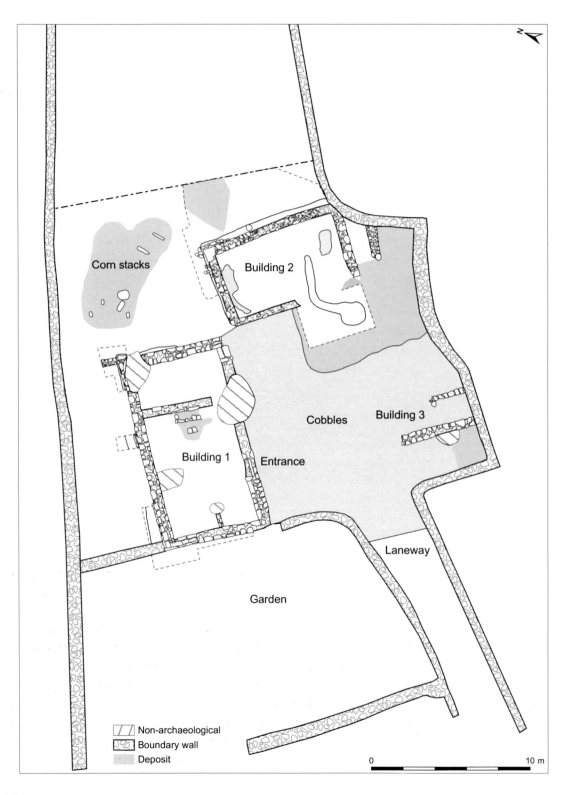

Corn stacks

Building 2

Cobbles

Building 3

Building 1

Entrance

Laneway

Garden

Non-archaeological
Boundary wall
Deposit

0   10 m

Illus. 2 (opposite page)—Interpretive post-excavation plan of the tenant farmstead excavated at Lavally, Co. Galway, on the N18 Oranmore to Gort road scheme (after F Delaney & Tierney 2011a).

Illus. 3 (above)—Locks and keys recovered from the farmstead at Lavally (John Sunderland).

2 & 3), and Sacred Heart devotional medals, objects which first appeared in the 17th century, the age of Counter-Reformation, and which probably—has there been work on this?—became part of the paraphernalia of domestic Catholicism in the penal age.

The very inclusion of all this 'later' heritage in the NRA volumes, integrated as it is into wider discussions of landscape evolution (see especially Rynne 2013b), is certainly contributing to the process of naturalising as archaeological the physical remains of recent, historically attested, populations. But I would argue that Post-Plantation Archaeology is not fully set up in the archaeological imagination in Ireland to challenge the grand narrative inherited from historians and geographers. I would identify the period of the plantations as one to which archaeologists have made a significant contribution, most notably through Horning's (2013) study of the Ulster Plantation in its Atlantic context but also, if a little less radically, through studies of south-western and midland Ireland by Colin Breen (2007) and James Lyttleton (2013) respectively. But once its coverage moves past 1650, an approximate end-date for the plantation period, Post-Medieval Archaeology in Ireland is still largely a subdiscipline that is focused on the collection, description and identification of data, and on the atomised, often site-specific, interpretation of those data. Generalisation is dangerous, of course, because there are always exceptions, not least in the *International Journal of Historical Archaeology*, an increasingly popular venue for Irish researchers with interesting things to say, but from my reading of post-medieval excavation literature, whether it originates with the NRA or any other organisation or agency, wider conceptual contextualisation is rarely attempted, except to reinforce the normative interpretations of the Irish past that are already heavily reliant on the work of non-archaeologists. For example, modernity, colonialism and capitalism, three of Chuck Orser's (1996) 'haunts' of global Historical (or Post-Medieval) Archaeology, are of central relevance to Ireland and Irish material, as scholars like Horning and Orser himself have shown, but the Irish post-medieval archaeological evidence is rarely refracted explicitly through those paradigmatic lenses, especially for the 18th and 19th centuries. Indeed, these very terms and concepts—modernity, colonialism and capitalism—barely featured a decade ago in the inaugural volume of the Irish Post-Medieval Archaeology Group (Horning et al. 2007), and I am not sure that they are any more a part of the conversation in Ireland now than they were back then. Equally, little attention is paid to the global context of Irish post-medieval archaeological evidence, even though Donnelly and Horning (2002, 560), reviewing the state of Post-Medieval Archaeology in Ireland about halfway through the Celtic Tiger years, insisted (absolutely correctly, by any measure) that 'post-medieval Ireland . . . be understood in its global context'.

One might argue that, as a field that has grown rapidly within the pressurised world of Contract Archaeology, it is too much to expect such themes to be developed in excavation reports. This would be a fair point. And one could argue that Contract Archaeology offers few opportunities to pursue research questions. This too would be a fair point. Thus, for example, had research been the driver of the excavation at Moyveela 3, Co. Galway, the dig would probably not have been confined to a small corner of the 'clachan' (Illus. 4 & 5). Excavation across the full extent of the site might have solved the key problem of chronology, left unsolved by the partial excavation. After all, the suggestion made by the excavation director, Linda Hegarty, that the 'clachan' was abandoned and the whole settlement relocated to a neighbouring townland is an important one (F Delaney & Tierney 2011a, 162), as it raises the possibility that, rather like what one finds in Scotland going back into the late Middle Ages, Moyveela itself was a relocation from an older 'clachan' (see O'Keeffe 2004, 21–5).

Lest this be seen as an attack on Contract Archaeology, much of the fault must lie in the university sector, where, in tandem with explaining the cultural-historical narrative, such themes as modernity, capitalism and colonialism might be explored and their relevance to Post-Medieval

Illus. 4 (opposite page)—Survey plan of the clachan at Moyveela 3, Co. Galway, on the N18 Oranmore to Gort road scheme, showing the excavated areas (outlined in red) at the northern end of the site (after F Delaney & Tierney 2011a).

0   30 m

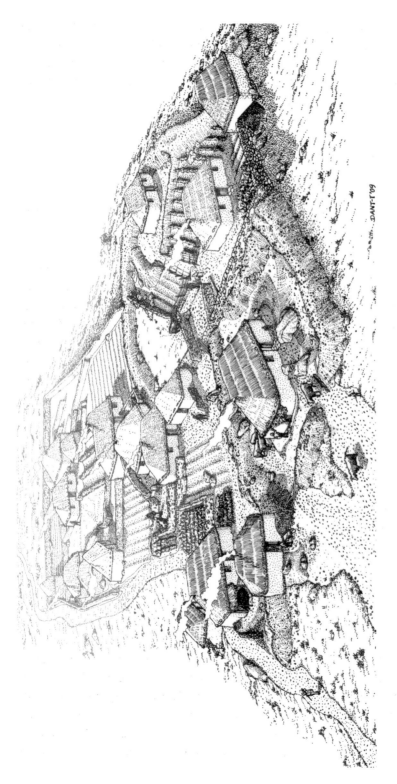

Illus. 5—Reconstruction drawing of the clachan at Moyveela, with the excavated areas in the foreground (Dan Tietzsch-Tyler).

Archaeology teased out much more. Twenty years on from the publication of Orser's *A Historical Archaeology of the Modern World* (1996), should those of us involved in teaching the archaeology of the recent past come together to discuss our role in the nascent subdiscipline? And should we include in our conversation the roles of oral history and collected memory in 'doing' archaeologies of the most recent past, which is the *remembered* past?

Contesting ownership of an over-familiar past

Prehistorians have a great advantage over historical archaeologists. They have no historical records. Their imaginations have great freedom. Historical evidence can be a safety net for those of us plying our trade in the second millennium AD, but it can just as easily imprison our imaginations.

The title of this section is borrowed in part from the title of a collection of essays entitled *The Familiar Past? Archaeologies of later historical Britain* (Tarlow & West 1999). The query at the end of the main title of that collection revealed the rhetorical intent common to those essays: the post-medieval centuries are familiar to us not only through historical documentation but also through our continued inhabitation of the world that was largely created during that period. Hitherto unrealised complexities in that world—our inherited world—can be revealed, it is argued in that volume, through closer scrutiny of the archaeological record. Now, few archaeologists in these islands and in many other parts of the world—though not really in continental Europe, oddly— would challenge this view. Most would agree with the principle that archaeological time, once confined to prehistory alone, now includes modernity and even contemporaneity, precisely because it is materiality and not temporality, subject *matter* rather than subject *period*, that defines the boundaries of archaeological praxis. Anecdotally, however, the extension of archaeology's remit into the recent past—from the 16th-century plantations in the Irish context to the present, basically—appears to make less sense to people who look in at archaeology from the outside. Those people include historians. Unlike medieval historians, all of whom would at least acknowledge the contribution that archaeology makes, historians of the modern period, starting with the plantations but especially of the post-Restoration period, express far more rarely any appreciation of archaeological research into that era. It may be the case, of course, that there is an unspoken admiration among them for what archaeology contributes and that one is only aware of negative comment, but the infrequency of references to archaeological research in the work of historians of modern (or post-medieval) Ireland must tell a story.

Negative comment by historians, when articulated, reveals what remains unrevealed when no comment is made at all. There are two types of negative comment. The first is the matter of disagreement. A good example is Nicholas Canny's criticism of Audrey Horning's book on colonialism in the British Atlantic (Horning 2013; Canny 2014). Canny simply disagrees with Horning's (revisionist) view that the archaeological evidence hints at considerable non-hostile interaction between natives and settlers in Plantation Ulster. It is an entirely acceptable point of view, and one can counter-argue. (I choose this example for a secondary reason: Canny not only disagreed with Horning but also, in my reading of the review, implicitly reprimanded her for not appreciating that only historians know the truth about such things! In so doing, he marked the cards of all archaeologists: research and investigate all you like, is the message, provided that you understand that, in the final analysis, documentary truth trumps whatever the material may say! Frankly, there is little the archaeological community can do about entrenched disciplinary allegiances. It just needs not to be deflected by such criticism.)

The second type of negative comment is one with which I have some sympathy. It is best expressed through an example, also in respect of the same period. The key figure is Edmund Spenser, an English undertaker in the Munster Plantation (who, incidentally, is known to have had cordial relations with some of the native inhabitants whom he encountered). Willy Maley, a specialist in English Renaissance literature, once wondered (somewhat sarcastically) what exactly Eric Klingelhofer was hoping to find in his archaeological excavation at Spenser's castle in Kilcolman, Co. Cork: 'What were they [the archaeologists] looking for? Spenser's reputation? The lost manuscripts of *The Faerie Queene*? The charred bones of the child who allegedly perished in the fire? A scorched manuscript decomposing in a foxhole?' (Maley 1997, 5). Maley comes from the field which gave birth to New Historicism and cultural materialism, so it is a field that recognises the rich potential of theory. What does it say, then, about our discipline and how it promotes its insights into the historical past that somebody like Maley should wonder why archaeologists should dig Kilcolman? No criticism of Klingelhofer's work is implied by drawing attention here to Maley's comments, and it should be noted for the record that Spenser's most recent biographer makes copious use of the excavation information (Hadfield 2012, 219–21), but the point is this: if archaeology's potential contribution to early modern research is not obvious (or made obvious), can it be any more obvious in respect of the more thoroughly documented 1800s and 1900s?

Although others may have different experiences, I have always had to explain to non-archaeologists, normally in the face of some puzzlement, why modern (especially from the 18th century) pasts would interest me, or anybody for that matter, *as an archaeologist*. It may well be a question that NRA archaeologists have been asked by visitors when excavating post-medieval sites. It is easy to dismiss such puzzlement as evidence that people outside our discipline simply do not understand the essence of what we do, but that would be an unfair dismissal, and it would be unwise for archaeologists in Ireland to be dismissive. Our pursuit of our interest in the past depends—now as much as ever, in the tailwind of a severe recession—to a considerable degree on public goodwill. After all, archaeology is an expensive business that always has an impact, directly or indirectly, on the public purse. In any case, the optics of expenditure, whether in the public or the private sector, matter hugely these days. If public goodwill is fragile when our pursuit of knowledge of distant (prehistoric) pasts potentially threatens infrastructural developments, the challenge is even greater when we spend time and resources exploring recent (historic) pasts that can be known, or are purported to be known already, without any intervention from us.

Were I invited to adopt the position of an unsympathetic historian in a debate on the need for and value of Post-Medieval Archaeology, I would alight on two specific issues. I raise these issues here not as evidence of some sort of existential crisis in our field—there is no such crisis—but as issues that require our attention, or at least some degree of self-examination.

First, the research questions of 'late period' archaeological study are not obvious in and of themselves, or at least are not articulated. What exactly is the archaeologist trying to find out when engaging with the recent archaeological record? What questions belong uniquely to the archaeologist as he or she walks across an estate landscape, looks at a Board of First Fruits church, excavates the foundations of a brick factory or handles a clay pipe? What is the specific interpretative context that justifies a specific type of question and provides a home for the answer to it?

Second, it is not obvious what, irrespective of a framework of questions, are the unique and demonstrably invaluable offerings of an archaeological methodology. Excavation is perhaps the quintessential archaeological methodology, since it is the methodology most exclusive to the discipline, but it is a method of data retrieval. Does it, in and of itself, offer something unique (other than, a cynic might argue, a privileging of broken objects of which complete examples might actually survive, and maybe even a privileging of the *context* of discovery over the actual thing that is discovered)? Yes, excavation provides contextual data, but that simply brings us back to the question of what exactly it is that we are trying to discover. How does one evaluate the revelation through excavation of some small detail on a lost 19th-century site when one can visit extant 19th-century sites and observe tens of thousands of other small details? And what, in any case, do we mean by 'context'? Archaeological things exist in a multiplicity of contexts, and the depositional context, which excavation unfolds, is but one. And how, in terms of the methods of identifying and dating 'late' objects, does the archaeologist differ from the experienced antiques dealer, who also handles 'late' things? This is a serious rather than a flippant question. Yes, there are huge differences between the values and conducts of both professions, not least in the concept of putting a fiscal evaluation on an item of heritage interest, but an archaeologist will appreciate an antiques dealer's skill in identifying types, in knowing places, dates and contexts of manufacture, in establishing function (at least in a narrow pragmatic sense) and in recognising rarity.

Moving forward

The concept that must be central to any response to the observations and questions raised above is context, specifically *archaeological* context. The term 'context' is almost self-explanatory, in that the end-stage of archaeological excavation is the contextualising of the information retrieved for the purpose of expanding our knowledge. The difference between prehistoric and historic archaeologies is that in the case of the former it is the archaeologist who has uncontested control over the construction of context and therefore ownership of the narrative, whereas once one moves into a historic period there is a narrative constructed by others—historians especially—that needs to be considered, even negotiated. By referring here to archaeological context (rather than simply to 'context') I am asserting the need for archaeologists of the later historic past to recognise that archaeological evidence requires its own bespoke framework of interpretation.

The concept of a 'bespoke framework of interpretation' sidelines the historical evidence. This is not to suggest that archaeological evidence should not be used to gloss historical accounts of the recent past but, rather, to stress that, if a central (ultimately Marxian) tenet of archaeological theory is that society is constituted materially and spatially, the archaeological narrative must emphasise the patterns and process of material and spatial formations. The historical record is by no means of secondary interest here, and it would be absurd to ignore the written record where it exists, but it is as an information technology that the written record is most germane to archaeological enquiry: societies that are literate, that reflect on and record their own histories, and possess the technology (publication) to transmit, are transformed by that literacy. So, it is not so much that historical sources *tell* us things but that they *are* things. Indeed, as John Moreland (2006, 135) puts it, 'a rapprochement between the disciplines [of archaeology and history] can be achieved only if we begin to think of texts and objects as having had efficacy in the past rather than just as evidence about it'.

I return, then, to the quotation at the start of the paper. Why, one might ask, is the archaeologist who is working in advance of motorway construction expected to dig, say, the foundations of a 19th-century cottage? If we are absolutely honest with ourselves, would we admit that it is simply 'because it's there'? If so, it is not a good enough answer. We need a philosophy. I think.

BIBLIOGRAPHY

Aalen, F H A, Whelan, K & Stout, M (eds) 2012 *Atlas of the Irish Rural Landscape* (2nd edn). Cork University Press, Cork.

Anderson, E 1993 'Appendix II. Lithic report', *in* G Walsh, *Archaeological Excavations on the N5 Swinford Bypass*, 37–40. Unpublished report for Mayo County Council.

Anderson-Whymark, H & Garrow, D 2015 'Seaways and shared ways: imaging and imagining the movement of people, objects and ideas over the course of the Mesolithic–Neolithic transition, c. 5000–3500 BC', *in* H Anderson-Whymark, D Garrow & F Sturt (eds), *Continental Connections*, 59–77. Oxbow, Oxford.

Anderson-Whymark, H, Garrow, D & Sturt, F 2015 'Microliths and maritime mobility: a continental European-style Late Mesolithic flint assemblage from the Isles of Scilly', *Antiquity*, Vol. 89, No. 346, 954–71.

Armit, I 2007 'Social landscapes and identities in the Irish Iron Age', *in* C Haselgrove & T Moore (eds), *The Later Iron Age in Britain and Beyond*, 130–9. Oxbow Books, Oxford.

Armit, I, Swindles, G & Becker, K 2013 'From dates to demography in later prehistoric Ireland? Experimental approaches to the meta-analysis of large ^{14}C data-sets', *Journal of Archaeological Science*, Vol. 40, No. 1, 433–8.

Armit, I, Swindles, G T, Becker, K, Plunkett, G & Blaauw, M 2014 'Rapid climate change did not cause population collapse at the end of the European Bronze Age', *Proceedings of the National Academy of Science USA*, Vol. 111, No. 48, 17045–9.

Baillie, M G L & Brown, D M 2011 'Dendrochronology and Deer Park Farms', *in* C J Lynn & J A McDowell, *Deer Park Farms: the excavation of a raised rath in the Glenarm Valley, Co. Antrim*, 558–67. Northern Ireland Archaeological Monographs 9. HMSO and Environment and Heritage Service, Belfast.

Barry, T B 1977 *The Medieval Moated Sites of South-east Ireland: counties Carlow, Kilkenny, Tipperary and Wexford*. British Archaeological Reports, British Series 35. Oxford.

Barry, T B 1981 'The shifting frontier: medieval moated sites in counties Cork and Limerick', *in* F A Aberg & A E Brown (eds), *Medieval Moated Sites in North-west Europe*, 71–85. British Archaeological Reports, International Series 121. Oxford.

Barry, T B 1987 *The Archaeology of Medieval Ireland*. Methuen, London.

Bayley, D 2008 *Final Report on the Excavations at Newtownbalregan 2, Site 113, Co. Louth.*

Unpublished report by Irish Archaeological Consultancy Ltd for Louth County Council and the National Roads Authority.

Bayley, D 2010 *M1 Dundalk Western Bypass. Site 127: Carn More 5.* Final report by Irish Archaeological Consultancy Ltd for Louth County Council and the National Roads Authority.

Bayliss, A & O'Sullivan, M 2013 'Interpreting chronologies for the Mound of the Hostages, Tara, and its contemporary contexts in Neolithic and Bronze Age Ireland', *in* M O'Sullivan, C Scarre & M Doyle (eds), *Tara—from the Past to the Future. Towards a new research agenda*, 26–104. Wordwell, Bray.

Bayliss, A, Healey, F, Whittle, A & Cooney, G 2011 'Neolithic narratives: British and Irish enclosures in their timescapes', *in* A Whittle, F Healey & A Bayliss, *Gathering Time: dating early Neolithic enclosures of southern Britain and Ireland*, 682–847. Oxbow, Oxford.

Becker, K, Armit, I & Swindles, G T (in prep.) *Mobility, Climate and Culture: remodelling the Irish Iron Age.*

Beckett, J F 2014 'A taphonomic assessment of the human bone assemblage', *in* A Lynch, *Poulnabrone: an Early Neolithic portal tomb in Ireland*, 56–61. Archaeological Monograph Series 9. The Stationery Office, Dublin.

Bergh, S & Hensey, R 2013 'Unpicking the chronology of Carrowmore', *Oxford Journal of Archaeology*, Vol. 32, No. 4, 343–66.

Bermingham, N 2013 'Prehistoric life and death', *in* N Bermingham, F Coyne, G Hull, F Reilly & K Taylor, *River Road: the archaeology of the Limerick Southern Ring Road*, 29–82. NRA Scheme Monographs 14. National Roads Authority, Dublin.

Bermingham, N, Hull, G & Taylor, K 2012a *Beneath the Banner: archaeology of the M18 Ennis Bypass and N85 Western Relief Road, Co. Clare.* NRA Scheme Monographs 10. National Roads Authority, Dublin.

Bermingham, N, Hull, G & Taylor, K 2012b 'Post-medieval and early modern excavations', *in* N Bermingham, G Hull & K Taylor, *Beneath the Banner: archaeology of the M18 Ennis Bypass and N85 Western Relief Road*, 91–102. NRA Scheme Monographs 10. National Roads Authority, Dublin.

Bogaard, A 2004 *Neolithic Farming in Central Europe.* Routledge, London.

Bogaard, A & Jones, G 2007 'Neolithic farming in Britain and central Europe: contrast or continuity?', *Proceedings of the British Academy*, Vol. 144, 357–75.

Bolger, T 2001 'Three sites on the northern motorway at Rathmullan, Co. Meath', *Ríocht na Midhe*, Vol. 7, 8–17.

Bolger, T 2011a *01E295 Rathmullan 7 Final Report.* Unpublished report by Irish Archaeological Consultancy Ltd for Meath County Council and the National Roads Authority.

Bolger, T 2011b 'Status, inheritance and land tenure: some thoughts on early medieval settlement in the light of recent archaeological excavations', *in* C Corlett & M Potterton (eds), *Settlement in Early Medieval Ireland in the Light of Recent Archaeological Excavations*, 1–10. Research Papers in Irish Archaeology 3. Wordwell, Dublin.

Bolger, T 2012 *00E0813 Rathmullan 10 Final Report*. Unpublished report by Irish Archaeological Consultancy Ltd for Meath County Council and the National Roads Authority.

Bolger, T (forthcoming) *Colonising a 'Royal' Landscape: the later medieval vill of Mullamast, Co. Kildare*. TII Heritage series. Transport Infrastructure Ireland, Dublin.

Bourke, L 2001 *Crossing the Rubicon: Bronze Age metalwork from Irish rivers*. Bronze Age Studies 5, Department of Archaeology, National University of Ireland, Galway.

Bradley, J 2011 'An early medieval crannog at Moynagh Lough, Co. Meath', *in* C Corlett & M Potterton (eds), *Settlement in Early Medieval Ireland in the Light of Recent Archaeological Excavations*, 11–34. Research Papers in Irish Archaeology 3. Wordwell, Dublin.

Bradley, R 2003 'A life less ordinary: the ritualization of the domestic sphere in later prehistoric Europe', *Cambridge Archaeological Journal*, Vol. 13, No. 1, 5–23.

Bradley, R 2005 *Ritual and Domestic Life in Prehistoric Europe*. Routledge, London.

Bradley, R 2007 *The Prehistory of Britain and Ireland*. Cambridge University Press, Cambridge.

Brady, C 2007 *A Landscape Survey of the Newgrange Environs: earlier prehistoric settlement at Brú na Bóinne, Co. Meath*. Unpublished PhD thesis, University College Dublin.

Brady, N 1988 'The plough pebbles of Ireland', *Tools and Tillage*, Vol. 6, No. 1, 47–60.

Brady, N 2006 'Mills in medieval Ireland: looking beyond design', *in* S Walton (ed.), *Wind and Water: the medieval mill*, 39–68. Arizona State University Press, Tempe.

Brady, N 2009 'Just how far can you go with a pebble? Taking another look at ploughing in medieval Ireland', *in* J Fenwick (ed.), *Lost and Found II: rediscovering Ireland's past*, 61–9. Wordwell, Bray.

Brady, N 2014 'Current research and future directions in medieval rural settlement in Ireland', *Præhistorica*, Vol. 31, No. 2, 297–308.

Breen, C 2007 *An Archaeology of Southwest Ireland, 1570–1670*. Four Courts Press, Dublin.

Breen, T 2009 *Kildare Town Bypass: archaeological resolution of a burnt spread*. Unpublished report by Valerie J Keeley Ltd for Kildare County Council and the National Roads Authority.

Breen, T 2012 'Farming and fighting on the frontier', *Seanda*, No. 7, 24–7.

Brindley, A 1999 'Irish Grooved Ware', *in* R Cleal & A MacSween (eds), *Grooved Ware in Britain and Ireland*, 23–35. Neolithic Studies Group Seminar Papers 3. Oxbow, Oxford.

Brindley, A L 2003 *Prehistoric Pottery from Rath (02E0638)*. Unpublished report for Margaret Gowen & Co. Ltd.

Brindley, A L 2007 *The Dating of Food Vessels and Urns in Ireland*. Bronze Age Studies 7, Department of Archaeology, National University of Ireland, Galway.

Brown, P 1981 *The Cult of Saints: its rise and function in Latin Christianity*. SCM Press, London.

Brück, J 1999 'Ritual and rationality: some problems of interpretation in European archaeology', *European Journal of Archaeology*, Vol. 2, No. 3, 313–44.

Buckley, L & McConway, C 2010 'Early medieval settlement and burial ground at Faughart Lower, Co. Louth', *in* C Corlett & M Potterton (eds), *Death and Burial in Early Medieval Ireland in the Light of Recent Archaeological Excavations*, 49–59. Research Papers in Irish Archaeology 2. Wordwell, Dublin.

Büntgen, U, Myglan, V S, Charpentier Ljungqvist, F, McCormick, M, Di Cosmo, N, Sigl, M, Jungclaus, J, Wagner, S, Krusic, P J, Esper, J, Kaplan, J O, de Vaan, M A C, Luterbacher, J, Wacker, L, Tegel, W & Kirdyanov, A V 2016 'Cooling and societal change during the Late Antique Little Ice Age from 536 to around 660 AD', *Nature Geoscience*, Vol. 9, No. 3, 1–7 (DOI: 10.1038/NGEO2652).

Burenhult, G 1984 *The Archaeology of Carrowmore: environmental archaeology and the megalithic tradition at Carrowmore, Co. Sligo, Ireland*. Theses and Papers in North-European Archaeology 14. Göran Burenhult, Stockholm.

Burenhult, G 2001 *The Megalithic Cemetery of Carrowmore, Co. Sligo*. Göran Burenhult, Tjörnarp.

Byrne, F J 1973 *Irish Kings and High-Kings*. Batsford, London.

Byrnes, E 2007 'Rath. Bronze Age enclosures', *in* E Grogan, L O'Donnell & P Johnston, *The Bronze Age Landscapes of the Pipeline to the West*, 329–30. Wordwell, Bray.

Cagney, L & O'Hara, R 2009 'An early medieval complex at Dowdstown 2', *in* M B Deevy & D Murphy (eds), *Places Along the Way: first findings on the M3*, 123–34. NRA Scheme Monographs 5. National Roads Authority, Dublin.

Cahill, M & Mullarkey, P 2010 'A tin bead from Sonnagh', *in* R F Gillespie & A Kerrigan, *Of Troughs and Tuyères: the archaeology of the N5 Charlestown Bypass*, 89–91. NRA Scheme Monographs 6. National Roads Authority, Dublin.

Cahill, M & Sikora, M (eds) 2012 *Breaking Ground, Finding Graves—Reports on the Excavations of Burials by the National Museum of Ireland, 1927–2006, Vol. 1*. National Museum of Ireland Monograph Series 4. Wordwell in association with the National Museum of Ireland, Dublin.

Canny, N 2014 'Reconciled to colonialism?', *The Irish Times*, 24 May 2014.

Carden, R F, McDevitt, A D, Zachos, F E, Woodman, P C, O'Toole, P, Rose, H, Monaghan, N T, Campana, M G, Bradley, D G & Edwards, C J 2012 'Phylogeographic, ancient DNA, fossil and morphometric analyses reveal ancient and modern human introductions of a large mammal: the complex case of red deer (*Cervus elaphus*) in Ireland', *Quaternary Science Reviews*, Vol. 42, 74–84.

Carlin, N 2012a *A Proper Place for Everything: the character and context of Beaker depositional practice in Ireland*. Unpublished PhD thesis, University College Dublin.

Carlin, N 2012b 'Into the West: placing Beakers within their Irish contexts', *in* A M Jones & G Kirkham (eds), *Beyond the Core: reflections on regionality in prehistory*, 87–100. Oxbow, Oxford.

Carlin, N 2013 '"Keep going, sure it's grand": understanding the Irish Late Neolithic–Early Bronze Age', *in* K Cleary (ed.), *The Archaeology of Disaster and Recovery: proceedings of the IAI autumn 2012 conference*, 18–27. Conference Proceedings Issue 1. Institute of Archaeologists of Ireland, Dublin (http://www.iai.ie/wp-content/uploads/2016/03/Proceedings-of-the-IAI-Autumn-2012-Conference-2.pdf; accessed May 2015).

Carlin, N (forthcoming) *The Beaker Phenomenon? Understanding the character and context of social practices in Ireland 2500–2000 BC*. Sidestone Press, Leiden.

Carlin, N (in press) 'Getting into the groove: exploring the relationship between Grooved Ware and developed passage tombs in Ireland c. 3000–2700 BC', *Proceedings of the Prehistoric Society*.

Carlin, N & Brück, J 2012 'Searching for the Chalcolithic: continuity and change in the Irish Final Neolithic/Early Bronze Age', *in* M J Allen, J Gardiner, A Sheridan & D McOmish (eds), *Is there a British Chalcolithic? People, place and polity in the later 3rd millennium*, 191–208. Prehistoric Society Research Paper No. 4. The Prehistoric Society, London.

Carlin, N, Clarke, L & Walsh, F 2008 *The Archaeology of Life and Death in the Boyne Floodplain: the linear landscape of the M4*. NRA Scheme Monographs 2. National Roads Authority, Dublin.

Carlin, N, O'Connell, T J & O'Neill, N 2015 'The Neolithic discoveries on the Carlow Bypass', *in* T Bolger, C Moloney & D Shiels (eds), *A Journey Along the Carlow Corridor: the archaeology of the M9 Carlow Bypass*, 95–109. NRA Scheme Monographs 16. National Roads Authority, Dublin.

Carroll, J 2008 *Archaeological Excavations at Rosepark, Balrothery, Co. Dublin*. Balrothery Excavations Volume 1. Environmental Publications, Dublin.

Carroll, J, Ryan, F & Wiggins, K 2008 *Archaeological Excavations at Glebe South and Darcystown, Balrothery, Co. Dublin*. Balrothery Excavations Volume 2. Environmental Publications, Dublin.

Carroll, M & Quinn, A 2009 'Appendix 8:2: copper-alloy dividers', *in* C Corlett & M Potterton (eds), *Rural Settlement in Medieval Ireland in the Light of Recent Archaeological Excavations*, 107–8. Research Papers in Irish Archaeology 1. Wordwell, Dublin.

Cassidy, L M, Martiniano, R, Murphy, E, Teasdale, M D, Mallory, J, Hartwell, B & Bradley, D G 2016 'Neolithic and Bronze Age migration to Ireland and establishment of the insular Atlantic genome', *Proceedings of the National Academy of Sciences*, Vol. 113, No. 2, 368–73 (DOI:10.1073/pnas.1518445113).

Charles-Edwards, T M 2000 *Early Christian Ireland*. Cambridge University Press, Cambridge.

Cherry, S 1990 'The finds from fulachta fiadh', *in* V Buckley (ed.), *Burnt Offerings: international contributions to burnt mound archaeology*, 49–54. Wordwell, Bray.

Chrobak, E, Kiely, J & McMorran, T 2012 *Archaeological Excavation Report, Busherstown, Co. Offaly: early medieval kilns and medieval moated site with associated annexe*. Unpublished report by Eachtra Archaeological Projects for Laois County Council and the National Roads Authority.

Clarke, L 2002 'An early medieval enclosure and burials, Johnstown, Co. Meath', *Archaeology Ireland*, Vol. 16, No. 4, 13–15.

Clarke, L & Carlin, N 2008 'Living with the dead at Johnstown 1: an enclosed burial, settlement and industrial site', *in* N Carlin, L Clarke & F Walsh, *The Archaeology of Life and Death in the Boyne Floodplain: the linear landscape of the M4*, 55–86. NRA Scheme Monographs 2. National Roads Authority, Dublin.

Clarke, L & Carlin, N 2009 'From focus to locus: a window upon the development of a funerary landscape', *in* M B Deevy & D Murphy (eds), *Places Along the Way: first findings on the M3*, 1–20. NRA Scheme Monographs 5. National Roads Authority, Dublin.

Clarke, L & Long, P 2009 *N7 Nenagh to Limerick High-Quality Dual Carriageway, Archaeological Resolution Project, Killalane Site 2 E2495, Co. Tipperary, Final Excavation Report*. Unpublished report by Headland Archaeology (Ireland) Ltd for Limerick County Council and the National Roads Authority.

Claudian 1956 *Claudian in Two Volumes*. Harvard University Press, Harvard.

Cleary, K 2016 'Burial practices in Ireland during the late third millennium BC connecting new ideologies with local expressions', *in* J Koch & B Cunliffe (eds), *Celtic from the West 3: Atlantic Europe in the metal ages—questions of shared language*, 139–79. Oxbow, Oxford.

Cleary, R 1983 'The ceramic assemblage', *in* M J O'Kelly, R Cleary & D Lehane, *Newgrange, Co. Meath, Ireland: the late Neolithic/Beaker period settlement*, 58–108. British Archaeological Reports, International Series 190. Oxford.

Cleary, R M 1993 'Appendix III. Metal, stone and glass from Lislackagh, Co. Mayo', *in* G Walsh, *Archaeological Excavations on the N5 Swinford Bypass*, 45–51. Unpublished report for Mayo County Council.

Cleary, R M & Kelleher, H 2011 *Archaeological Excavations at Tullahedy, County Tipperary: Neolithic settlement in north Munster*. Collins Press, Cork.

Clinton, M 2014 'The Viking *longphort* of Linn Duachaill: a first report', *Peritia*, Vols 24–5 (2013– 14), 123–40.

Cody, E 2002 *Survey of the Megalithic Tombs of Ireland, Vol. VI: County Donegal*. The Stationery Office, Dublin.

Collins, T 2009 'Hermitage, Ireland: life and death on the western edge of Europe', *in* S McCartan, P C Woodman, R Schulting & G M Warren (eds), *Mesolithic Horizons: papers presented at the Seventh International Conference on the Mesolithic in Europe, Belfast 2005, Vol. 2*, 876–9. Oxbow, Oxford.

Comber, M 2002 'M.V. Duignan's excavations at the ringfort of Rathgurreen, Co. Galway, 1948– 9', *Proceedings of the Royal Irish Academy*, Vol. 102C, 137–97.

Comber, M & Hull, G 2008 'Caherconnell, Co. Clare, and cashel chronology', *Archaeology Ireland*, Vol. 22, No. 4, 30–3.

Comber, M & Hull, G 2010 'Excavations at Caherconnell Cashel, the Burren, Co. Clare: implications for cashel chronology and Gaelic settlement', *Proceedings of the Royal Irish Academy*, Vol. 110C, 133–12.

Condit, T & Simpson, D 1998 'Irish hengiform enclosures and related monuments: a review', *in* A Gibson & D Simpson (eds), *Prehistoric Ritual and Religion*, 45–61. Sutton, Stroud.

Cooney, G 2000 *Landscapes of Neolithic Ireland*. Routledge, London.

Cooney, G 2002 'From Lilliput to Brobdingnag: traditions of enclosure in the Irish Neolithic', *in* G Varndell & P Topping (eds), *Enclosures in Neolithic Europe*, 69–72. Oxbow, Oxford.

Cooney, G 2006 'Newgrange—a view from the platform', *Antiquity*, Vol. 80, No. 309, 697–708.

Cooney, G 2014 'The role of cremation in mortuary practice in the Irish Neolithic', *in* I Kuijt, C P Quinn & G Cooney (eds), *Transformation by Fire: the archaeology of cremation in cultural context*, 198–206. University of Arizona Press, Tucson.

Cooney, G (forthcoming) 'Mortuary practices at Knowth', *in* G Eogan & K Cleary (eds), *Excavations at Knowth 6: the Great Mound at Knowth (Tomb 1) and its passage tomb archaeology*. Royal Irish Academy, Dublin.

Cooney, G & Grogan, E 1999 *Irish Prehistory: a social perspective*. Wordwell, Bray.

Cooney, G & Mandal, S 1998 *The Irish Stone Axe Project*. Monograph 1. Wordwell, Bray.

Cooney, G, Bayliss, A, Healy, F, Whittle, A, Danaher, E, Cagney, L, Mallory, J, Smyth, J, Kador, T & O'Sullivan, M 2011 'Ireland', *in* A Whittle, F Healy & A Bayliss (eds), *Gathering Time: dating the early Neolithic enclosures of southern Britain and Ireland*, 562–669. Oxbow, Oxford.

Corlett, C 2006 'Medieval Dalkey in the 1760s', *Archaeology Ireland*, Vol. 20, No. 1, Heritage Guide 33.

Corlett, C 2009 'Wicklow's emerging archaeology', *Archaeology Ireland*, Vol. 23, No. 1, 26–30.

Cotter, E 2005 'Bronze Age Ballybrowney, Co. Cork', *in* J O'Sullivan & M Stanley (eds), *Recent Archaeological Discoveries on National Road Schemes 2004*, 25–35. Archaeology and the National Roads Authority Monograph Series No. 2. National Roads Authority, Dublin.

Cotter, E 2006 *Excavations at Kilbride, Co. Mayo*. Unpublished final report by Archaeological Consultancy Services Ltd.

Cotter, E 2009 'The medieval moated site at Ballinvinny South, Co. Cork', *in* C Corlett & M Potterton (eds), *Rural Settlement in Medieval Ireland in the Light of Recent Archaeological Excavations*, 49–58. Research Papers in Irish Archaeology 1. Wordwell, Dublin.

Cotter, E 2013a 'Killalough 1—*fulacht fia*', *in* K Hanley & M F Hurley (eds), *Generations: the archaeology of five national road schemes in County Cork. Vol. 1: prehistoric sites*, 124–8. NRA Scheme Monographs 13. National Roads Authority, Dublin.

Cotter, E 2013b 'Ballybrowney Lower 1—nucleated settlement', *in* K Hanley & M F Hurley (eds), *Generations: the archaeology of five national road schemes in County Cork. Vol. 1: prehistoric sites*, 93–104. NRA Scheme Monographs 13. National Roads Authority, Dublin.

Cotter, E 2013c 'Ballybrowney Lower 1—settlement', *in* K Hanley & M F Hurley (eds), *Generations: the archaeology of five national road schemes in County Cork. Vol. 1: prehistoric sites*, 130–2. NRA Scheme Monographs 13. National Roads Authority, Dublin.

Cotter, E 2013d 'Mitchelstown 1—settlement (three houses)', *in* K Hanley & M F Hurley (eds), *Generations: the archaeology of five national road schemes in County Cork. Vol. 1: prehistoric sites*, 110–13. NRA Scheme Monographs 13. National Roads Authority, Dublin.

Cotter, E 2013e 'Ballinvinny South AR16—mid 17th- to mid 18th-century rural settlement', *in* K Hanley & M F Hurley (eds), *Generations: the archaeology of five national road schemes in County Cork, Vol. 2: historic sites, artefactual and environmental evidence and radiocarbon dates*, 281–92. NRA Scheme Monographs 13. National Roads Authority, Dublin.

Cramp, L J E, Jones, J R, Sheridan, A, Smyth, J, Whelton, H, Mulville, J, Sharples, N & Evershed, R P 2014 'Immediate replacement of fishing with dairying by the earliest farmers of the northeast Atlantic archipelagos', *Proceedings of the Royal Society B*, Vol. 281 (DOI: 10.1098/rspb.2013.2372).

Danaher, E 2007 *Monumental Beginnings: the archaeology of the N4 Sligo Inner Relief Road*. NRA Scheme Monographs 1. National Roads Authority, Dublin.

Danaher, E 2013 'Curraheen 1—settlement: conjoined enclosures', *in* K Hanley & M F Hurley (eds), *Generations: the archaeology of the national road schemes of County Cork. Volume 2: historic sites, artefactual and environmental evidence and radiocarbon dates*, 215–22. NRA Scheme

Monographs 13. National Roads Authority, Dublin.

Danaher, E & Cagney, L 2004 *Report on the Archaeological Excavation of a Multi-phased Site at Ballinaspig More 5, Ballincollig, Co. Cork.* Unpublished report by Archaeological Consultancy Services Ltd for Cork County Council and the National Roads Authority.

Deery, S 2005 'Archaeology and cultural heritage', *in* McCarthy Hyder Carl Bro (eds), *N8 Cashel to Mitchelstown Proposed Road Development, Environmental Impact Statement, Vol. 2*, 1–88. South Tipperary County Council, Clonmel.

Deevy, M B 2005 'The M3 Clonee to North of Kells Road Scheme, County Meath', *in* J O'Sullivan & M Stanley (eds), *Recent Archaeological Discoveries on National Road Schemes 2004*, 83–92. Archaeology and the National Roads Authority Monograph Series No. 2. National Roads Authority, Dublin.

Deevy, M B 2006 'The hidden archaeological landscapes of the M3', *Seanda*, No. 1, 10–11.

Deevy, M B 2008 'The M3 research framework and the Lismullin discovery in County Meath', *in* J O'Sullivan & M Stanley (eds), *Roads, Rediscovery and Research*, 71–82. Archaeology and the National Roads Authority Monograph Series No. 5. National Roads Authority, Dublin.

Deevy, M B & Murphy, D (eds) 2009 *Places Along the Way: first findings on the M3.* NRA Scheme Monographs 5. National Roads Authority, Dublin.

Delaney, F 2014 'Ringfort with round-house, souterrain and *cillín* burials at Mackney', *in* J McKeon & J O'Sullivan (eds), *The Quiet Landscape: archaeological investigations on the M6 Galway to Ballinasloe national road scheme*, 187–200. National Roads Authority, Dublin.

Delaney, F & Silke, Z 2011 'Owenbristy: towards an understanding', *in* F Delaney & J Tierney, *In the Lowlands of South Galway: archaeological excavations on the N18 Oranmore to Gort national road scheme*, 98–109. NRA Scheme Monographs 7. National Roads Authority, Dublin.

Delaney, F & Tierney, J 2011a *In the Lowlands of South Galway: archaeological excavations on the N18 Oranmore to Gort national road scheme.* NRA Scheme Monographs 7. National Roads Authority, Dublin.

Delaney, F & Tierney, J 2011b 'Burnt mounds in the Bronze Age landscape', *in* F Delaney & J Tierney, *In the Lowlands of South Galway: archaeological excavations on the N18 Oranmore to Gort national road scheme*, 33–44. NRA Scheme Monographs 7. National Roads Authority, Dublin.

Delaney, F, O'Sullivan, J & Toscano, M 2011 'Introduction', *in* F Delaney & J Tierney, *In the Lowlands of South Galway: archaeological excavations on the N18 Oranmore to Gort national road scheme*, 1–25. NRA Scheme Monographs 7. National Roads Authority, Dublin.

Delaney, S 2010 'An early medieval landscape at Balriggan, Co. Louth', *in* C Corlett & M Potterton (eds), *Death and Burial in Early Medieval Ireland in the Light of Recent Archaeological Excavations*, 91–102. Research Papers in Irish Archaeology 2. Wordwell, Dublin.

Delaney, S & Roycroft, N 2003 'Early medieval enclosure at Balriggan, Co. Louth', *Archaeology Ireland*, Vol. 17, No. 2, 16–19.

Delaney, S, Bayley, D, Lyne, E, McNamara, S, Nunan, J & Molloy, K 2012a *Borderlands: archaeological investigation on the route of the M18 Gort to Crusheen road scheme.* NRA Scheme Monographs 9. National Roads Authority, Dublin.

Delaney, S, Bayley, D, Lyne, E, Nunan, J & McNamara, S 2012b 'Burnt mounds: kitchen sinks of the Bronze Age', *in* S Delaney, D Bayley, E Lyne, S McNamara, J Nunan & K Molloy, *Borderlands: archaeological investigation on the route of the M18 Gort to Crusheen road scheme*, 57–79. NRA Scheme Monographs 9. National Roads Authority, Dublin.

Dempsey, C 2013 'An analysis of stone axe petrography and production at Lough Gur, Co. Limerick', *Journal of Irish Archaeology*, Vol. 22, 23–50.

Dennehy, E 2007a '122a. Cahiracon', *in* E Grogan, L O'Donnell & P Johnston, *The Bronze Age Landscapes of the Pipeline to the West*, 188–9. Wordwell, Bray.

Dennehy, E 2007b '135. Carrahil', *in* E Grogan, L O'Donnell & P Johnston, *The Bronze Age Landscapes of the Pipeline to the West*, 197–8. Wordwell, Bray.

Dennehy, E 2007c '145. Cloonagowan', *in* E Grogan, L O'Donnell & P Johnston, *The Bronze Age Landscapes of the Pipeline to the West*, 199–200. Wordwell, Bray.

Dennehy, E 2007d '148. Cloonagowan', *in* E Grogan, L O'Donnell & P Johnston, *The Bronze Age Landscapes of the Pipeline to the West*, 201. Wordwell, Bray.

Dennehy, E & Halpin, E 2011 'Newrath 9—Middle Bronze Age settlement', *in* J Eogan & E Shee Twohig (eds), *Cois tSiúire—Nine Thousand Years of Human Activity in the Lower Suir Valley: archaeological excavations on the N25 Waterford City Bypass, Vol. 1*, 110–12. NRA Scheme Monographs 8. National Roads Authority, Dublin.

Dennehy, E & Sutton, B 2007 'Gortaficka. Hilltop complex', *in* E Grogan, L O'Donnell & P Johnston, *The Bronze Age Landscapes of the Pipeline to the West*, 206. Wordwell, Bray.

de Paor, L 1993 *Saint Patrick's World*. Four Courts Press, Dublin.

Dingwall, K 2010 *Final Report on Excavations at Site 4, Armalughey, Co. Tyrone*. Unpublished report by Headland UK.

Ditchfield, P 2014 'Stable isotope analysis', *in* A Lynch, *Poulnabrone, Co. Clare: excavation of an Early Neolithic portal tomb in Ireland*, 86–93. Archaeological Monograph Series 9. The Stationery Office, Dublin.

Doherty, C 1980 'Exchange and trade in early medieval Ireland', *Journal of the Royal Society of Antiquaries of Ireland*, Vol. 110, 67–89.

Doherty, C 1985 'The monastic towns in early medieval Ireland', *in* H Clarke & A Simms (eds), *The Comparative History of Urban Origins in Non-Roman Europe: Ireland, Wales, Denmark, Germany, Poland and Russia from the ninth to the thirteenth century, part 1*, 45–75. British Archaeological Reports, International Series 255. Oxford.

Doherty, C 1998 'The Vikings in Ireland: a review', *in* H B Clarke, M Ní Mhaonaigh & R Ó Floinn (eds), *Ireland and Scandinavia in the Early Viking Age*, 288–330. Four Courts Press, Dublin.

Doherty, C 2000 'Settlement in early medieval Ireland: a review', *in* T B Barry (ed.), *A History of Settlement in Ireland*, 50–80. Routledge, London.

Donnelly, C J & Horning, A 2002 'Post-medieval and industrial archaeology in Ireland: an overview', *Antiquity*, Vol. 76, 557–61.

Doody, M 2000 'Bronze Age houses in Ireland', *in* A Desmond, G Johnson & M McCarthy (eds),

New Agendas in Irish Prehistory: papers in commemoration of Liz Anderson, 135–59. Wordwell, Bray.

Doody, M 2009 'Templenoe, Co. Tipperary. Flat cemetery. Site 163.1 (E2290)', *in* M McQuade, B Molloy & C Moriarty, *In the Shadow of the Galtees: archaeological excavations along the N8 Cashel to Mitchelstown Road Scheme*, 130–3. NRA Scheme Monographs 4. National Roads Authority, Dublin.

Dooley, A 2007 'The plague and its consequences in Ireland', *in* L K Little (ed.), *Plague and the End of Antiquity: the pandemic of 541–750*, 215–28. Cambridge University Press, Cambridge.

Dowd, M A 2008 'The use of caves for funerary and ritual practices in Neolithic Ireland', *Antiquity*, Vol. 82, No. 316, 305–17.

Dowd, M 2015 *The Archaeology of Caves in Ireland*. Oxbow, Oxford.

Dowling, D 2014 'Landscape and settlement in Late Iron Age Ireland: some emerging trends', *Discovery Programme Reports*, Vol. 8, 151–74.

Doyle, I W 2009 'Mediterranean and Frankish pottery imports in early medieval Ireland', *Journal of Irish Archaeology*, Vol. 18, 17–62.

Dyer, C 1997 'Peasants and coins: the uses of money in the Middle Ages', *British Numismatic Journal*, Vol. 67, 30–47.

Elder, S 2009 *Report on the Archaeological Excavation of Raynestown 1, Co. Meath. M3 Clonee–North of Kells, Contract 1 Clonee–Dunshaughlin*. Unpublished report by Archaeological Consultancy Services Ltd for Meath County Council and the National Roads Authority.

Elder, S & Ginn, V 2009a *Report on the Archaeological Excavation of Johnstown 1, Co. Meath*. Unpublished report by Archaeological Consultancy Services Ltd for Meath County Council and the National Roads Authority.

Elder, S & Ginn, V 2009b *Report on the Archaeological Excavation of Johnstown 4, Co. Meath*. Unpublished report by Archaeological Consultancy Services Ltd for Meath County Council and the National Roads Authority.

Elliott, R 2009 *Excavations at Paulstown 2, Co. Kilkenny*. Unpublished preliminary report by Irish Archaeological Consultancy for Kilkenny County Council and the National Roads Authority.

Empey, E 1982 'Medieval Knocktopher: a study in manorial settlement—Part 1', *Old Kilkenny Review*, Vol. 2, No. 4, 329–42.

Eogan, G 1964 'The Later Bronze Age in Ireland in the light of recent research', *Proceedings of the Prehistoric Society*, Vol. 14, 268–350.

Eogan, G 1974 'Regionale Gruppierungen in der Spätbronzezeit Irlands', *Archäologisches Korrespondenzblatt*, Vol. 4, 319–27.

Eogan, G 1983 *Hoards of the Irish Later Bronze Age*. University College, Dublin.

Eogan, G 1984 *Excavations at Knowth (1)*. Royal Irish Academy, Dublin.

Eogan, G 1993 'The Late Bronze Age: customs, crafts and cults', *in* E Shee Twohig & M Ronayne (eds), *Past Perceptions: the prehistoric archaeology of south-west Ireland*, 121–33. University College, Cork.

Eogan, G 2000 *The Socketed Bronze Axes in Ireland*. Prähistorische Bronzefunde, Abteilung 9, 22.

Band, Stuttgart.

Eogan, G 2012 *The Archaeology of Knowth in the First and Second Millennia AD.* Excavations at Knowth 5. Royal Irish Academy, Dublin.

Eogan, G & Roche, H 1997 *Excavations at Knowth (2).* Royal Irish Academy, Dublin.

Eogan, G & Roche, H 1999 'Grooved Ware from Brugh na Bóinne and its wider context', *in* R Cleal & A MacSween (eds), *Grooved Ware in Britain and Ireland*, 98–111. Neolithic Studies Group Seminar Papers 3. Oxbow, Oxford.

Eogan, J 1999 'Bettystown prehistoric/multiperiod site', *in* I Bennett (ed.), *Excavations 1998: summary accounts of archaeological excavations in Ireland*, 161. Wordwell, Dublin.

Eogan, J 2005 *Excavations at Bettystown, Co. Meath [98E0072].* Unpublished report for Archaeological Development Services Ltd.

Eogan, J 2009 'A betagh settlement at Attyflin, Co. Limerick', *in* C Corlett & M Potterton (eds), *Rural Settlement in Medieval Ireland in the Light of Recent Archaeological Excavations*, 67–77. Research Papers in Irish Archaeology 1. Wordwell, Dublin.

Eogan, J 2011a 'Introduction', *in* J Eogan & E Shee Twohig (eds), *Cois tSiúire—Nine Thousand Years of Human Activity in the Lower Suir Valley: archaeological excavations on the N25 Waterford City Bypass, Vol. 1*, 1–19. NRA Scheme Monographs 8. National Roads Authority, Dublin.

Eogan, J 2011b 'The later prehistory of the Lower Suir Valley (2400 BC–AD 400)', *in* J Eogan & E Shee Twohig (eds), *Cois tSiúire—Nine Thousand Years of Human Activity in the Lower Suir Valley: archaeological excavations on the N25 Waterford City Bypass, Vol. 1*, 253–83. NRA Scheme Monographs 8. National Roads Authority, Dublin.

Eogan, J & Kelly, B 2016 'New roads to medieval Wexford', *in* I W Doyle & B Browne (eds), *Medieval Wexford—Essays in Memory of Billy Colfer*, 212–40. Four Courts Press, Dublin.

Eogan, J & Shee-Twohig, E (eds) 2011 *Cois tSiúire—Nine Thousand Years of Human Activity in the Lower Suir Valley: archaeological excavations on the N25 Waterford city bypass.* NRA Scheme Monographs 8. National Roads Authority, Dublin.

Fegan, G 2009 'Discovery and excavation of a medieval moated site at Coolamurry, Co. Wexford', *in* C Corlett & M Potterton (eds), *Rural Settlement in Medieval Ireland in the Light of Recent Archaeological Excavations*, 91–108. Research Papers in Irish Archaeology 1. Wordwell, Dublin.

Finan, T & O'Conor, K 2002 'The moated site at Cloonfree, Co. Roscommon', *Journal of the Galway Archaeological and Historical Society*, Vol. 54, 72–87.

FitzPatrick, E 2009 'Native enclosed settlement and the problem of the Irish "ring-fort"', *Medieval Archaeology*, Vol. 53, 271–307.

Flynn, C 2011 '2011:066—Level crossing XE82, Gortaficka, Clare', *Excavations.ie: Database of Irish Excavation Reports* (http://www.excavations.ie/report/2011/Clare/0022127/, accessed August 2015).

Flynn, C 2012 'Camlin: the archaeology of a townland in County Tipperary', *in* B Kelly, N Roycroft & M Stanley (eds), *Encounters Between Peoples*, 31–48. Archaeology and the National Roads Authority Monograph Series No. 9. National Roads Authority, Dublin.

Gardiner, M F 2014 'An archaeological approach to the development of the late medieval peasant house', *Vernacular Architecture*, Vol. 45, 16–28.

Garrow, D 2012 'Concluding discussion: pits and perspective', *in* H Anderson-Whymark & J Thomas (eds), *Regional Perspectives on Neolithic Pit Deposition: beyond the mundane*, 216–25. Neolithic Studies Group Seminar Papers 12. Oxbow, Oxford.

Garrow, D & Sturt, F 2011 'Grey waters bright with Neolithic argonauts? Maritime connections and the Mesolithic–Neolithic transition within the "western seaways" of Britain, c. 5000–3500 BC', *Antiquity*, Vol. 85, No. 327, 59–72.

Gibson, A M 2010 'Excavation and survey at the Dyffryn Lane Henge Complex, Powys, and a reconsideration of the dating of henges', *Proceedings of the Prehistoric Society*, Vol. 76, 213–48.

Gibson, D B 2012 *From Chiefdom to State in Early Ireland*. Cambridge University Press, Cambridge.

Gillespie, R 2010 'A multi-period archaeological complex at Lowpark', *in* R Gillespie & A Kerrigan, *Of Troughs and Tuyères: the archaeology of the N5 Charlestown Bypass*, 155–317. NRA Scheme Monographs 6. National Roads Authority, Dublin.

Gillespie, R & Kerrigan, A 2010 *Of Troughs and Tuyères: the archaeology of the N5 Charlestown Bypass*. NRA Scheme Monographs 6. National Roads Authority, Dublin.

Ginn, V 2011 'The fusion of settlement and identity in dispersed and nucleated settlements in Bronze Age Ireland', *Journal of Irish Archaeology*, Vol. 20, 27–44.

Ginn, V 2013 'Power to the people: reinterpreting Bronze Age society', *Emania*, Vol. 21, 47–58.

Ginn, V 2014a 'Who lives in a roundhouse like this? Going through the keyhole on Bronze Age domestic identity', *in* V Ginn, R Enlander & R Crozier (eds), *Exploring Prehistoric Identity in NW Europe: our construct or theirs?*, 72–84. Oxbow, Oxford.

Ginn, V 2014b *Settlement Structure in Middle–Late Bronze Age Ireland*. Unpublished PhD thesis, Queen's University, Belfast.

Ginn, V & Rathbone, S (eds) 2012 *Corrstown: a coastal community. Excavations of a Bronze Age village in Northern Ireland*. Oxbow Books, Oxford.

Glasscock, R E 1968 'Kilmagoura', *Medieval Archaeology*, Vol. 12, 196–7.

Glasscock, R E 1970 'Moated sites and deserted boroughs and villages: two neglected aspects of Anglo-Norman settlement in Ireland', *in* N Stephens & R E Glasscock (eds), *Irish Geographical Studies*, 162–77. Queen's University, Belfast.

Gleeson, P 2014 'Assembly and élite culture in late Antique Europe: a case study of Óenach Clochair, Co. Limerick', *Journal of Irish Archaeology*, Vol. 23, 171–87.

Gleeson, P 2015 'Kingdoms, communities, and Óenaig: Irish assembly practices in their northwest European context', *Journal of the North Atlantic*, Vol. 8, 33–51.

Gnecco, C & Schmidt Dias, A S 2015 'On Contract Archaeology', *International Journal of Historical Archaeology*, Vol. 19, No. 4, 687–98.

Gowen, M, Ó Néill, J & Phillips, M (eds) 2005 *The Lisheen Mine Archaeological Project 1996–8*. Wordwell, Bray.

Graham, B J 1993 'Early medieval Ireland: settlement as an indicator of economic and social transformation *c.* AD 500–1100', *in* B J Graham & L J Proudfoot (eds), *An Historical Geography* of Ireland, 19–57. Academic Press, London.

Graham-Campbell, J & Valor, M (eds) 2007 *The Archaeology of Medieval Europe, Vol. 1: eighth to twelfth centuries AD.* Århus University Press, Århus.

Gregory, N & Sheehan, G 2011 'Dunkitt 8—*fulacht fia*, Iron Age pits, kiln and post-medieval agricultural activity', *in* J Eogan & E Shee Twohig (eds), *Cois tSiúire—Nine Thousand Years of Human Activity in the Lower Suir Valley: archaeological excavations on the N25 Waterford City Bypass, Vol. 1*, 106–9. NRA Scheme Monographs 8. National Roads Authority, Dublin.

Grogan, E 1990 'Bronze Age cemetery at Carrig, Co. Wicklow', *Archaeology Ireland*, Vol. 4, No. 4, 12–14.

Grogan, E 2004 'Middle Bronze Age burial traditions in Ireland', *in* H Roche, E Grogan, J Bradley, J Coles & B Raftery (eds), *From Megaliths to Metals: essays in honour of George Eogan*, 61–71. Oxbow, Oxford.

Grogan, E 2005a *The North Munster Project, Vol. 1: the later prehistoric landscape of south-east Clare.* Discovery Programme Monograph No. 6. Wordwell, Bray.

Grogan, E 2005b *The North Munster Project, Vol. 2: the prehistoric landscape of North Munster.* Discovery Programme Monograph No. 6. Wordwell, Bray.

Grogan, E 2006 'The place of routeways in later prehistory', *in* F Coyne, *Islands in the Clouds: an upland archaeological study of Mount Brandon and the Paps, County Kerry*, 74–82. Kerry County Council/Aegis Archaeology Ltd, Tralee.

Grogan, E 2008 *The Rath of the Synods, Tara, Co. Meath: excavations by Seán P. Ó Ríordáin.* Wordwell, Bray.

Grogan, E 2012 'Stone artefacts', *in* V Ginn & S Rathbone (eds), *Corrstown: a coastal community. Excavations of a Bronze Age village in Northern Ireland*, 186–94. Oxbow Books, Oxford.

Grogan, E 2013 'The development of the Neolithic and Bronze Age landscape in the Tara region', *in* M O'Sullivan, C Scarre & M Doyle (eds), *Tara—from the Past to the Future. Towards a new research agenda*, 335–62. Wordwell in association with the UCD School of Archaeology, Dublin.

Grogan, E 2014 'High and low: identity and status in Late Bronze Age Ireland', *in* V Ginn, R Enlander & R Crozier (eds), *Exploring Prehistoric Identity in NW Europe: our construct or theirs?*, 60–71. Oxbow, Oxford.

Grogan, E & Eogan, G 1987 'Lough Gur excavations by Seán P. Ó Ríordáin: further Neolithic and Beaker habitations on Knockadoon', *Proceedings of the Royal Irish Academy*, Vol. 87C, 299–506.

Grogan, E & Roche, H 2006 *The Prehistoric Pottery from Pit C12, Mitchelstown, Co. Cork (04E1071). N8 Mitchelstown Relief Road.* Unpublished report for Eachtra Archaeological Projects.

Grogan, E & Roche, H 2009a 'Appendix 6. The prehistoric pottery from Raynestown 1', *in* S Elder, *Report on the Archaeological Excavation of Raynestown 1, Co. Meath. M3 Clonee–North of Kells, Contract 1 Clonee–Dunshaughlin*, 1–26. Unpublished report for Archaeological Consultancy Services Ltd.

Grogan, E & Roche, H 2009b *The Prehistoric Pottery Assemblage from Burtown Little, Co. Kildare (E2989)*. Unpublished report for Headland Archaeology (Ireland) Ltd.

Grogan, E & Roche, H 2010a 'Clay and fire: the development and distribution of pottery traditions in prehistoric Ireland', *in* M Stanley, E Danaher & J Eogan (eds), *Creative Minds*, 27–45. Archaeology and the National Roads Authority Monograph Series 7. National Roads Authority, Dublin.

Grogan, E & Roche, H 2010b 'A Bronze Age funerary crisis', *in* M Davies, U MacConville & G Cooney (eds), *A Grand Gallimaufry: collection in honour of Nick Maxwell*, 15–17. Wordwell, Bray.

Grogan, E & Roche, H 2012 'Prehistoric pottery', *in* S Delaney, D Bayley, E Lyne, S McNamara, J Nunan & K Molloy, *Borderlands: archaeological investigation on the route of the M18 Gort to Crusheen road scheme*, 47–9. NRA Scheme Monographs 9. National Roads Authority, Dublin.

Grogan, E & Roche, H 2013a 'Appendix 2.1 Prehistoric pottery report', *in* P Wierbicki & T Coughlan, *E3858 Kellymount 5 Final Report*, xxiii–xxvii. Unpublished report for Irish Archaeological Consultancy Ltd.

Grogan, E & Roche, H 2013b 'Prehistoric pottery and the development of the prehistoric landscape in the Cork region', *in* K Hanley & M F Hurley (eds), *Generations: the archaeology of five national road schemes in County Cork. Vol. 2: historic sites, artefactual and environmental evidence and radiocarbon dates*, 305–22. NRA Scheme Monographs 13. National Roads Authority, Dublin.

Grogan, E, Dunne, N & Moloney, C 2016 'The Burtown Lady: personal adornment in Early Bronze Age Ireland', *in* M Stanley (ed.), *Above and Below: the archaeology of roads and light rail*, 1–11. TII Heritage 3. Transport Infrastructure Ireland, Dublin.

Grogan, E, O'Donnell, L & Johnston, P 2007 *The Bronze Age Landscapes of the Pipeline to the West: an integrated and environmental assessment*. Wordwell, Bray.

Hackett, L 2009 *Kilcullen to Waterford Scheme: Phase 3; Kilcullen to Carlow. Archaeological Services Contract No. 5—Resolution Kilcullen to Moone and Athy Link Road. Preliminary Report on Archaeological Excavations at Site E2980 in the Townland of Moone, Co. Kildare*. Unpublished report by Headland Archaeology (Ireland) Ltd for Kildare County Council and the National Roads Authority.

Hadfield, A 2012 *Edmund Spenser: a life*. Oxford University Press, Oxford.

Hall, D N & Wrathmell, S 2012 'Field systems and landholdings', *in* S Wrathmell (ed.), *A History of Wharram Percy and its Neighbours*, 278–88. York University Archaeological Publications, York.

Hall, D N, Hennessy, M & O'Keeffe, T 1985 'Medieval agriculture and settlement in Castlewarden and Oughterard', *Irish Geography*, Vol. 18, 16–25.

Hamerow, H 2002 *Early Medieval Settlements: the archaeology of rural communities in northwest Europe, AD 400–900*. Oxford University Press, Oxford.

Hamerow, H 2009 'Early medieval settlements in northwest Europe, *c.* AD 400–900: the social aspects of settlement layout', *in* J A Quirós Castillo (ed.), *The Archaeology of Early Medieval Villages in Europe*, 68–76. Universidad del País Vasco, Bilbao.

Hamerow, H 2012 *Rural Settlements and Society in Anglo-Saxon England*. Oxford University Press,

Oxford.

Hanley, K   2011   'Profiting from the land: mixed fortunes in the historic landscapes of north Cork', *in* S Conran, E Danaher & M Stanley (eds), *Past Times, Changing Fortunes*, 31–56. Archaeology and the National Roads Authority No. 8. National Roads Authority, Dublin.

Hartnett, P J   1951   'A Neolithic burial from Martinstown, Kiltale, Co. Meath', *Journal of the Royal Society of Antiquaries of Ireland*, Vol. 81, 19–23.

Hartwell, B   1998   'The Ballynahatty complex', *in* A Gibson & D Simpson (eds), *Prehistoric Ritual and Religion*, 32–44. Sutton, Stroud.

Hay, G & Carlin, N   2014   'Translating ceramics: Neolithic to digital, to contemporary social objects', *Ceramics Ireland*, Vol. 34, 44–7.

Henry, F   1965   *Irish Art in the Early Christian Period (to 800 AD)*. Methuen Press, London.

Hensey, R   2015   *First Light: the origins of Newgrange*. Oxbow, Oxford.

Hensey, R, Meehan, P, Dowd, M & Moore, S   2013   'A century of archaeology—historical excavation and modern research at the Carrowkeel passage tombs, County Sligo', *Proceedings of the Royal Irish Academy*, Vol. 114C, 1–31.

Higham, R & Barker, P   1992   *Timber Castles*. Batsford, London.

Hodder, I   2012   *Entangled: an archaeology of the relationships between humans and things*. Wiley and Blackwell, Oxford.

Holmes, P & Molloy, B   2006   'The Charlesland (Wicklow) Pipes', *in* E Hickman, A A Both & R Eichmann (eds), *Studies in Music Archaeology V: music archaeology in contexts*, 15–40. Verlag Marie Leidorf, Rahden/Westfalen.

Horning, A   2012   'Ireland: medieval identities, settlement and land use', *in* N Christie & P Stamper (eds), *Medieval Rural Settlement: Britain and Ireland AD 800–1600*, 174–85. Windgather Press, Oxford.

Horning, A   2013   *Ireland in the Virginian Sea: colonialism in the British Atlantic*. University of North Carolina Press, Chapel Hill.

Horning, A, Ó Baoill, R, Donnelly, C & Logue, P (eds)   2007   *The Post-Medieval Archaeology of Ireland, 1550–1850*. Wordwell, Bray.

Hughes, J & Ó Droma, M   2011   'Finding the plot: urban and rural settlement in 13th-century Cashel, Co. Tipperary', *in* S Conran, E Danaher & M Stanley (eds), *Past Times, Changing Fortunes*, 17–29. Archaeology and the National Roads Authority Monograph Series No. 8. National Roads Authority, Dublin.

Hughes, J, Wilkins, B & Price, J   2011   'Newrath 35—Neolithic ritual and Iron Age metalworking', *in* J Eogan & E Shee Twohig (eds), *Cois tSiúire—Nine Thousand Years of Human Activity in the Lower Suir Valley: archaeological excavations on the N25 Waterford City Bypass*, Vol. 1, 128–36. NRA Scheme Monographs 8. National Roads Authority, Dublin.

Hull, G   2007   '153. Cragbrien, burnt mound and human skull parts', *in* E Grogan, L O'Donnell & P Johnston, *The Bronze Age Landscapes of the Pipeline to the West*, 202–3. Wordwell, Bray.

Hull, G   2016   'A 9,000-year-long story: archaeological discoveries on the M11 Gorey to Enniscorthy motorway', *in* M Stanley (ed.), *Above and Below: the archaeology of roads and light rail*, 73–93. TII Heritage 3. Transport Infrastructure Ireland, Dublin.

Ivens, R J 1987 'The Early Christian monastic enclosure at Tullylish, Co. Down', *Ulster Journal of Archaeology*, Vol. 50, 55–121.

Jackman, N, Moore, C & Rynne, C 2013 *The Mill at Kilbegly: an archaeological investigation on the route of the M6 Ballinasloe to Athlone national road scheme*. NRA Scheme Monographs 12. National Roads Authority, Dublin.

Johnston, P & Carlin, N (forthcoming) 'The significance of the prehistoric settlement and communal places', *in* P Johnston & J Kiely, *Hidden Voices—the Archaeology of the M8 Fermoy–Mitchelstown Motorway*. TII Heritage series. Transport Infrastructure Ireland, Dublin.

Johnston, P, Kiely, J & Tierney, J 2008 *Near the Bend in the River: the archaeology of the N25 Kilmacthomas Realignment*. NRA Scheme Monographs 3. National Roads Authority, Dublin.

Kador, T, Geber, J, Hensey, R, Meehan, P & Moore, S 2015 'New dates from Carrowkeel', *PAST*, Vol. 79, 12–14.

Kelly, A 2008 'A Turkish import in County Meath: Mediterranean pottery on the M3', *Seanda*, No. 3, 16–18.

Kelly, A 2010a *E3123: Grange 3 Final Report. M3 Clonee–North of Kells Motorway Scheme*. Unpublished report by Irish Archaeological Consultancy Ltd for Meath County Council and the National Roads Authority.

Kelly, A 2010b 'The discovery of Phocaean Red slip-ware (PRSW) form 3 and Bii ware (LR1 amphorae) on sites in Ireland: an analysis within a broader framework', *Proceedings of the Royal Irish Academy*, Vol. 110C, 35–88.

Kelly, R L 1995 *The Foraging Spectrum: diversity in hunter-gatherer lifeways*. Smithsonian Institute Press, London.

Kerr, T R 2009 'The height of fashion: raised raths in the landscape of north-west Ulster', *Journal of Irish Archaeology*, Vol. 17, 63–76.

Kerr, T R & McCormick, F 2013 'Statistics, sunspots and settlement: influences on sum of probability curves', *Journal of Archaeological Science*, Vol. 41, 493–501.

Kerr, T R, Doyle, M, Seaver, M, McCormick, F & O'Sullivan, A 2015 *Early Medieval Crafts and Production in Ireland, AD 400–1100: the evidence from rural settlements*. British Archaeological Reports, International Series 2707. Oxford.

Kerr, T, Harney, L, Kinsella, J, O'Sullivan, A & McCormick, F 2009 *Early Medieval Dwellings and Settlements in Ireland, AD 400–1100, Vol. 2: gazetteer of site descriptions, version 1*. Early Medieval Archaeology Project (EMAP) Report 3.2 (http://www.emap.ie/documents/EMAP_Report_3.2_WEB.pdf, accessed March 2015).

Kerr, T R, Swindles, G T & Plunkett, G 2009 'Making hay while the sun shines? Socio-economic change, cereal production and climatic deterioration in early medieval Ireland', *Journal of Archaeological Science*, Vol. 36, No. 12, 2868–74.

Kerrigan, A 2011 '6.1.12 Ballyglass West (E3870)—burnt mound', *in* F Delaney & J Tierney, *In the Lowlands of South Galway: archaeological excavations on the N18 Oranmore to Gort national road scheme*, 134–41. NRA Scheme Monographs 7. National Roads Authority, Dublin.

Kerrigan, A & Gillespie, R F 2010a 'Introduction', *in* R F Gillespie & A Kerrigan, *Of Troughs and Tuyères: the archaeology of the N5 Charlestown Bypass*, 1–22. NRA Scheme Monographs 6. National Roads Authority, Dublin.

Kerrigan, A & Gillespie, R F 2010b 'Relics of the Irish rural landscape', *in* R F Gillespie & A Kerrigan, *Of Troughs and Tuyères: the archaeology of the N5 Charlestown Bypass*, 341–64. NRA Scheme Monographs 6. National Roads Authority, Dublin.

Kilbride-Jones, H E 1950 'The excavation of a composite early Iron Age monument with "henge" features at Lugg, Co. Dublin', *Proceedings of the Royal Irish Academy*, Vol. 53C, 311–32.

Kinsella, J 2008 'New discoveries and fresh insights: researching the early medieval archaeology of the M3 in County Meath', *in* J O'Sullivan & M Stanley (eds), *Roads, Rediscovery and Research*, 95–107. Archaeology and the National Roads Authority Monograph Series No. 5. National Roads Authority, Dublin.

Kuijt, I & Quinn, C P 2013 'Biography of the Neolithic body: tracing pathways to cist II, Mound of the Hostages, Tara', *in* M O'Sullivan, C Scarre & M Doyle (eds), *Tara—from the Past to the Future. Towards a new research agenda*, 130–43. Wordwell in association with the UCD School of Archaeology, Dublin.

Laidlaw, G 2008 *Final Report on Excavations at Scart North, Co. Kilkenny (E3021). N9/N10 Dunkitt to Sheepstown.* Unpublished report by Valerie J Keeley Ltd for Kilkenny County Council and the National Roads Authority.

Laidlaw, G 2009 'Breaking pots: the grooved ware assemblage from Scart, Co. Kilkenny', *Old Kilkenny Review*, No. 61, 37–46.

Larsson, E 2009 *R158 Realignment Scheme Summerhill to Kilcock. Road Improvement Scheme; Final Report, Site 10, Garadice, Co. Meath.* Unpublished report by CRDS Ltd for Meath County Council and the National Roads Authority.

Lawton-Matthews, E & Warren, G M 2015 'Pits in the Irish Mesolithic', *in* N Bicho, C Detry, T D Price & E Cunha (eds), *Muge 150th: the 150th anniversary of the discovery of Mesolithic shellmiddens—Volume 2*, 139–52. Cambridge Scholars Publishing, Newcastle.

Lemonnier, P 2012 *Mundane Objects: materiality and non-verbal communication.* Left Coast, Walnut Creek, CA.

Lennon, A.M 2006 'Excavation of a ringfort at Leggetsrath West, County Kilkenny', *in* J O'Sullivan & M Stanley (eds), *Settlement, Industry and Ritual*, 43–52. Archaeology and the National Roads Authority Monograph Series No. 3. National Roads Authority, Dublin.

Lévi-Strauss, C 1983 *The Way of the Masks.* Jonathan Cape, London.

Linnane, S & Kinsella, J 2009 'Military lords and defensive beginnings: a preliminary assessment of the social role of an impressive rath at Baronstown', *in* M B Deevy & D Murphy (eds), *Places Along the Way: first findings on the M3*, 101–22. NRA Scheme Monographs 5. National Roads Authority, Dublin.

Little, L K (ed.) 2007 *Plague and the End of Antiquity: the pandemic of 541–750.* Cambridge University Press, Cambridge.

Liversage, G D 1968 'Excavations at Dalkey Island, Co. Dublin, 1956–1959', *Proceedings of the*

Royal Irish Academy, Vol. 66C, 53–233.

Loveluck, C   2013   *Northwest Europe in the Early Middle Ages c. AD 600–1150: a comparative archaeology*. Cambridge University Press, Cambridge.

Loveluck, C & O'Sullivan, A   2016   'Travel, transport and communication to and from Ireland, *c.* 400–1100: an archaeological perspective', *in* R Flechter & S Meeder (eds), *The Irish in Early Medieval Europe: identity, culture and religion*, 19–37. Palgrave Macmillan, London.

Lynch, A   2014   *Poulnabrone: an Early Neolithic portal tomb in Ireland*. Archaeological Monograph Series 9. The Stationery Office, Dublin.

Lynch, L   2003   *Osteoarchaeological Report on Cremated Remains from Thirteen Sites Along the Gas Pipeline to the West*. Unpublished report by Aegis Archaeology Ltd for Margaret Gowen & Co. Ltd.

Lynch, L & O'Donnell, L   2007   'Cremation in the Bronze Age: practice, process and belief', *in* E Grogan, L O'Donnell & P Johnston, *The Bronze Age Landscapes of the Pipeline to the West*, 105–14. Wordwell, Bray.

Lynch, M   2013   '2013:11—Fanore More, Clare', *Excavations.ie: Database of Irish Excavation Reports* (http://www.excavations.ie/report/2013/Clare/0022650/, accessed July 2015).

Lynch, P   2011   *E3158: Cakestown Glebe 2. Ministerial Direction Ref. No.: A029/. Final Report.* Unpublished report by Irish Archaeological Consultancy Ltd for Meath County Council and the National Roads Authority.

Lynn, C J   1988   'A thousand-year-old farm: Ballywee, Co. Antrim', *in* A Hamlin & C J Lynn (eds), *Pieces of the Past: archaeological excavations by the Department of the Environment for Northern Ireland, 1970–1986*, 32–5. HMSO, Belfast.

Lynn, C J   2005   'Settlement and disease: a plague on your raths', *Archaeology Ireland*, Vol. 19, No. 4, 14–17.

Lynn, C J & McDowell, J A   2011   *Deer Park Farms: the excavation of a raised rath in the Glenarm Valley, Co. Antrim*. HMSO and Environment and Heritage Service, Belfast.

Lyons, S & O'Donnell, L   2009   'Wood identification and analysis', *in* J Eogan & E Shee Twohig (eds), *Cois tSiúire—Nine Thousand Years of Human Activity in the Lower Suir Valley: archaeological excavations on the N25 Waterford City Bypass, Vol. 1*, 124–6. NRA Scheme Monographs 8. National Roads Authority, Dublin.

Lyttleton, J   2013   *The Jacobean Plantations in Seventeenth-Century Offaly: an archaeology of a changing world*. Four Courts Press, Dublin.

McClatchie, M   2014   'Food production in the Bronze Age: analysis of plant macro-remains from Haughey's Fort, Co. Armagh', *Emania*, Vol. 22, 33–48.

McClatchie, M, Bogaard, A, Colledge, S, Whitehouse, N J, Schulting, R J, Barratt, P & McLaughlin, T R   2014   'Neolithic farming in north-western Europe: archaeobotanical evidence from Ireland', *Journal of Archaeological Science*, Vol. 51, 206–15.

McClatchie, M, Bogaard, A, Colledge, S, Whitehouse, N J, Schulting, R J, Barratt, P & McLaughlin, R   2016   'Farming and foraging in Neolithic Ireland: a review of the evidence from plant macro-remains', *Antiquity*, Vol. 90, No. 350, 302–18.

McClatchie, M, McCormick, F, Kerr, T R & O'Sullivan, A 2015 'Early medieval farming and food production: a review of the archaeobotanical evidence from archaeological excavations in Ireland', *Vegetation History and Archaeobotany*, Vol. 24, 179–86.

McCormick, F 2007 'Mammal bones from prehistoric Irish sites', *in* E M Murphy & N J Whitehouse (eds), *Environmental Archaeology in Ireland*, 76–101. Oxbow, Oxford.

McCormick, F 2008 'The decline of the cow: agricultural and settlement change in early medieval Ireland', *Peritia*, Vol. 20, 210–25.

McCormick, F 2012 'Cows, milk and religion: the use of dairy produce in early societies', *Anthropozoologica*, Vol. 47, No. 2, 99–112.

McCormick, F 2014 'Agriculture, settlement and society in early medieval Ireland', *Quaternary International*, Vol. 346, 119–30.

McCormick, F, Kerr, T R, McClatchie, M & O'Sullivan, A 2014 *Early Medieval Agriculture, Livestock and Cereal Production in Ireland, AD 400–1100*. British Archaeological Reports, International Series 2647. Archaeopress, Oxford.

McCormick, M 2001 *Origins of the European Economy*. Cambridge University Press, Cambridge.

McCormick, M 2002 'New light on the "Dark Ages": how the slave trade fuelled the Carolingian economy', *Past and Present*, Vol. 177, 17–54.

McCormick, M 2003 'Complexity, chronology and context in the early medieval economy', *Early Medieval Europe*, Vol. 12, 307–23.

McCormick, M 2007 'Towards a molecular history of the Justinianic Pandemic', *in* L K Little (ed.), *Plague and the End of Antiquity: the pandemic of 541–750*, 290–312. Cambridge University Press, Cambridge.

McCormick, M 2015 'Tracking mass death during the fall of Rome's empire (I)', *Journal of Roman Archaeology*, Vol. 28, 325–57 (DOI: https://doi.org/10.1017/S1047759415002512).

McCutcheon, C 2009 'Appendix 8.1: the medieval pottery', *in* C Corlett & M Potterton (eds), *Rural Settlement in Medieval Ireland in the Light of Recent Archaeological Excavations*, 102–7. Research Papers in Irish Archaeology 1. Wordwell, Dublin.

McCutcheon, W A 1980 *The Industrial Archaeology of Northern Ireland*. HMSO, Belfast.

McGonigle, M 2013 'Early Neolithic houses on site 1, area B, at Upper Campsie, Co. Derry', *Journal of Irish Archaeology*, Vol. 22, 1–21.

McKenzie, C, Murphy, E & Donnelly, C J (eds) 2015 *The Science of a Lost Medieval Gaelic Graveyard: the Ballyhanna Research Project*. TII Heritage 2. Transport Infrastructure Ireland, Dublin.

McKeon, J & O'Sullivan, J (eds) 2014 *The Quiet Landscape: archaeological investigations on the M6 Galway to Ballinasloe national road scheme*. NRA Scheme Monographs 15. National Roads Authority, Dublin.

McKinstry, L 2011 *N11 Gorey to Arklow Link: archaeological resolution. Final Report. Ministerial Direction: A003/022. Excavation Number: E3478. Site 13, Moneylawn Lower Townland, Co. Wexford*. Unpublished report by Valerie J Keeley Ltd for Wexford County Council and the National Roads Authority.

McKitterick, R (ed.) 2001 *The Early Middle Ages, Europe 400–1000*. Oxford University Press, Oxford.

McLaughlin, T R, Whitehouse, N J, Schulting, R J, McClatchie, M, Barratt, P & Bogaard, A 2016 'The changing face of Neolithic and Bronze Age Ireland: a big data approach to the settlement and burial records', *Journal of World Prehistory*, Vol. 29, 117–53.

McLoughlin, G 2010 *Final Excavation Report, Site 13 Haggardstown, Co. Louth 06E0485*. Unpublished report for Irish Archaeological Consultancy Ltd.

McNeill, T E 1997 *Castles in Ireland—Feudal Power in a Gaelic World*. Routledge, London and New York.

McNeill, T E 2007 'Where should we place the boundary between the medieval and post-medieval periods in Ireland?', *in* A Horning, R Ó Baoill, C Donnelly & P Logue (eds), *The Post-Medieval Archaeology of Ireland, 1550–1850*, 15–23. Wordwell, Dublin.

McQuade, M 2005 'Archaeological excavation of a multi-period prehistoric settlement at Waterunder, Mell, Co. Louth', *County Louth Archaeological and Historical Journal*, Vol. 26, 31–66.

McQuade, M 2009 'Ballydrehid, Co. Tipperary. Two structures. Site 185.5 (E2267)', *in* M McQuade, B Molloy & C Moriarty, *In the Shadow of the Galtees: archaeological excavations along the N8 Cashel to Mitchelstown Road Scheme*, 51–7. NRA Scheme Monographs 4. National Roads Authority, Dublin.

McQuade, M & O'Donnell, L 2007 'Late Mesolithic fish traps from the Liffey estuary, Dublin, Ireland', *Antiquity*, Vol. 81, 569–84.

McQuade, M, Molloy, B & Moriarty, C 2009 *In the Shadow of the Galtees: archaeological excavations along the N8 Cashel to Mitchelstown Road Scheme*. NRA Scheme Monographs 4. National Roads Authority, Dublin.

McSparron, C 2008 'Have you no homes to go to?', *Archaeology Ireland*, Vol. 22, No. 3, 18–21.

MacSween, A, Hunter, J, Sheridan, A, Bond, J, Bronk Ramsey, C, Reimer, P, Bayliss, A, Griffiths, S & Whittle, A 2015 'Refining the chronology of the Neolithic settlement at Pool, Sanday, Orkney', *Proceedings of the Prehistoric Society*, Vol. 81, 283–310.

Maley, W 1997 *Salvaging Spenser: colonialism, culture and identity*. Macmillan, Basingstoke.

Mallory, J P, Nelis, E & Hartwell, B 2011 *Excavations on Donegore Hill, Co. Antrim*. Wordwell, Dublin.

Marshall, J W & Rourke, G D 2000 *High Island: an Irish monastery in the Atlantic*. Town House and Country House, Dublin.

Marshall, J W & Walsh, C 2005 *Illaunloughan Island: an early medieval monastery in County Kerry*. Wordwell, Bray.

Martin, K 2009 'Boyerstown: a rediscovered medieval farmstead', *in* M B Deevy & D Murphy (eds), *Places Along the Way: first findings on the M3*, 135–51. NRA Scheme Monographs 5. National Roads Authority, Dublin.

Masterson, B 1999 'Archaeological applications of modern survey techniques', *Discovery Programme Reports*, Vol. 5, 131–46.

Meiklejohn, C & Woodman, P M 2012 'Radiocarbon dating of Mesolithic human remains in

Ireland', *Mesolithic Miscellany*, Vol. 22, No. 1, 22–41.

Meyer, K   1894   *Hibernica Minora*. Clarendon Press, Oxford.

Molloy, B   2007a   'N8 Cashel to Mitchelstown Road Improvement Scheme final archaeological excavation report: (E2341) Knockcommane', *in* M McQuade, B Molloy & C Moriarty, *In the Shadow of the Galtees: archaeological excavations along the N8 Cashel to Mitchelstown Road Scheme* (CD-ROM). National Roads Authority, Dublin.

Molloy, B   2007b   'N8 Cashel to Mitchelstown Road Improvement Scheme final archaeological excavation report: (E2342) Knockcommane', *in* M McQuade, B Molloy & C Moriarty, *In the Shadow of the Galtees*: *archaeological excavations along the N8 Cashel to Mitchelstown Road Scheme* (CD-ROM). National Roads Authority, Dublin.

Molloy, B   2009a   'Clonmore North, Co. Tipperary. Structures and *fulacht fia*. Site 92.3 (E2294)', *in* M McQuade, B Molloy & C Moriarty, *In the Shadow of the Galtees: archaeological excavations along the N8 Cashel to Mitchelstown Road Scheme*, 45–8. NRA Scheme Monographs 4. National Roads Authority, Dublin.

Molloy, B   2009b   'Clonmore North, Co. Tipperary. Structures and associated *fulacht fia*. Site 92.3 (E2294)', *in* M McQuade, B Molloy & C Moriarty, *In the Shadow of the Galtees: archaeological excavations along the N8 Cashel to Mitchelstown Road Scheme*, 107–8. NRA Scheme Monographs 4. National Roads Authority, Dublin.

Molloy, B   2009c   'Raheen, Co. Tipperary. *Fulachta fia*. Site 92.2 (E2295)', *in* M McQuade, B Molloy & C Moriarty, *In the Shadow of the Galtees: archaeological excavations along the N8 Cashel to Mitchelstown Road Scheme*, 97–8. NRA Scheme Monographs 4, Dublin.

Molloy, K   2005   'Holocene vegetation and land-use history at Mooghaun, south-east Clare, with particular reference to the Bronze Age', *in* E Grogan, *The North Munster Project, Vol. 1: the later prehistory of south-east Clare*, 255–87. Discovery Programme Monographs 6. Wordwell, Bray.

Molloy, K & O'Connell, M   2012   'Prehistoric farming in western Ireland: pollen analysis at Caheraphuca, Co. Clare', *in* S Delaney, D Bayley, E Lyne, S McNamara, J Nunan & K Molloy, *Borderlands: archaeological investigation on the route of the M18 Gort to Crusheen road scheme*, 109–22. NRA Scheme Monographs 9. National Roads Authority, Dublin.

Monk, M A & Power, O   2012   'More than a grain of truth emerges from a rash of corn-drying kilns?', *Archaeology Ireland*, Vol. 26, No. 2, 38–41.

Monteith, J   2008   *Final Report on Excavations at Scart 1, Co. Kilkenny (E3001). N9/N10 Dunkitt to Sheepstown*. Unpublished report by Valerie J Keeley Ltd for Kilkenny County Council.

Moore, C   2008   'Old routes to new research: the Edercloon wetland excavations in County Longford', *in* J O'Sullivan & M Stanley (eds), *Roads, Rediscovery and Research*, 1–12. Archaeology and the National Roads Authority Monograph Series No. 5. National Roads Authority, Dublin.

Moore, D G   2007   'Kilshane. Neolithic segmented enclosure', *in* I Bennett (ed.), *Excavations 2003: summary accounts of archaeological excavations in Ireland*, 143–6. Wordwell, Bray.

Moreland, J   2006   'Archaeology and texts: subservience or enlightenment', *Annual Review of Anthropology*, Vol. 35, 135–51.

Moriarty, C   2009   'Cloghabreedy, Co. Tipperary. Circular structures. Site 125.4 (E2274)', *in* M McQuade, B Molloy & C Moriarty, *In the Shadow of the Galtees: archaeological excavations along the N8 Cashel to Mitchelstown Road Scheme*, 35–42. NRA Scheme Monographs 4. National Roads Authority, Dublin.

Moriarty, C   2011   'The medieval vill of Portmarnock', *in* S Duffy (ed.), *Medieval Dublin XI: proceedings of the Friends of Medieval Dublin Symposium 2009*, 229–74. Four Courts Press, Dublin.

Mossop, M   2009   'Lakeside developments in County Meath, Ireland: a Late Mesolithic fishing platform and possible mooring at Clowanstown 1', *in* S McCartan, P C Woodman, R Schulting & G M Warren (eds), *Mesolithic Horizons: papers presented at the Seventh International Conference on the Mesolithic in Europe, Belfast 2005, Vol. 2*, 895–9. Oxbow, Oxford.

Mossop, M & Mossop, E   2009   *M3 Clonee–North of Kells. Contract 2 Dunshaughlin–Navan. Report on the archaeological excavation of Clowanstown 1, Co. Meath.* Unpublished report by Archaeological Consultancy Services Ltd for Meath County Council and the National Roads Authority.

Mount, C   1995   'New research on Irish Early Bronze Age cemeteries', *in* J Waddell & E Shee Twohig (eds), *Ireland in the Bronze Age*, 97–112. The Stationery Office, Dublin.

Mount, C   1997   'Early Bronze Age burial in south-east Ireland in the light of recent research', *Proceedings of the Royal Irish Academy*, Vol. 97C, 101–93.

Mullins, G   2014   'A hillfort, ringforts and field system at Rahally', *in* J McKeon & J O'Sullivan (eds), *The Quiet Landscape: archaeological investigations on the M6 Galway to Ballinasloe national road scheme*, 105–15. NRA Scheme Monographs 15. National Roads Authority, Dublin.

Murphy, D   2013a   'Archaeological investigations (pre-construction)', *in* K Hanley & M F Hurley (eds), *Generations: the archaeology of five national road schemes in Cork. Vol. 1: prehistoric sites*, 17. NRA Scheme Monographs 13. National Roads Authority, Dublin.

Murphy, D   2013b   'Ballynora 1—late 17th-/early 18th-century brick kilns', *in* K Hanley & M F Hurley (eds), *Generations: the archaeology of five national road schemes in County Cork Vol. 2: historic sites, artefactual and environmental evidence and radiocarbon dates*, 277. NRA Scheme Monographs 13. National Roads Authority, Dublin.

Murphy, D & Ginn, V   2013   'The M3 motorway excavations and Tara', *in* M O'Sullivan, C Scarre & M Doyle (eds), *Tara—from the Past to the Future. Towards a new research agenda*, 312–35. Wordwell in association with the UCD School of Archaeology, Dublin.

Murphy, D & Rathbone, S   2006   'Excavations of an early medieval vertical watermill at Killoteran, County Waterford', *in* J O'Sullivan & M Stanley (eds), *Settlement, Industry and Ritual*, 19–28. Archaeology and the National Roads Authority Monograph Series No. 3. National Roads Authority, Dublin.

Murphy, M & Potterton, M   2010   *The Dublin Region in the Middle Ages: settlement, land-use and economy.* Four Courts Press, Dublin.

Murray, E V & McCormick, F   2012   'Doonloughan: a seasonal settlement site on the Connemara coast', *Proceedings of the Royal Irish Academy*, Vol. 112C, 95–146.

Needham, S P 2004 'Migdale-Marnoch: sunburst of Scottish metallurgy', *in* I A G Shepherd & G J Barclay (eds), *Scotland in Ancient Europe: the Neolithic and Early Bronze Age of Scotland in their European context*, 217–45. Society of Antiquaries of Scotland, Edinburgh.

Nelis, D 2011 *01E433 Rathmullan 8 Final Report*. Unpublished report by Irish Archaeological Consultancy Ltd for Meath County Council and the National Roads Authority.

Newman, C 1997 *Tara: an archaeological survey*. Discovery Programme Monographs No. 2. Royal Irish Academy/Discovery Programme, Dublin.

Ní Lionáin, C 2007 'Life, death and food production in Bronze Age Ireland: recent excavations at Stamullin, Co. Meath', *Archaeology Ireland*, Vol. 21, No. 2, 18–21.

Nicholls, K W 1987 'Gaelic society and economy in the High Middle Ages', *in* A Cosgrove (ed.), *A New History of Ireland, Vol. 2. Medieval Ireland, 1169–1534*, 397–438. Clarendon Press, Oxford.

Nixon, C E V (ed.) 1987 *Panegyric to the Emperor Theodosius/Pacatus*. Liverpool University Press, Liverpool.

Noonan, D 2013 'Ballynacarriga AR12—settlement, rectangular enclosure complex', *in* K Hanley & M F Hurley (eds), *Generations: the archaeology of the national road schemes of County Cork. Vol. 2: historic sites, artefactual and environmental evidence and radiocarbon dates*, 222–37. NRA Scheme Monographs 13. National Roads Authority, Dublin.

Northover, P, O'Brien, W & Stos, S 2001 'Lead isotopes and metal circulation in Beaker/Early Bronze Age Ireland', *Journal of Irish Archaeology*, Vol. 10, 25–48.

O'Brien, E 2009 'Pagan or Christian? Burial in Ireland during the 5th to 8th centuries A.D', *in* N Edwards (ed.), *The Archaeology of Early Medieval Celtic Churches*, 135–54. Society for Medieval Archaeology Monograph 29. Maney, Leeds.

O'Brien, W 1999 *Sacred Ground: megalithic tombs in coastal south-west Ireland*. Bronze Age Studies 4. Department of Archaeology, National University of Ireland, Galway.

O'Brien, W 2004 *Ross Island: mining, metal and society in early Ireland*. Bronze Age Studies 6. Department of Archaeology, National University of Ireland, Galway.

O'Brien, W 2009 *Local Worlds: upland farming and early settlement landscapes in southwest Ireland*. Collins Press, Cork.

O'Brien, W 2012a 'The Chalcolithic in Ireland: a chronological and cultural framework', *in* M J Allen, J Gardiner & A Sheridan (eds), *Is there a British Chalcolithic? People, places and polity in the late 3rd millennium*, 211–25. Prehistoric Society Research Paper No. 4. Oxbow and the Prehistoric Society, Oxford.

O'Brien, W 2012b 'Stone circle or proto-cashel? An Iron Age enclosure in south-west Ireland', *in* C Corlett & M Potterton (eds), *Life and Death in Iron Age Ireland in the Light of Recent Archaeological Excavations,* 199–212. Research Papers in Irish Archaeology 4. Wordwell, Dublin.

O'Byrne, E 2002 'On the frontier: Carrickmines Castle and Gaelic Leinster', *Archaeology Ireland*, Vol. 16, No. 3, 13–15.

O'Callaghan, N 2012 'Archaeological excavation report 03E1717—Kilbane, Castletroy, Co.

Limerick. A ring-ditch, three cremation cemeteries and four *fulachta fiadh*', *Eachtra Journal*, Vol. 13, 118–24.

Ó Carragáin, T 2003 'The architectural setting of the cult of relics in early medieval Ireland', *Journal of the Royal Society of Antiquaries of Ireland*, Vol. 133, 130–76.

Ó Carragáin, T 2009 'Cemetery settlements and local churches in pre-Viking Ireland in light of comparisons with England and Wales', *in* J Graham-Campbell & M Ryan (eds), *Anglo-Saxon/Irish Relations Before the Vikings*, 329–65. Proceedings of the British Academy 157. Oxford University Press, Oxford.

Ó Carragáin, T 2010a 'From family cemeteries to community cemeteries in Viking Age Ireland?', *in* C Corlett & M Potterton (eds), *Death and Burial in Early Medieval Ireland in the Light of Recent Archaeological Excavations*, 217–26. Research Papers in Irish Archaeology 2. Wordwell, Dublin.

Ó Carragáin, T 2010b *Churches in Early Medieval Ireland*. Yale University Press, London.

O Carroll, E & Cobain, S 2012 'Wood and charcoal', *in* S Delaney, D Bayley, E Lyne, S McNamara, J Nunan & K Molloy, *Borderlands: archaeological investigation on the route of the M18 Gort to Crusheen road scheme*, 67–74. NRA Scheme Monographs 9. National Roads Authority, Dublin.

O'Connell, A 2004 'Recent archaeological investigations at Kill St Lawrence, Waterford, carried out as part of the realignment of the R708 airport road', *Decies*, Vol. 60, 27–64.

O'Connell, A 2006 'The many lives of Castlefarm', *Seanda*, No. 1, 19–24.

O'Connell, A 2009 'Excavations at Castlefarm—director's first findings', *in* M B Deevy & D Murphy (eds), *Places Along the Way: first findings on the M3*, 43–56. NRA Scheme Monographs 5. National Roads Authority, Dublin.

O'Connell, A 2013 *Harvesting the Stars: a pagan temple at Lismullin, Co. Meath*. NRA Scheme Monographs 11. National Roads Authority, Dublin.

O'Conor, K 1998 *The Archaeology of Medieval Rural Settlement in Ireland*. Royal Irish Academy, Dublin.

O'Conor, K 1999 'Anglo-Norman castles in Co. Laois', *in* P G Lane & W Nolan (eds), *Laois: history and society*, 183–212. Geography Publications, Dublin.

O'Conor, K 2000 'The ethnicity of Irish moated sites', *Ruralia*, Vol. 3, 92–101.

O'Conor, K 2001 'The morphology of Gaelic lordly sites in north Connacht', *in* P J Duffy, D Edwards & E FitzPatrick (eds), *Gaelic Ireland c. 1250–c. 1650: land, lordship and settlement*, 329–45. Four Courts Press, Dublin.

O'Conor, K 2002a 'Housing in later medieval Gaelic Ireland', *Ruralia*, Vol. 4, 197–206.

O'Conor, K 2002b 'Motte castles in Ireland: permanent fortresses, residences and manorial centres', *Château Gaillard*, Vol. 20, 173–82.

O'Conor, K 2014 'Castles', *in* R Moss (ed.), *Art and Architecture of Ireland. Volume I. Medieval, c. 400–c. 1600*, 341–5. Royal Irish Academy and Yale University Press, Dublin, New Haven and London.

Ó Corráin, D 2005 'Ireland *c*. 800: aspects of society', *in* D Ó Cróinín (ed.), *A New History of*

Ireland, Vol. 1: prehistoric and early Ireland, 549–608. Oxford University Press, Oxford.

Ó Cróinín, D 1995 *Early Medieval Ireland, 400–1200.* Longman, London.

O'Donnabhain, B & Tesorieri, M 2014 'Bioarchaeology', *in* A Lynch, *Poulnabrone, Co. Clare: excavation of an Early Neolithic portal tomb in Ireland*, 61–86. Archaeological Monograph Series 9. The Stationery Office, Dublin.

Ó Donnchadha, B & Grogan, E 2010 *M1 Dundalk Western Bypass, Site 116: Balregan 1 and 2. Final report.* Unpublished report by Irish Archaeological Consultancy Ltd for Louth County Council and the National Roads Authority.

O'Donnell, L 2007a 'Environmental archaeology: identifying patterns of exploitation in the Bronze Age', *in* E Grogan, L O'Donnell & P Johnston, *The Bronze Age Landscapes of the Pipeline to the West*, 27–79. Wordwell, Bray.

O'Donnell, L 2007b 'Appendix 6: Charcoal analysis', *in* B Molloy, 'N8 Cashel to Mitchelstown Road Improvement Scheme final archaeological excavation report: (E2342) Knockcommane', *in* M McQuade, B Molloy & C Moriarty, *In the Shadow of the Galtees: archaeological excavations along the N8 Cashel to Mitchelstown Road Scheme* (CD-ROM). National Roads Authority, Dublin.

O'Donnell, L, Halwas, S & Geber, J 2009 'The environmental and faunal evidence', *in* M McQuade, B Molloy & C Moriarty, *In the Shadow of the Galtees: archaeological excavations along the N8 Cashel to Mitchelstown Road Scheme*, 241–86. NRA Scheme Monographs 4. National Roads Authority, Dublin.

Ó Drisceoil, C 2002 'Recycled ringforts: the evidence from archaeological excavation for the conversion of pre-existing monuments to motte castles in medieval Ireland', *Journal of the Louth Archaeological and Historical Society*, Vol. 25, No. 2, 189–201.

Ó Drisceoil, C 2006 'A Neolithic disc-bead necklace from Carrickmines Great, Co. Dublin', *Journal of the Royal Society of Antiquaries of Ireland*, Vol. 136, 141–57.

Ó Drisceoil, C 2007a 'A preliminary report concerning the archaeological excavation of Neolithic houses at Coolfore, County Louth', *Journal of the County Louth Archaeological and Historical Society*, Vol. 26, No. 3, 360–85.

Ó Drisceoil, C 2007b 'Life and death in the Iron Age at Carrickmines Great, County Dublin', *Journal of the Royal Society of Antiquaries of Ireland*, Vol. 137, 5–28.

Ó Drisceoil, C 2009 'Archaeological excavation of a late Neolithic Grooved Ware site at Balgatheran, County Louth', *Journal of the County Louth Archaeological and Historical Society*, Vol. 27, No. 1, 77–102.

Ó Droma, M 2008 'Archaeological investigations at Twomileborris, Co. Tipperary', *in* J O'Sullivan & M Stanley (eds), *Roads, Rediscovery and Research*, 45–59. Archaeology and the National Roads Authority Monograph Series No. 5. National Roads Authority, Dublin.

Ó Floinn, R 2011 'Annagh, Co. Limerick, 1992E047', *in* M Cahill & M Sikora (eds), *Breaking Ground, Finding Graves—Reports on the Excavations of Burials by the National Museum of Ireland, 1927–2006, Vol. 1*, 17–47. National Museum of Ireland Monograph Series 4. Wordwell, Dublin.

O'Hara, R 2007 'Roestown 2, Co. Meath: an excavation on the M3 Clonee to North of Kells motorway scheme', *in* J O'Sullivan & M Stanley (eds), *New Routes to the Past*, 141–51. Archaeology and the National Roads Authority Monograph Series No. 4. National Roads Authority, Dublin.

O'Hara, R 2009a *Report on the Archaeological Excavation of Roestown 2, Co. Meath*. Unpublished report by Archaeological Consultancy Services Ltd for Meath County Council and the National Roads Authority.

O'Hara, R 2009b 'Early medieval settlement at Roestown 2', *in* M B Deevy & D Murphy (eds), *Places Along the Way: first findings on the M3*, 57–82. NRA Scheme Monographs 5. National Roads Authority, Dublin.

O'Hara, R 2010 *An Iron Age and Early Medieval Cemetery at Collierstown 1, Co. Meath: interpreting the changing character of a burial ground*. Early Medieval Archaeology Project (EMAP) Report 4.4. University College Dublin and Queen's University Belfast, Dublin and Belfast.

O'Keeffe, T 2000 *Medieval Ireland: an archaeology*. Tempus, Stroud.

O'Keeffe, T 2004 *The Gaelic Peoples and their Archaeological Identities, AD 1000–1650*. Quiggin Pamphlets on the Sources of Mediaeval Gaelic History 7. Department of Anglo-Saxon, Norse and Celtic, University of Cambridge, Cambridge.

O'Kelly, M J 1954 'Excavations and experiments in Irish cooking-places', *Journal of the Royal Society of Antiquaries of Ireland*, Vol. 84, 105–56.

Ó Maolduin, R 2014 *Exchange in Chalcolithic and Early Bronze Age (EBA) Ireland: connecting people, objects and ideas*. Unpublished PhD thesis, Department of Archaeology, NUI, Galway.

Ó Néill, J 2005 'Killoran 240', *in* M Gowen, J Ó Néill & M Phillips (eds), *The Lisheen Mine Archaeological Project 1996–8*, 267–9. Wordwell, Bray.

O'Neill, T 2006 *Final Report on Archaeological Excavation of Curraghprevin 3*. Unpublished report by Archaeological Consultancy Services Ltd for Cork County Council and the National Roads Authority.

O'Neill, T 2007 'Medieval enclosure', *in* E Danaher, *Monumental Beginnings: the archaeology of the N4 Sligo Inner Relief Road* (CD-ROM). NRA Scheme Monographs 1. National Roads Authority, Dublin.

O'Neill, T 2010 'The changing character of early medieval burial at Parknahown 5, Co. Laois, AD 400–1200', *in* C Corlett & M Potterton (eds), *Death and Burial in Early Medieval Ireland in the Light of Recent Archaeological Excavations*, 251–60. Research Papers in Irish Archaeology 2. Wordwell, Dublin.

Ó Ríordáin, B & Waddell, J 1993 *The Funerary Bowls and Vases of the Irish Bronze Age*. Galway University Press, Galway.

Ó Ríordáin, S P 1949 'Lough Gur excavations: Carrig Aille and the "Spectacles"', *Proceedings of the Royal Irish Academy*, Vol. 52C, 39–111.

Ó Ríordáin, S P 1951 'Lough Gur excavations: the Great Stone Circle (B) in Grange townland', *Proceedings of the Royal Irish Academy*, Vol. 54C, 37–74.

Ó Ríordáin, S P 1954 'Lough Gur excavations: Neolithic and Bronze Age houses on

Knockadoon', *Proceedings of the Royal Irish Academy*, Vol. 56C, 297–459.

Orser, C E 1996 *A Historical Archaeology of the Modern World*. Springer, New York.

O'Sullivan, A 1998 *The Archaeology of Lake Settlement in Ireland*. Royal Irish Academy, Dublin.

O'Sullivan, A 2001 'Crannogs in late medieval Gaelic Ireland, *c.* 1350–*c.* 1600', *in* P J Duffy, D Edwards & E FitzPatrick (eds), *Gaelic Ireland: land, lordship and settlement, c. 1250–c. 1660*, 397–417. Four Courts Press, Dublin.

O'Sullivan, A 2008 'Early medieval houses in Ireland: social identity and dwelling places', *Peritia*, Vol. 20, 226–56.

O'Sullivan, A 2009 'Early medieval crannogs and imagined islands', *in* G Cooney, K Becker, J Coles, M Ryan & S Sievers (eds), *Relics of Old Decency: archaeological studies in later prehistory. Festschrift for Barry Raftery*, 79–87. Wordwell, Dublin.

O'Sullivan, A 2011 'Daily life and practice in an early medieval rath: encountering early Irish society through archaeology, history and palaeoecology', *in* C Corlett & M Potterton (eds), *Settlement in Early Medieval Ireland in the Light of Recent Archaeological Excavations*, 345–55. Research Papers in Irish Archaeology 3. Wordwell, Dublin.

O'Sullivan, A & Kinsella, J 2013 'Living by a sacred landscape: interpreting the early medieval archaeology of the Hill of Tara and its environs, AD 400–1100', *in* M O'Sullivan, C Scarre & M Doyle (eds), *Tara—from the Past to the Future. Towards a new research agenda*, 321–44. Wordwell, Dublin.

O'Sullivan, A & Nicholl, T 2011 'Early medieval settlement enclosures in Ireland: dwellings, daily life and social identity', *Proceedings of the Royal Irish Academy*, Vol. 111C, 59–90.

O'Sullivan, A, McCormick, F, Kerr, T R & Harney, L 2014a *Early Medieval Ireland AD 400–1100: the evidence from archaeological excavations*. Royal Irish Academy, Dublin.

O'Sullivan, A, McCormick, F, Kerr, T R, Harney, L & Kinsella, J 2014b *Early Medieval Dwellings and Settlements in Ireland, AD 400–1100*. British Archaeological Reports, International Series 2604. Archaeopress, Oxford.

O'Sullivan, M 2005 *Duma na nGiall. The Mound of the Hostages, Tara*. Wordwell in association with UCD School of Archaeology, Bray.

O'Sullivan, M & Downey, L 2007 'Ridges and furrows', *Archaeology Ireland*, Vol. 21, No. 2, 34–7.

O'Sullivan, M, Davis, S & Stout, G 2012 'Henges in Ireland: new discoveries and emerging issues', *in* A Gibson (ed.), *Enclosing the Neolithic: recent studies in Britain and Europe*, 37–53. British Archaeological Reports, International Series 2440. Oxford.

Otway-Ruthven, J 1951 'The organization of Anglo-Irish agriculture in the Middle Ages', *Journal of the Royal Society of Antiquaries of Ireland*, Vol. 81, 1–13.

Parker Pearson, M 2007 'The Stonehenge Riverside Project: excavations at the east entrance of Durrington Walls', *in* M Larsson & M Parker Pearson (eds), *From Stonehenge to the Baltic: living with cultural diversity in the third millennium BC*, 125–44. British Archaeological Reports, International Series 1692. Oxford.

Parker Pearson, M 2012 *Stonehenge: exploring the greatest Stone Age mystery*. Simon and Schuster,

London.

Peters, C N   2016   'Translating food shortages in the Irish chronicles, AD 500–1170', *Cambrian Medieval Celtic Studies*, Vol. 71, 29–58.

Pioffet, H   2014   *Sociétés et Identités du Premier Néolithique de Grande-Bretagne et d'Irlande dans leur Contexte Ouest Européen: caractérisation et analyses comparatives des productions céramiques entre Manche, Mer d'Irlande et Mer du Nord*. Unpublished PhD thesis, Durham University.

Raftery, B   1976   'Rathgall and Irish hillfort problems', *in* D Harding (ed.), *Hillforts: later prehistoric earthworks in Britain and Ireland*, 339–57. Academic Press, London.

Raftery, B   1983   *A Catalogue of Irish Iron Age Antiquities*. Veröffentlichungen des Vorgeschichtlichen Seminars Marburg, Sonderband 1. Marburg.

Raftery, B   1994   *Pagan Celtic Ireland: the enigma of the Irish Iron Age*. Thames and Hudson, London.

Raftery, B   1996   *Trackway Excavations in the Mountdillon Bogs, Co. Longford, 1985–1991*. Irish Archaeological Wetland Unit Transactions 3. Crannog Publications, Dublin.

Reilly, F   2013   'Bridges, bricks and lime', *in* N Bermingham, F Coyne, G Hull, F Reilly & K Taylor, *River Road: the archaeology of the Limerick Southern Ring Road*, 115–40. NRA Scheme Monographs 14. National Roads Authority, Dublin.

Rensink, E   2006   'Stones or bones: on Mesolithic fieldwork in the Netherlands and the potential of buried and surface sites for the preservation of bone and antler remains', *in* C-J Kind (ed.), *After the Ice: settlements, subsistence and social development in the Mesolithic of Central Europe. Proceedings of the international conference 9th to 12th of September 2003 Rottenburg/Neckar, Baden-Württemberg, Germany*, 101–18. Konrad Thesis Verlag, Stuttgart.

Richards, C   2005   *Dwelling Among the Monuments: the Neolithic village of Barnhouse, Maeshowe passage grave and surrounding monuments at Stenness, Orkney*. McDonald Institute for Archaeological Research, Cambridge.

Robb, J E   2013   'Material culture, landscapes of action, and emergent causation', *Current Anthropology*, Vol. 54, 657–83.

Robertson, A, Lochrie, J & Timpany, S   2013   'Built to last: Mesolithic and Neolithic settlement at two sites beside the Forth estuary, Scotland', *Proceedings of the Society of Antiquaries of Scotland*, Vol. 143, 73–136.

Roche, H   1995   *Style and Context for Grooved Ware in Ireland with Special Reference to the Assemblage at Knowth, Co. Meath*. Unpublished MA thesis, University College Dublin.

Roche, H   2004   'The dating of the embanked stone circle at Grange, Co. Limerick', *in* H Roche, E Grogan, J Bradley, J Coles & B Raftery (eds), *From Megaliths to Metals: essays in honour of George Eogan*, 109–16. Oxbow, Oxford.

Roche, H & Eogan, G   2001   'Late Neolithic activity in the Boyne Valley, Co. Meath', *in* C T L Roux (ed.), *Du Monde des Chasseurs à Celui des Métallurgistes: hommage scientifique à la mémoire de Jean L'Helgouach et mélanges offerts à Jacques Briard*, 125–40. Revue Archéologiques de l'Ouest, Supplement 9. Pôle éditorial archéologique de l'Ouest, Rennes.

Roche, H & Eogan, G   2007   'A re-assessment of the enclosure at Lugg, County Dublin, Ireland', *in* C Gosden, H Hamerow, P de Jersey & G Lock (eds), *Communities and Connections: essays in honour of Barry Cunliffe*, 154–68. Oxford University Press, Oxford.

Rolfe, J C (ed.) 1950 *Ammianus Marcellinus*. Wm Heinemann Ltd, London.

Rowley-Conwy, P 2004 'How the West was lost: a reconsideration of agricultural origins in Britain, Ireland, and southern Scandinavia', *Current Anthropology*, Vol. 45, 83–113.

Roycroft, N 2005 'Around the bay on the Great North Road: the archaeology of the M1 Dundalk Western Bypass', *in* J O'Sullivan & M Stanley (eds), *Recent Archaeological Discoveries on National Road Schemes 2004*, 65–82. Archaeology and the National Roads Authority Monograph Series No. 2. National Roads Authority, Dublin.

Russell, I & Ginn, V 2011a 'Adamstown 1—Bronze Age structures, iron-working activity', *in* J Eogan & E Shee Twohig (eds), *Cois tSiúire—Nine Thousand Years of Human Activity in the Lower Suir Valley: archaeological excavations on the N25 Waterford City Bypass, Vol. 1*, 25–30. NRA Scheme Monographs 8. National Roads Authority, Dublin.

Russell, I & Ginn, V 2011b 'Adamstown 3—Bronze Age settlement', *in* J Eogan & E Shee Twohig (eds), *Cois tSiúire—Nine Thousand Years of Human Activity in the Lower Suir Valley: archaeological excavations on the N25 Waterford City Bypass, Vol. 1*, 30–7. NRA Scheme Monographs 8. National Roads Authority, Dublin.

Russell, I & Harrison, S H 2011 'Woodstown 6—Viking Age enclosed settlement and grave', *in* J Eogan & E Shee Twohig (eds), *Cois tSiúire—Nine Thousand Years of Human Activity in the Lower Suir Valley: archaeological excavations on the N25 Waterford City Bypass, Vol. 1*, 53–72. NRA Scheme Monographs 8. National Roads Authority, Dublin.

Russell, I & Hurley, M F (eds) 2014 *Woodstown: a Viking-age settlement in Co. Waterford*. Four Courts Press, Dublin.

Ryan, M 1983 'Metalworking and style in the Early Christian period, 7th to 10th centuries AD', *in* M Ryan (ed.), *Treasures of Early Irish Art, 1500 BC to 1500 AD*, 34–45. Royal Irish Academy, Dublin.

Ryan, M 1988 'Fine metalworking and early Irish monasteries: the archaeological evidence', *in* J Bradley (ed.), *Settlement and Society in Medieval Ireland*, 33–48. Boethius Press, Kilkenny.

Ryan, M 1989 'Church metalwork in the eighth and ninth centuries', *in* S Youngs (ed.), *'The Work of Angels': masterpieces of Celtic metalwork, 6th to 9th centuries AD*, 125–69. British Museum Publications in association with the National Museum of Ireland and the National Museums of Scotland, London.

Ryan, M 2002 *Studies in Medieval Irish Metalwork*. Pindar Press, London.

Rynne, C 2013a 'Mills and milling in early medieval Ireland', *in* N Jackman, C Moore & C Rynne, *The Mill at Kilbegly: an archaeological investigation on the route of the M6 Ballinasloe to Athlone national road scheme*, 115–47. NRA Scheme Monographs 12. National Roads Authority, Dublin.

Rynne, C 2013b 'Overview of the second millennium AD (later and post-medieval)', *in* K Hanley & M F Hurley (eds), *Generations: the archaeology of five national road schemes in County Cork. Vol. 2: historical sites, artefactual and environmental evidence and radiocarbon dates*, 299–304. NRA Scheme Monographs 13. National Roads Authority, Dublin.

Sahlins, M   1968   'Notes on the original affluent society', *in* R Lee & I DeVore (eds), *Man the Hunter*, 85–9. Alidine, Chicago.

Scarre, C (ed.)   2002   *Monuments and Landscape in Atlantic Europe: perception and society during the Neolithic and Bronze Age*. Routledge, London.

Schulting, R J   2011   'The radiocarbon dates from Tullahedy', *in* R M Cleary & H Kelleher, *Excavations at Tullahedy, Co. Tipperary: Neolithic settlement in north Munster*, 145–61. Collins Press, Cork.

Schulting, R J   2013   'On the northwestern fringes: earlier Neolithic subsistence in Britain and Ireland as seen through faunal remains and stable isotopes', *in* S Shennan, K Dobney, S Colledge & J Connolly (eds), *The Origins and Spread of Stock-keeping in the Near East and Europe*, 313–38. Left Coast Press, Walnut Creek, CA.

Schulting, R J   2014   'The dating of Poulnabrone, Co. Clare', *in* A Lynch, *Poulnabrone, Co. Clare: excavation of an Early Neolithic portal tomb in Ireland*, 93–113. Archaeological Monograph Series 9. The Stationery Office, Dublin.

Schulting, R J, Bronk Ramsey, C, Reimer, P J, Eogan, G, Cleary, K, Cooney, G & Sheridan, A (forthcoming) 'Dating the human remains from Knowth', *in* G Eogan & K Cleary (eds), *Excavations at Knowth 6: the Great Mound at Knowth (Tomb 1) and its passage tomb archaeology*. Royal Irish Academy, Dublin.

Schulting, R, McClatchie, M, Sheridan, A, McLaughlin, R, Barratt, P & Whitehouse, N   2017   'Radiocarbon dates for a multi-phase passage tomb on Baltinglass Hill, Co. Wicklow', *Proceedings of the Prehistoric Society*, 1–19 (DOI: https://doi.org/10.1017/ppr.2017.1).

Schulting, R J, Murphy, E, Jones, C & Warren, G   2012   'New dates from the north, and a proposed chronology for Irish court tombs', *Proceedings of the Royal Irish Academy*, Vol. 112C, 1–60.

Schulting, R, Sheridan, A, Clarke, S & Bronk Ramsey, C   2008   'Largantea and the dating of Irish wedge tombs', *Journal of Irish Archaeology*, Vol. 17, 1–18.

Schulting, R J, Sheridan, A, Crozier, R & Murphy, E   2010   'Revisiting Quanterness: new AMS dates and stable isotope data from an Orcadian chamber tomb', *Proceedings of the Society of Antiquaries of Scotland*, Vol. 140, 1–50.

Schweitzer, H   2009   'A medieval farmstead at Moneycross Upper, Co. Wexford', *in* C Corlett & M Potterton (eds), *Rural Settlement in Medieval Ireland in the Light of Recent Archaeological Excavations*, 175–88. Research Papers in Irish Archaeology 1. Wordwell, Dublin.

Scully, O B M   1997   'Domestic architecture: introduction and discussion', *in* M Hurley, O B M Scully & S J McCutcheon, *Late Viking and Medieval Waterford: excavations 1986–1992*, 34–9. Waterford Corporation, Waterford.

Seaver, M   2005   'Run of the mill? Excavation of an early medieval site at Raystown, Co. Meath', *Archaeology Ireland*, Vol. 19, No. 4, 9–12.

Seaver, M   2006   'Through the mill: excavation of an early medieval settlement at Raystown, County Meath', *in* J O'Sullivan & M Stanley (eds), *Settlement, Industry and Ritual*, 73–87. Archaeology and the National Roads Authority Monograph Series No. 3. National Roads Authority, Dublin.

Seaver, M   2010   'Against the grain: early medieval settlement and burial on the Blackhill: excavations at Raystown, Co. Meath', *in* C Corlett & M Potterton (eds), *Death and Burial in Early Medieval Ireland in the Light of Recent Archaeological Excavations*, 261–79. Research Papers in Irish Archaeology 2. Wordwell, Dublin.

Seaver, M 2016   *Meitheal: the archaeology of lives, labours and beliefs at Raystown, Co. Meath*. TII Heritage 4. Transport Infrastructure Ireland, Dublin.

Seaver, M & Keeley, V J   2007   *Final Report on the Archaeological Excavation of an Archaeological Complex, Laughanstown townland, Co. Dublin*. Unpublished report by Valerie J Keeley Ltd for Dún Laoghaire–Rathdown County Council and the National Roads Authority.

Sheehan, C & Leahy, D   2011   'Cloone 3—*fulachtaí fia* and a late medieval kiln', *in* J Eogan & E Shee Twohig (eds), *Cois tSiúire—Nine Thousand Years of Human Activity in the Lower Suir Valley: archaeological excavations on the N25 Waterford City Bypass, Vol. 1*, 146–53. NRA Scheme Monographs 8. National Roads Authority, Dublin.

Sheehan, J   1998   'Early Viking Age silver hoards from Ireland and their Scandinavian elements', *in* H Clarke, M Ní Mhaonaigh & R Ó Floinn (eds), *Ireland and Scandinavia in the Early Viking Age*, 166–202. Four Courts Press, Dublin.

Sheridan, J A   1989   'Pottery production in Neolithic Ireland: a petrological and chemical study', *in* J Henderson (ed.), *Scientific Analysis in Archaeology and its Interpretation*, 112–35. Oxford University Committee for Archaeology Monograph No. 19 and UCLA Institute of Archaeology, Archaeological Research Tools 5. Oxford University Committee for Archaeology and UCLA Institute of Archaeology, Oxford.

Sheridan, J A   1995   'Irish Neolithic pottery: the story in 1995', *in* I Kinnes & G Varndell (eds), *'Unbaked Urns of Rudely Shape': essays on British and Irish pottery for Ian Longworth*, 3–21. Oxbow Monograph 55. Oxbow, Oxford.

Sheridan, J A   2004a   'Neolithic connections along and across the Irish Sea', *in* V Cummings & C Fowler (eds), *The Neolithic of the Irish Sea: materiality and traditions of practice*, 9–21. Oxbow, Oxford.

Sheridan, J A   2004b   'Going round in circles? Understanding the Irish Grooved Ware "complex" in its wider context', *in* H Roche, E Grogan, J Bradley, J Coles & B Raftery (eds), *From Megaliths to Metals: essays in honour of George Eogan*, 26–37. Oxbow, Oxford.

Sheridan, J A   2006   'A non-megalithic funerary tradition in early Neolithic Ireland', *in* M Meek (ed.), *The Modern Traveller to our Past: festschrift in honour of Ann Hamlin*, 24–31. DPK, Rathfriland.

Sheridan, [J] A   2007a   'From Picardie to Pickering and Pencraig Hill? New information on the "Carinated Bowl Neolithic" in northern Britain', *in* A W R Whittle & V Cummings (eds), *Going Over: the Mesolithic–Neolithic transition in north-west Europe*, 441–92. Proceedings of the British Academy 144. Oxford University Press, Oxford.

Sheridan, [J] A   2007b   'The beads from the Bronze Age graves at Caltragh', *in* E Danaher, *Monumental Beginnings: the archaeology of the N4 Sligo Inner Relief Road* (CD-ROM). NRA Scheme Monographs 1. National Roads Authority, Dublin.

Sheridan, J A 2010 'The Neolithization of Britain and Ireland: the "Big Picture"', *in* B Finlayson & G Warren (eds), *Landscapes in Transition*, 89–105. Oxbow, Oxford.

Sheridan, J A 2013 'Early Neolithic habitation structures in Britain and Ireland: a matter of circumstance and context', *in* D Hoffman & J Smyth (eds), *Tracking the Neolithic House in Europe: sedentism, architecture and practice*, 283–300. Springer, New York.

Sheridan, J A 2014 'Little and large: the miniature "carved stone ball" beads from the eastern tomb at Knowth, Ireland, and their broader significance', *in* R M Arbogast & A Greffier-Richard (eds), *Entre Archéologie et Écologie: une préhistoire de tous les milieux. Mélanges offerts à Pierre Pétrequin*, 303–14. Presses Universitaires de Franche-Comté, Besançon.

Sheridan, J A & Brophy, K (eds) 2012 *Neolithic Scotland: ScARF Panel Report*. Scottish Archaeological Research Framework, Society of Antiquaries of Scotland (http://www.scottishheritagehub.com/sites/default/files/u12/ScARF%20Neolithic%20June%202012%20v2%20.pdf; accessed May 2015).

Simpson, L 2012 'The *longphort* of Dublin: lessons from Woodstown, County Waterford, and Annagassan, County Louth', *in* S Duffy (ed.), *Medieval Dublin XII: proceedings of the Friends of Medieval Dublin symposium 2010*, 94–112. Four Courts Press, Dublin.

Smith, J M H 2005 *Europe after Rome: a new cultural history, AD 500–1000*. Oxford University Press, Oxford.

Smyth, J 2012 'Breaking ground: an overview of pits and pit-digging in Neolithic Ireland', *in* H Anderson-Whymark & J Thomas (eds), *Regional Perspectives on Neolithic Pit Deposition: beyond the mundane*, 13–29. Neolithic Studies Group Seminar Papers 12. Oxbow, Oxford.

Smyth, J 2013 'Tides of change? The house through the Irish Neolithic', *in* D Hoffman & J Smyth (eds), *Tracking the Neolithic House in Europe: sedentism, architecture and practice*, 321–7. Springer, New York.

Smyth, J 2014 *Settlement in the Irish Neolithic: new discoveries at the edge of Europe*. Prehistoric Society Research Paper No. 6. Oxbow, Oxford.

Smyth, J & Evershed, R P 2015a 'Milking the megafauna: using organic residue analysis to understand early farming practice', *Journal of Environmental Archaeology*, Vol. 21, No. 3 (DOI: http://dx.doi.org/10.1179/1749631414Y.0000000045).

Smyth, J & Evershed, R P 2015b 'The molecules of meals: new insight into Neolithic foodways', *Proceedings of the Royal Irish Academy*, Vol. 115C, 27–46.

Soderberg, J 2004 'Wild cattle: red deer in the religious texts, iconography, and archaeology of early medieval Ireland', *International Journal of Historical Archaeology*, Vol. 8, No. 3, 167–83.

Squatriti, P 2002 'Digging ditches in early medieval Europe', *Past and Present*, Vol. 176, No. 1, 11–65.

Stafford, E 2012 *00E0914 Lagavooren 7 Final Report*. Unpublished report to the National Monuments Service, Department of the Environment, Heritage and Local Government.

Sternke, F 2009 'APPENDIX 14: Lithics report', *in* L Cagney, R O'Hara, G Kelleher & R Morkan, *Report on the Archaeological Excavation of Dowdstown 2, Co. Meath*. Unpublished report by Archaeological Consultancy Services Ltd for Meath County Council and the National

Roads Authority.

Sternke, F 2010 'From boy to man:'rights' of passage and the lithic assemblage from a Neolithic mound in Tullahedy, Co. Tipperary', *in* M Stanley, E Danaher & J Eogan (eds), *Creative Minds: production, manufacturing and invention in ancient Ireland*, 1–14. Archaeology and the National Roads Authority Monograph Series No. 7. National Roads Authority, Dublin.

Stevens, C & Fuller, D 2012 'Did Neolithic farming fail? The case for a Bronze Age agricultural revolution in the British Isles', *Antiquity*, Vol. 86, No. 333, 707–22.

Stevens, P 2006 'A monastic enclosure site at Clonfad, Co. Westmeath', *Archaeology Ireland*, Vol. 20, No. 2, 8–11.

Stevens, P 2007 'Clonfad 3: a unique glimpse into early monastic life in County Westmeath', *Seanda*, No. 2, 42–3.

Stevens, P 2010 'For whom the bell tolls: the monastic site at Clonfad 3, Co. Westmeath', *in* M Stanley, E Danaher & J Eogan (eds), *Creative Minds: production, manufacturing and invention in ancient Ireland*, 85–94. Archaeology and the National Roads Authority Monograph Series No. 7. National Roads Authority, Dublin.

Stevens, P & Channing, J 2012 *Settlement and Community in the Fir Tulach Kingdom: archaeological excavation on the M6 and N52 road schemes*. National Roads Authority and Westmeath County Council, Dublin.

Stout, G 1991 'Embanked enclosures of the Boyne region', *Proceedings of the Royal Irish Academy*, Vol. 91C, 245–84.

Stout, G & Stout, M 2008 *Newgrange*. Cork University Press, Cork.

Stout, G & Stout, M 2011 'Early landscapes: from prehistory to plantation', *in* F H A Aalen, K Whelan & M Stout (eds), *Atlas of the Irish Rural Landscape* (2nd edn), 31–65. Cork University Press, Cork.

Sutton, B 2013 'Mitchelstown 2—the "Mitchelstown Face Cup" deposit and nearby burnt mound', *in* K Hanley & M F Hurley (eds), *Generations: the archaeology of five national road schemes in County Cork. Vol. 1: prehistoric sites*, 80–4. NRA Scheme Monographs 13. National Roads Authority, Dublin.

Sweetman, P D 1976 'An earthen enclosure at Monknewtown, Slane, Co. Meath', *Proceedings of the Royal Irish Academy*, Vol. 76C, 25–72.

Sweetman, P D 1981 'Excavations of a medieval moated site at Rigsdale, County Cork, 1977–8', *Proceedings of the Royal Irish Academy*, Vol. 81C, 103–205.

Sweetman, P D 1985 'A Late Neolithic/Early Bronze Age pit circle at Newgrange, Co. Meath', *Proceedings of the Royal Irish Academy*, Vol. 85C, 195–221.

Swift, C 1997 *Ogam Stones and the Earliest Irish Christians*. Department of Old and Middle Irish, St Patrick's College, Maynooth.

Tarlow, S & West, S (eds) 1999 *The Familiar Past? Archaeologies of later historical Britain*. Routledge, London.

Taylor, K 2007 'Inchagreenoge. *Fulachta fiadh*, ritual deposit of a human skull, wooden artefacts, post-medieval trackway', *in* E Grogan, L O'Donnell & P Johnston, *The Bronze Age Landscapes of the Pipeline to the West*, 281–4. Wordwell, Bray.

Taylor, K 2010a *N7 Nenagh to Limerick High Quality Dual Carriageway Archaeological Resolution Project, E2903, Gortnaskehy Site 1, Co. Tipperary (A026/238, 275 & 276), Final Archaeological Excavation Report*. Unpublished report by TVAS (Ireland) Ltd for Limerick County Council and the National Roads Authority.

Taylor, K 2010b 'An early medieval enclosure and cemetery at Carrigatogher (Harding), Co. Tipperary', *in* C Corlett & M Potterton (eds), *Death and Burial in Early Medieval Ireland in the Light of Recent Archaeological Excavations*, 281–93. Research Papers in Irish Archaeology 2. Wordwell, Dublin.

Thomas, G 2011 'Overview: craft production and technology', *in* H Hamerow, D A Hinton & S Crawford (eds), *The Oxford Handbook of Anglo-Saxon Archaeology*, 405–22. Oxford University Press, Oxford.

Thomas, J 2004 'Current debates on the Mesolithic–Neolithic transition in Britain and Ireland', *Documenta Praehistorica*, Vol. 31, 113–30.

Thomas, J 2007 'The internal features at Durrington Walls: investigations in the Southern Circle and Western Enclosures 2005–6', *in* M Larsson & M Parker Pearson (eds), *From Stonehenge to the Baltic: living with cultural diversity in the third millennium BC*, 145–57. British Archaeological Reports, International Series 1692. Oxford.

Thomas, J 2010 'The return of the Rinyo-Clacton folk? The cultural significance of the Grooved Ware Complex in later Neolithic Britain', *Cambridge Archaeological Journal*, Vol. 20, No. 1, 1–15.

Thomas, J 2013 *The Birth of Neolithic Britain*. Oxford University Press, Oxford.

Tierney, J 2009 'Excavating feudalism? A medieval moated site at Carrowreagh [*sic*], Co. Wexford', *in* C Corlett & M Potterton (eds), *Rural Settlement in Medieval Ireland in the Light of Recent Archaeological Excavations*, 189–200. Research Papers in Irish Archaeology 1. Wordwell, Dublin.

Tierney, J & Logan, E 2008 'Bronze Age *fulacht fiadh*: Area 30, Graigueshoneen Td, Licence No. 98E0575', *in* P Johnston, J Kiely & J Tierney, *Near the Bend in the River: the archaeology of the N25 Kilmacthomas realignment*, 86–9. NRA Scheme Monographs 3. National Roads Authority, Dublin.

Timpany, S 2011 'The changing landscape of the Lower Suir Valley', *in* J Eogan & E Shee Twohig (eds), *Cois tSiúire—Nine Thousand Years of Human Activity in the Lower Suir Valley: archaeological excavations on the N25 Waterford City Bypass, Vol. 1*, 187–98. NRA Scheme Monographs 8. National Roads Authority, Dublin.

Tresset, A 2003 'French Connections II: of cows and men', *in* I Armit, E Murphy, E Nelis & D Simpson (eds), *Neolithic Settlement in Ireland and Western Britain*, 18–30. Oxbow, Oxford.

Waddell, J 1990 *The Bronze Age Burials of Ireland*. Galway University Press, Galway.

Waddell, J 1998 *The Prehistoric Archaeology of Ireland* (1st edn). Galway University Press, Galway.

Waddell, J 2010 *The Prehistoric Archaeology of Ireland* (3rd edn). Wordwell, Bray.

Wagner, D M, Klunk, J, Harbeck, M, Devault, A, Waglechner, N, Sahl, J W, Enk, J, Birdsell, D N,

Kuch, M, Lumibao, C, Poinar, D, Pearson, T, Fourment, M, Golding, B, Riehm, J M, Earn, D J D, DeWitte, S, Rouillard, J M, Grupe, G, Wiechmann, I, Bliska, J B, Keim, P S, Scholz, H C, Holmes, E C & Poinar, H 2014 'Yersinia pestis and the Plague of Justinian 541–543 AD: a genomic analysis', *The Lancet*, Vol. 14, No. 4, 319–26.

Wallace, P F 1987 'The economy and commerce of Viking Age Dublin', *in* K Duwel, H Jankuhn, H Siems & D Timpe (eds), *Untersuchungen zu Handel und Verkehr der Vor- und Frühgeschichtlichen Zeit in Mittel- und Nordeuropa Vol. 4*, 200–45. Vandenhoeck und Ruprech, Gottingen.

Wallace, P 2016 *Viking Dublin: the Wood Quay excavations*. Irish Academic Press, Dublin.

Walsh, C 1997 *Archaeological Excavation of a Development Site to the Southeast of St Maelruan's, Tallaght, Co. Dublin (96E188)*. Unpublished report submitted to the National Monuments Service, Dublin.

Walsh, F 2006 'Neolithic Monanny, County Monaghan', *in* J O'Sullivan & M Stanley (eds), *Settlement, Industry and Ritual*, 7–17. Archaeology and the National Roads Authority Monograph Series No. 3. National Roads Authority, Dublin.

Walsh, F 2008 'Killickaweeny 1: high-class early medieval living', *in* N Carlin, L Clarke & F Walsh, *The Archaeology of Life and Death in the Boyne Floodplain: the linear landscape of the M4*, 27–54. National Roads Authority, Dublin.

Walsh, F 2009 *Site 110, Monanny 1: N2 Carrickmacross–Aclint Road Re-alignment*. Unpublished report by Irish Archaeological Consultancy Ltd for Monaghan County Council and the National Roads Authority.

Walsh, F 2011 'Archaeology of two townlands (Part 1)', *Clogher Record*, Vol. 20, No. 3, 500–20.

Walsh, F & Harrison, J 2003 'Early medieval enclosure at Killickaweeny, Co. Kildare', *Archaeology Ireland*, Vol. 17, No. 1, 33–6.

Walsh, G 1993 *Archaeological Excavations on the N5 Swinford Bypass*. Unpublished report for Mayo County Council.

Walsh, G 1995 'Iron Age settlement in Co. Mayo', *Archaeology Ireland*, Vol. 9, No. 2, 7–8.

Walsh, P 1993 'In circle and row: Bronze Age ceremonial monuments', *in* E Shee Twohig & M Ronayne (eds), *Past Perceptions: the prehistoric archaeology of south-west Ireland*, 101–13. University College Cork, Cork.

Walsh, P 1995 'Structure and deposition in Irish wedge tombs: an open and shut case?', *in* J Waddell & E Shee Twohig (eds), *Ireland in the Bronze Age*, 113–27. The Stationery Office, Dublin.

Warren, G M 2013 'The adoption of agriculture in Ireland: perceptions of key research challenges', *Journal of Archaeological Method and Theory*, Vol. 20, No. 4, 525–51 (DOI:10.1007/s10816-012-9129-4).

Warren, G M 2015a ' "Mere food gatherers they, parasites upon nature . . .": food and drink in the Mesolithic of Ireland', *Proceedings of the Royal Irish Academy*, Vol. 115C, 1–26.

Warren, G M 2015b 'Britain and Ireland inside Mesolithic Europe', *in* H Anderson-Whymark, D Garrow & F Sturt (eds), *Continental Connections: exploring cross-Channel relationships from the Mesolithic to the Iron Age*, 43–58. Oxbow, Oxford.

Warren, G M & Kador, T   2013 'What did the Hill of Tara mean in the Mesolithic?', *in* M O'Sullivan, C Scarre & M Doyle (eds), *Tara—from the Past to the Future. Towards a new research agenda*, 15–25. Wordwell, Dublin.

Webster, L & Brown, M   1997   *The Transformation of the Roman World, AD 400–900*. British Museum, London.

Whitehouse, N J, Schulting, R J, McClatchie, M, Barratt, P, McLaughlin, T R, Bogaard, A, Colledge, S, Marchant, R, Gaffrey, J & Bunting, M J   2014 'Neolithic agriculture on the European western frontier: the boom and bust of early farming in Ireland', *Journal of Archaeological Science*, Vol. 51, 181–205 (DOI: http://dx.doi.org/10.1016/j.jas.2013.08.009).

Whittaker, J   2009   *Peatland Excavations 2001–2002: Mountdillon group of bogs, Co. Longford*. ADS Monograph 3. Archaeological Development Services Ltd, Dublin.

Whittle, A   2003   *The Archaeology of People: dimensions of Neolithic life*. Routledge, London.

Whittle, A, Healy, F & Bayliss, A (eds)   2011   *Gathering Time: dating the early Neolithic enclosures of southern Britain and Ireland*. Oxford, Oxbow.

Whitty, Y   2012 'An Iron Age ring-ditch complex at Holdenstown 1, Co. Kilkenny', *in* C Corlett & M Potterton (eds), *Life and Death in Iron Age Ireland in the Light of Recent Archaeological Excavations*, 313–26. Research Papers in Irish Archaeology 4. Wordwell, Dublin.

Wickham, C   2005   *Framing the Early Middle Ages: Europe and the Mediterranean, 400–800*. Oxford University Press, Oxford.

Wierbicki, P & Coughlan, T   2013   *E3858 Kellymount 5 Final Report*. Unpublished report by Irish Archaeological Consultancy Ltd for Kilkenny County Council and the National Roads Authority.

Wiggins, K, Duszynski, B & Ginn, V   2009   *Report on the Archaeological Excavation of Ross 1, Co. Meath*. Unpublished report by Archaeological Consultancy Services Ltd for Meath County Council and the National Roads Authority.

Wilkins, B, Timpany, S, Drum, M & Price, J   2009 'Newrath 34—Mesolithic activity, wooden trackways and platforms, *fulacht fia* and brock kiln', *in* J Eogan & E Shee Twohig (eds), *Cois tSiúire—Nine Thousand Years of Human Activity in the Lower Suir Valley: archaeological excavations on the N25 Waterford City Bypass, Vol. 1*, 113–28. NRA Scheme Monographs 8. National Roads Authority, Dublin.

Wooding, J M   1996   *Communication and Commerce Along the Western Sea-lanes AD 400–800*. British Archaeological Reports, International Series 654. Tempus Reparatum, Oxford.

Woodman, P C   1978   *The Mesolithic in Ireland: hunter-gatherers in an insular environment*. British Archaeological Reports, British Series 58. Oxford.

Woodman, P C   2009a 'Challenging times: reviewing Irish Mesolithic chronologies', *in* P Crombé, M Van Strydonck, J Sergant, M Boudin & M Bats (eds), *Chronology and Evolution Within the Mesolithic of North-west Europe: proceedings of an international meeting, Brussels, May 30th–June 1st 2007*, 195–216. Cambridge Scholars Publishing, Newcastle.

Woodman, P C   2009b 'Ireland's place in the European Mesolithic: why it's ok to be different', *in* S McCartan, R Schulting, G M Warren & P C Woodman (eds), *Mesolithic Horizons: papers presented at the Seventh International Conference on the Mesolithic in Europe, Belfast 2005, Vol. 1,* xxxvi–xlvi. Oxbow, Oxford.

Woodman, P C   2011   'The significance of the lithic assemblages from the archaeological excavations on the N25 Waterford City Bypass', *in* J Eogan & E Shee Twohig (eds), *Cois tSiúire—Nine Thousand Years of Human Activity in the Lower Suir Valley: archaeological excavations on the route of the N25 Waterford City Bypass*, 199–206. NRA Scheme Monographs 8. National Roads Authority, Dublin.

Woodman, P C   2015   *Ireland's First Settlers: time and the Mesolithic*. Oxbow, Oxford.

Woodman, P C & Johnson, G   1996   'Excavations at Bay Farm 1, Carnlough, Co. Antrim, and the study of the "Larnian" technology', *Proceedings of the Royal Irish Academy*, Vol. 96C, 137–235.

Woodman, P C, Anderson, E & Finlay, N   1999   *Excavations at Ferriter's Cove, 1983–95: last foragers, first farmers in the Dingle Peninsula*. Wordwell, Bray.

Woodman, P C, Finlay, N & Anderson, E   2006   *The Archaeology of a Collection: the Keiller–Knowles collection of the National Museum of Ireland*. Wordwell, Dublin.

Wren, J & Halpin, E   2011   'Kilmurry C—standing stones, pit circle and cist', *in* J Eogan & E Shee Twohig (eds), *Cois tSiúire—Nine Thousand Years of Human Activity in the Lower Suir Valley: archaeological excavations on the N25 Waterford City Bypass, Vol. 1*, 160–4. NRA Scheme Monographs 8. National Roads Authority, Dublin.

Wren, J & Price, J   2011   'Newrath 37—Neolithic building and Early Bronze Age cemetery', *in* J Eogan & E Shee Twohig (eds), *Cois tSiúire—Nine Thousand Years of Human Activity in the Lower Suir Valley: archaeological excavations on the N25 Waterford City Bypass, Vol. 1*, 135–46. NRA Scheme Monographs 8. National Roads Authority, Dublin.

INDEX

Note: Page numbers in *italics* refer to illustrations; '*t*' following a page number indicates a table.